NAVY DIVER

NAVY DIVER

JOSEPH SIDNEY KARNEKE

as told to

VICTOR BOESEN

AN AUTHORS GUILD BACKINPRINT.COM EDITION

AN AUTHORS GUILD BACKINPRINT.COM EDITION

Published by iUniverse.com, Inc.

For information address:
iUniverse.com, Inc.
5220 S 16th, Ste. 200
Lincoln, NE 68512
www.iuniverse.com

Originally published by GP Putnam

ISBN: 0-595-14212-5

Printed in the United States of America

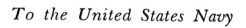

To the United States Navy

Contents

Prologue

A dummy first got me interested in deep-sea diving. I was a boot at the Naval Training Station, Newport, Rhode Island, and the dummy, in full diving gear, caught my eye as I stepped through the classroom door to begin a course in gunnery. I stopped to look him over.

"This is a course in gunnery!" barked Gunner Waldo, my instructor. "If you ever make a diver you'll have to learn to concentrate—starting right now, with gunnery."

During class my attention kept wandering to the undersea figure by the door. When the class was over, Gunner Waldo said, "Seaman Karneke, since you're so interested in diving and not gunnery, I'm going to give you a little extra duty. Come back this evening after you're secured from drill and shine up Jake."

That evening I spent two hours polishing Jake's brass and scrubbing his canvas. This did cool me off a little, but diving lingered in my mind, and when I got the chance to try it out after finishing boot camp, as you will discover later in this book, I was hooked. And while I was qualifying for second-class diver, I read up on the subject and found I was involved in a field with quite an interesting history.

The first written reference to diving occurs in Homer's *Iliad*, in which Patroculus speaks of the fall of Hector's chariot as reminding him of a diver going after oysters. At the siege of Syracuse, divers went down to cut away the underwater barriers which had been erected to keep Greek ships from entering the harbor. Later Aristotle spoke of a device to bring air down to the diver, and a metallic affair to go over his head.

But it took hundreds of years before somebody invented a suit. The first, devised by an Englishman, John Lethbridge, in 1715, was made of leather. The suit was watertight and contained air—without ventilation. This carbon-dioxide deathtrap is believed to have been the first outfit to make underwater salvage work possible.

Nearly another century passed before a suit, which somewhat resembled today's diving dress, appeared. Invented by a German named Kleingert, it consisted of tight-fitting leather jacket and drawers, with a cylinder coming over the diver's head and down to his hips. Fresh air was supplied through a pipe with an ivory mouthpiece at the lower end and a bladder at the top to keep it afloat.

The biggest forward step came when Augustus Siebe, in 1819, added a pump to a diving outfit, so that air could be circulated under pressure to the diver. The suit that went with this improvement included a helmet formed to a shoulder plate, which in turn was attached to a waterproof leather jacket. The air was pumped down into the helmet through a tube, and exhausted under the edge of the jacket. The air in the helmet kept the water below the diver's chin, thus using the same principle as the diving bell. A good outfit for its time, it allowed the diver to do things he hadn't been able to do before, as long as he didn't bend over. Siebe went on experimenting, and in another dozen years he introduced a rig with both intake and exhaust valves in the helmet. With, of course, many refinements, this is the diving dress used all over the world today.

The oceans, covering 71 per cent of the earth's surface, are still our biggest and least-known frontier. To keep learning more of how to go deeper into it, the Navy maintains its Experimental Diving School, at the Naval Gun Factory, in Washington, D. C. It is to these contemporary Navy divers, pioneers of the modern world, and to all those who served under the seas in the two wars of my time, that this book is dedicated.

1. All I Wanted Was a Trip

I never really meant to get into the Navy. All I had in mind was a trip. The Navy was a kind of government tour organization, as I understood it, which specialized in arranging travel for young men of my age who were interested in seeing the world.

While the arrangement proved to have some reciprocal features that hadn't been clear to me, the part about seeing the world certainly came out just as I had heard. The very first time out we kept going for 100,000 miles. During the twenty years the Navy and I were together, I got to see not only most of the dry parts of the world and the seventy-one per cent that is under water, but also the bottom side of the flooded section. Finally, the tour took in the time of the biggest war in history, making it extra stimulating. All in all, I couldn't have asked for more.

I was a farm boy in western Pennsylvania, and I was bored with the rustic life. I had had enough of milking, plowing, hoeing and all the rest of it. Going into Cherry Valley on Saturday nights and mingling with other farm folk, in town like ourselves to buy the week's groceries, wasn't doing much for me. Nor was there much kick any longer in hooking a ride into Pittsburgh on the milk truck once in a while. Here I was, twenty years old, and the most exciting experience I could remember was the time I fell off the silo while I was putting a roof on it. It had been a carom shot—from the roof to the scaffold, which springboarded me up and out, and then to the ground, fifty feet away.

Things hadn't been the same since the year they found oil in our part of the country. The roughnecks of the drill crews that came to drive the wells were men of the world who lived dangerously. They chewed tobacco on the job instead of smoking, showing how hazardous their work was, and they told tales of faraway places. To us ten-and-twelve-year-olds, these were plainly men to imitate. We collected the emptied sacks of Beech Nut and Pay Car Scrap they threw away, and salvaged the few flakes of tobacco that remained. Then on Sunday we went hiking in the woods to chew these dregs, carelessly letting the juice run down the corners of our mouths, and spitting importantly. After a while we decided to pool our resources and buy a pack of our own.

The procurement came off fine, and everything went well in the woods—even to seeing how long we could hold back the juice after the manner of our idols, before letting it go in gleaming yellow geysers at the nearest bush. But for me there came a recession in fortune after we got home. My mother anxiously remarked that I looked pale. I tossed it off as nothing, but when I went to bed uncommonly early and presently lost my supper, my position became precarious. Next day at school I got sick all over again, declining so badly that the teacher sent me home under escort. At home I passed out, and for two days was delirious, intermittently crying out, "I don't want any more chewing tobacco!" and naming my colleagues in delinquency. This included poor Steve, my brother, who instantly caught flailing hell with a harness strap. As for myself, though, I was in such pitiful shape that my parents decided to spare the leather, feeling I was already well taken care of. They could not have guessed how right they were. So well in mind did I have the message about the weed that it wasn't until the war, many years later, that I even tried smoking the stuff. Tobacco then seemed a relatively minor hazard.

While the affair of the tobacco cured me of chewing, it did not end my urge for adventure. Each time I rode into Pittsburgh on the milk pickup truck, decked out in freshly laundered overalls and my Sunday shoes, I would carry on to the driver about how I wanted to take a trip, but couldn't because I didn't have the money. Often, as we passed the post office, the driver would nod absently toward the Navy recruiting poster in front and remark, "There're the people that can fix you up. They're in the business." One hot day as we waited for the traffic light, the driver suddenly stabbed a finger toward the poster and said sternly, "I'm tired of hearing you yapping about wanting to go someplace! Go in there and sign up for a trip! They'll give it to you for nothing. I'll pick you up on my way back."

I kept sitting, undecided. "God damn!" said the driver. "This traffic is going to start moving in a minute! Better get out while you can."

I climbed down from the truck and slowly crossed the street to the post office. At the stamp window I asked, "Where can I get one of these Navy trips?"

"The recruiting office is on the next floor," replied the man impersonally. "There's a sign up there that'll tell you where to go."

As I rounded onto the second floor from the stairs, I was met by a man in a blue uniform—some employee of the post office, I thought, since there were no white stripes on his collar. "Can I get a trip with the Navy?" I asked cautiously. If I didn't see it through, I would be in trouble with the milk driver on the way home.

The man looked me over. "Well, yes and no," he said. "It depends whether you qualify." He kept measuring me up and down. "Everybody wants to take a cruise with the Navy," he went on. "We just take a select few."

"What have I got to do?" I asked.

"First I gotta give you some tests," he replied. He led the way to his desk and handed me a form from a sheaf of papers on top. "Fill this out," he directed, standing by as I laid the form on the desk and began to write. I wrote in my name and address, when and where I was born, my height and weight, the name of my school, and other such personal data. This, explained the man in blue, was to make sure they only got the elite. Next came an examination test. "Don't be nervous," he said. "Just answer the ones you know. The thing is timed, so if you don't know the answer, skip it and go on to the next one."

The questions were the same as I was used to in high school, and gave me no trouble. "What do I do next?" I asked, gaining confidence.

"Go home and wait—we'll contact you," he said. "And it may be some time. We got a big waiting list."

After I had waited a week, I decided I hadn't made the grade and took a job as an apprentice coal miner. I moved into a boardinghouse in Westland, fifteen or twenty miles from home, and as time passed forgot all about the formalities I had been through that morning at the Pittsburgh post office. I was making forty dollars a week, and beginning to think of going to college, maybe becoming a mining engineer. Then one evening as I came in from work I found a telephone message from my mother. I called her at once.

"What kind of trouble are you in, son?" she asked suspiciously. "What did you do?"

"Why, nothing," I replied, puzzled.

"You must have done something," she insisted. "There was some man here looking for you. He was wearing a uniform. He said he was from the government."

"Government?" I echoed. "What do you mean?"

"He said he was from the Navy Department or something. He said it was very important. He wants to see you in Pittsburgh first thing in the morning." She gave me an address.

Still the dawn didn't come for me. Navy? Pittsburgh? I remembered about signing up for a trip, but there had been no urgency about that. In fact, the man had said I would be lucky if I got it.

Just the same, I thought, it might be well to find out. Next morning I told the boss I would need the day off. "I should be back early this afternoon," I said.

"Good," said the boss. "We'll leave a note at the lamp shack so you can pick up your lamp for the rest of the shift." Little did either of us suspect that I would need no miner's lamp for what I would be doing later that day—or on any other day, forevermore.

Not until the bus dropped me in front of the Pittsburgh post office did I tie in present developments with those on the morning of my last ride to town on the milk truck. At the desk on the second floor sat my old friend of my previous visit, who had so kindly taken an interest in my travel problems. "What's this all about?" I asked as I came up, grinning genially.

He had changed. "Where've you been?" he demanded sharply. "We've been looking for you."

"Why?" I asked.

"I don't have time to tell you now," he said briskly. "Get in that next room there." He pointed to a door. "They're waiting for you." He hustled me over to the door and shoved me inside.

I stood in the rear of the room, gaping curiously as I heard the man up in front, undoubtedly an officer because he wore a uniform with braid, call out to the gathering before me. "All right, you men, raise your right hand and repeat after me . . ."

I nudged the fellow standing next to me. "What's going on?" I asked.

He held a finger to his mouth. "Sh-sh-sh! Raise your right hand!" he whispered. "I'll tell you later."

I raised my hand and joined the rest in mumbling something about defending the country. The next thing I knew, an officer was shaking my hand, and beaming: "Only one in ten makes it." Just what it was I had made I still wasn't sure, although I was beginning to have a disturbed feeling that I was in the grip of forces beyond my control. Bewildered, I turned back to the man I had nudged when I came in, repeating the question I had asked then. From his answer, he clearly thought I was up on events to the present and only wanted to know what came next. "I don't know," he replied. "The guy said he'd tell us everything we needed to know."

The truth of this appeared as my friend from the desk in the corridor walked in and blew our chattering little groups apart with a loud "Okay, hold down the noise and follow me!"

As we shuffled after him, I hurried up to the front of the line and tapped our bellwet;the on the shoulder. "You were going to tell me what this was all about," I reminded him in a voice of growing alarm.

He gave me a glance of disgust. "Look," he said, "you don't want to start as a troublemaker, do you? You've already been late for the swearing-in ceremony. You still haven't signed all your papers." He motioned toward the desk in the corridor. "Go over there and wait for me," he ordered.

There was now a new man at the desk and he took me in hand. "Oh, yes, you gotta sign these," he said, spreading some papers before me. I seemed to be doing everything backward. "Now step over here," he directed when I was finished with the papers. He led me into a small side room. "You're supposed to have had your physical long before this," he said. "Take your clothes off."

"What for?" I asked.

"We can't give you a physical with your clothes on," he explained grimly.

"I think there's some mistake," I said. We were extending our remarks on the matter when the first man joined us. "What's the trouble?" he asked.

"This guy doesn't want to take his clothes off," replied the other.

"I figured that," said the first man. "He's a wise guy. We're going to have trouble with him." He turned to me and said, "Do you have any reason why you don't want to take your clothes off?"

"Of course not," I retorted.

"Okay, then take 'em off!"

I passed this inspection and soon was back at the desk in the corridor, where the first man gave me a handful of chits. "Sign these," he directed. "They're for your hotel and meals."

"I got a place to stay," I said, having in mind my boarding-house back in Westland. "I just came here to find out what you wanted to see me about."

The man at the desk studied me. Then he leaned forward and said intently, "Let me give you a little friendly advice. You're in the Navy now. You can save yourself a lot of trouble by doing as you're told and not asking questions. You got everybody mad at you already." He jammed a finger down on the chits, still lying on the desk. "Eat and sleep where you want to tonight," he said, "but sign these damn chits anyway, and be sure to be at that hotel at four o'clock in the morning. That's when we're shoving off. If you're not there, you'll be AWOL."

"What about my job?" I asked.

"Don't worry about that. They'll square you away in boot camp." He waved an arm toward the other recruits. "Now go over there with the rest of the men."

I joined the others, still not quite comprehending what had happened. I pursued the subject with one of my mates, who proved to be an ex-Marine. "Don't you know you're in the Navy?" he asked with disbelief. "You signed all these papers, didn't you? You were in the swearing-in ceremony. You're in the Navy, man!" He asked how I got involved.

"I just wanted to take a trip," I said.

"Well, here's your chance," replied my new friend knowingly. "Stick around."

By the next afternoon I was already farther from home than I had ever been. We were in boot camp at Newport, Rhode Island, arriving in time for evening chow. The miner's lamp waiting for me back at Westland, Pennsylvania, belonged in a world remarkably distant in time and place. The following morning, after breakfast, our conversion from civilians to fighting men of the sea was at least symbolically complete: we were in the middy blouses and bell-bottom pants of the United States Navy.

As far as I was concerned, however, the uniform made for a flagrant case of misbranding. The first day on the drill field, as we stood lined up like two rows of corn before Chief Petty Officer Fraser, our company commander, I was suddenly excited to hear him open an escape route. "If you have any problems," he said after he had introduced himself, "don't hesitate to come to me. If I can't solve them I'll send you to the chaplain."

I shot my hand up like a man sighting rescuers as he is going down for the third time, waving it wildly. "Good," said Chief Fraser, looking past me, "I'm glad to see there are no crybabies in this outfit. I'll see that this is the best company that ever went out of here." He clicked his heels. "Ten-SHUN!"

At home, meanwhile, my family knew nothing of this turn in my affairs. It was first heralded when the bundle containing my old clothes arrived. To my father this meant nothing good. "I always knew he'd end up in serious trouble," he remarked dourly.

"How do you know he's in trouble?" my mother demanded loyally.

"They sent his clothes home, didn't they?" my father returned. "That means he's someplace where he doesn't need
them."

By now my mother had found the note from the Red Cross
which accompanied the bundle, explaining that I was in the
Navy. She read it aloud.

My father nodded thoughtfully. "Well," he said after a
while, "maybe those people will straighten him out."

2. In Deep

Rain splattered the decks of the light cruiser *Savannah* as she slid from her berth at the Philadelphia Navy Yard under the raw sky of early spring, bound for the warm blue waters of the Caribbean. As the city's skyline faded into the mists off the fantail and the world dissolved into a universe of water, it became a struggle for us youngsters fresh from boot camp, hats shoved rakishly forward over an eye, to keep up the bored, worldly-wise bearing of seasoned salts. The air was charged with the promise of exciting things to come.

What some of these might be was hinted by the presence of deep-sea diving equipment aboard, brought up the gangplank in crates and dumped on the fantail just before we weighed anchor. With studied casualness, I mentioned to Turret Captain Watkins that I had seen it. This seemed to interest him. "Do you know anything about diving?" he asked, looking me over.

I told him about the Jakes—dummy divers—we had in boot camp. Watkins became conversational. "I'm a qualified diver myself," he confided with pride. A qualified diver, I was to learn, is a diver of the second class, limited in his descents to fifteen fathoms or ninety feet. Watkins was being

22

remarkably chummy toward a boot, and I would learn why soon enough.

After a couple of days, a damage control gang broke out the diving equipment to inspect it, and to try it on in some dry-run diving practice. They laboriously got into the suits, pulled on the heavy leaded shoes, and lowered the helmets over their heads, clamping them in place on the breastplate. Fully outfitted, they clomped heavily around the deck with the uncertainty of earthmen newly landed on the moon. I watched their activities for a time, and then went looking for Watkins. I found him in a turret and reported what was happening on the fantail.

He replied scornfully, "You can put anybody in a diving dress and have him get his picture taken, but getting him down in the water is something else. You want to be a diver?" he asked suddenly.

"No," I said, "just being on top of the water is enough for me. I don't want to go under it." But I was tempted. I had qualified in several specialties, putting the insignia on my sleeve so these attainments wouldn't go unnoticed, but I didn't want Watkins to think that this boot considered himself good enough to be a diver. He dropped the matter and pointed down the barrels of the guns sticking from the turret. "Better go out and touch up those muzzles a little," he ordered. "We want 'em to look good when we get there."

With warm breezes sweeping across the deck, we threaded down through the Bahama Islands, treated to pyrotechnic sunsets and butterball moons rising behind palm trees. We passed into the broad Windward Channel dividing Cuba and Haiti, and dropped anchor on the Haiti side, in the cobalt sea of Gonaïves Bay. The water was as clear as the springs back home, and when there came a call for volunteers to qualify for diving, at least two dozen stepped forward, eager to explore these clean, friendly depths. For a couple of days the fantail became the center of interest as these diver candidates practiced putting on the suits, and received instructions from

Watkins in how to operate them. They could hardly wait to get into the water.

Then a rumor went around the ship that barracuda had been seen. From older hands aboard I learned that barracuda are more dangerous than sharks. They strike at anything that moves, ripping it with razorlike teeth, and are often the real culprits in attacks on humans in which sharks get the blame. This sobering news was followed by a new rumor: that a crewman, plunging into the water in a devil-may-care short cut back to the ship after a damp shore leave, was bitten by a barracuda. Disquieting as these reports were, open-mindedness prevailed until there came a third rumor. This one had it that a deck hand, falling out of a boat alongside the ship, had been attacked by a barracuda which snapped a boat hook in two as the deck hand was pulled to safety. There followed a general retirement from diver candidacy.

Abruptly finding himself with no one to instruct, Watkins again asked if I wanted to be a diver. I stalled. "What about all those rated guys that have been practicing on the fantail?" I parried, not letting on that I knew they had quit.

"They changed their minds," said Watkins, saying nothing about the reasons.

"Yeah, I know why," I said, repeating the rumors about the barracuda.

"Oh, don't worry about that," replied Watkins. "Go down to sick bay and get your physical this afternoon, and in the morning you'll be all set to go."

I hedged. "I don't know about that," I said. "It looks to me like those sharks and barracudas mean business."

Watkins looked shocked. "You're not afraid of sharks, are you?" he demanded, as if he had never heard of such a thing.

"No," I said, "but I don't want to go down there and bother them."

"They won't mind," said Watkins. "I assure you they won't give you any trouble."

"How you going to assure me?" I asked.

"If I go down first . . . ?"

"That will assure me," I said. "If they don't eat you, I don't see why they should want to eat me."

Early next morning, in a motor launch rigged for diving, we went out where the water was the required five fathoms deep, a half dozen miles from the *Savannah*. I noted that there were sixteen men in the work party to operate the pump sending air down to the man in the water, manning it in four-man relays. In those days motors were not considered reliable and no diver would think of diving on mechanized air. That it took this many men to do the job didn't seem to me to reflect much confidence in manpower, either.

True to his word, Watkins went down first. He returned intact and with a kind of see-there's-nothing-to-it bearing. Next to go was his only other recruit, a little man about five feet tall. Moments after he had disappeared, he came scrambling back up the descending line like an animal going up a tree to escape the dogs. He was obviously in difficulty. "The trouble with him, he's too small," Watkins said hastily, adding, as the man's helmet was lifted off, "And he's probably not in physical condition to be a diver."

Whatever the poor fellow's physical state may have been a little while before, it was clearly not so good now. He was spitting blood, and blood was oozing from his nose, ears and eyes. At the sick bay later, his injuries were found to include two broken eardrums, ruptured blood vessels in the ears and nose, and near-inblown eyeballs.

His size and the state of his health of course had nothing to do with all this, although in those days not many people knew better. He had simply been lowered too fast. The pressure of the water around him had increased faster than the pumpers topside had been able to offset it with the air they were pumping down into his suit. He had gotten a "squeeze."

Knowing none of this, though, I pretty well ran out of the assurance I had been given by Watkins' dive. The sharks and barracudas I at least understood. As I was being dressed, I sensed a feeling in everybody but Watkins that once I went over the side, I would never be seen again. My tenders treated me as if this was their last act of kindness toward me.

"All you have to do," said Watkins, "is follow instructions. Then nothing will happen."

"What about my valves?" I asked, referring to the means for letting the fresh air into my suit and the exhaust air out.

"I'll set them before you go down, so you won't have to touch them," Watkins answered.

"What'll I do if I don't get enough air?" I asked. I didn't know it but this was a good question. Without enough air I would get squeezed like the man before me.

"Signal for some more," said Watkins.

"What signal is that?" I asked. Telephones in the helmet were still in the future.

"Give three jerks on your air hose," Watkins instructed.

"What if I'm getting too much air?" I persisted, unwittingly asking another good one. Too much air would mean overbuoyancy, maybe floating me off the bottom.

Watkins laughed. "Don't worry about getting too much air," he said. He waved an arm at the pumping crew. "In this heat these sailors won't pump that fast."

The helmet was lifted over my head and fastened in place. As each turn of the bolts trapped me in my prison, I grew more desperate. I was choosing death before dishonor—death in the water before the dishonor of backing out—and I wasn't sure of my choice. The crew helped me over the side, and keeping a white-knuckled grip on the descending line, I let myself cautiously into the water. It came up my body, rose over my faceplate, and then over my head. I was agreeably surprised to find myself not being killed but, instead, able to breathe normally, and keeping nicely dry and comfortable. With the inrush of air to my helmet roaring in my ears, I slid down the line inches at a time, unaware that in this slow progress I was giving the pumpers time to keep up and sparing myself the fate of the first diver.

I was beginning to feel that there had been some mistake about the depth when at last my feet touched bottom. There I stood, staring stonily straight ahead like a cigar-store Indian, looking neither right nor left for fear of what I might see. I was vaguely aware of a few bright colored fish drifting idly in and out among tall streamers of seaweed waving in the amber twilight before me, but my interest in marine biology was nil. I was concentrating on the four tugs on my air hose which would be the signal to come up. When they came, I answered with the prescribed four from myself so fast that I nearly interrupted the incoming signal.

When I broke surface, the crew looked at me with awe and, as I was pulled into the boat, pounded me on the back. By chow time back on the *Savannah*, I was the best-known man aboard. I only wished I could be sure it was all right for heroes to be scared.

I was glad when a new day came, bringing an opportunity to improve my technique. To qualify as a second-class diver took four dives, each deeper and longer than the last. My second dive called for doubling the depth to ten fathoms and staying down an hour. To find the new depth needed, we went out several miles farther than on the first day and anchored near a coral garden, showing dimly through the translucent water. With the pumpers looking on admiringly, I bore myself with the detached air becoming a hero as I was being dressed. For today's dive I wore a shallow-water helmet, forerunner of the mask for shallow water. The helmet worked on the same principle as the diving bell, the air in the top keeping the water from rising around the diver's face. I confined my requests for instructions from Watkins to the single one of what he wanted me to do when I got to the bottom. "Just walk around a little and get used to the suit," he said.

This took more out of me than I would have cared to admit after I found myself once more standing on the ocean floor, gazing rigidly forward. After a while I got enough control of myself to steal a look to the side. What I saw startled and amazed me. I was in a coral wonderland of strange shapes and brilliant colors. Gradually I became more curious than scared. I let go of the descending line and slowly began walking, learning to lean into the water, as in walking against a high wind. Except for some small fish as on the day before, I seemed to have things to myself, and I proceeded with growing boldness, ignorantly unmindful of the snags and corners that could foul my lines.

When I had gone some sixty feet, I came to a pair of coral mounds, standing like a gateway to new wonders beyond. I walked between them, and as I did so, a shadow drifted across my path. I retreated like a housebreaker who suddenly discovers he is not alone. As I turned to go, I looked into the face of an enormous fish, inches away. He was hanging in the water like a moored airship, with myself the mooring mast, and he seemed about as big, reaching back out of sight. He was staring at me through eyes the size of chow plates, and slowly opened and closed his mouth, which was wide enough to take me in at one gulp.

As I stood staring back, the fish slowly drifted backward, widening the gap between us. I was starting to unfreeze when the drifting reversed and the fish began to come forward again. I stopped breathing. The fish came so close that my entire outlook on the world was confined to a panorama of teeth. He kept coming until he touched my helmet. Then he shot backward and disappeared so fast he roiled the water around me. Apparently there was something about the feel of metal that offended him. I took a deep breath that nearly brought the water up to my mouth. What kind of fish he was I never knew.

I hurried back to my descending line, lying forward into the water almost horizontal to make time. When I got there, I gave four powerful tugs on the line. I wanted to go up at once, even though my hour wasn't finished and this would lose me the dive. I received four jerks back, approving my request. Then came a single tug, asking if I was all right. By now I had got hold of myself and I replied with a single pull of my own, meaning everything was fine. But the adventure was all gone from me, and I returned to my cigar-store Indian stance by the line for the rest of my hour on the bottom.

When at last I got back to the top, I found the crew bursting with excitement. Watkins asked, "Did you see something unusual down there?"

"Why?" I asked shiftily.

"Well, you gave us four tugs on the line," Watkins reminded me.

"I thought it was time to come up," I said.

Watkins was relieved. "I'm glad to hear you didn't see anything," he said. "We saw a bunch of sharks swimming around the boat. We thought they might be bothering you."

I then told about my meeting with the big fish, and I was a hero all over again. Watkins gloated. "I told you they wouldn't bother you, didn't I?"

Back on the *Savannah* that night the story of my dive flashed around the ship, picking up embellishment as it went. It took only a few relays of the tale to have me deliberately diving into the presence of sharks, defiantly glaring back at death on the bottom, and finally coming up with my knife unsheathed, challenging any shark to come near me. Nor did this illusion of derring-do lose anything from my refusal to tell of my adventures firsthand, indifferently shrugging them off as nothing.

My final two dives were uneventful and I became a full-fledged diver, second class. The captain extended congratulations, and my standing as a brave man was secure. Much of the credit, however, should really have gone to Turret Captain Watkins; he had talked me into wearing the suit, and personally broken trail for me in the water, making his point about the dietary inclinations of sharks and barracudas.

"So now you're a deep-sea diver, too," remarked a sailor one day, eying my new insignia. He read off the markings crowding my sleeve. "Qualified diver, qualified gun captain, qualified pointer, qualified small arms . . . Boy, you sure are qualified!" he exclaimed. Whereupon I was of course nicknamed Qualified. "Yeah, we know you're qualified," I would hear whenever I spoke up on practically any subject.

I went on diving for the next couple of years, going down hundreds of times. I was then asked if I wanted to make a full-time job of it, dropping my regular duties as a gunner's mate. The Navy was anxious to advance diving beyond its then experimental state and wanted twelve or fifteen of us for special training in the field. There could be no extra inducements—only the wish to get into the work for its own sake. It was 1940. War was in the air. War meant sunken ships, and sunken ships meant sunken treasures—the dream of every diver. I became the quota of one from the cruiser battle force, and along with the ten others the Navy had been able to round up in three or four months, was enrolled at the Navy's Deep Sea Diving School at Washington, D. C.

For a fellow who hadn't planned to get into the Navy, I was getting in pretty deep.

3. Death Presses Down

"You know what to do," said Chief John Lavesque gruffly as the crew finished dressing me. "So go down there and do it."

We were on a sound barge tied up in the Anacostia River, near the Navy's underwater sound laboratories, in Washington, D. C. With three wells extending down through it, the craft was used to test sonar equipment. The equipment was mounted in the wells, and after each test, before a new piece could be installed, the well had to be emptied of water. The usual procedure was to seal it from the bottom and pump it dry. My job on this occasion was to seal the after well. As Chief Lavesque said, I did know what to do—we divers from the Navy's Deep Sea Diving School nearby had done the chore many times. But there was something new I would know when I got through, one of the best lessons of my schooling: Don't get cocky because you've done a thing before.

The crew slid me feet first into the middle well. This was the best way to reach the well to be sealed, since the barge lay sandwiched between the river piling on one side and our diving boat on the other. In a moment I was on the bottom, sitting in soft mud studded with rock and pieces of scrap iron.

31

Directly above, a few inches from my head, the well outlined a dull halo from the light showing faintly through the murky water, while out to the sides all was total blackness. To make sure of my bearings, I ran a hand over the bottom of the barge and found a seam in the steel plates. With this to guide me, and digging my feet and elbows into the mud, I propelled myself backward, squidlike, to the well I was to close.

Sitting under it, I felt out the cover plate, carried at the side of the opening. With my lug wrench I removed the bolt holding it and swung the plate under the hole, blocking out my last thin bond with the daylight world above. I began fishing bolts one by one from my tool bag, resting in the muddy darkness at my side, and putting them in place over my head, working by touch.

The work went smoothly. The coating of preservative smeared into the boltholes to prevent corrosion when the well was opened was still good, allowing the bolts to turn easily. The water gave buoyancy to my arms, and as I leaned back a little each time I reached up, I felt a support behind which I took to be my lifeline and air hose.

As I worked, Skill, my telephone man, heckled me from above. "Silly Skilly" we called him, because of his quick laughter.

"How're you doing?" Skill would say every few moments, his friendly twang mixing with the whistling roar of the air entering my helmet and the bubbling at the exhaust valve. He was trying to relieve the feeling of isolation that a man often gets on the bottom.

By my answers I told of my progress and the state of my spirits. "Ten more bolts to go," I replied at one point.

"Well, speed it up," Skill said, keeping the conversation going.

"What do you think I'm doing down here—looking for mermaids?" I shot back.

Suddenly I noticed that the barge was no longer at arm's

length above me, but in front of my face, inches away. "That's funny," I mumbled.

"What's funny?" Skill asked suspiciously.

"Nothing—just checking," I said. I ran a hand over the bottom of the barge again. *It was parallel to my body! I was lying flat on my back!* Without knowing it, I had leaned farther and farther back until I was now stretched out like a man working under a car.

"Hey, this barge is sinking!" I yelled.

"What'd you say?" Skill asked.

"This barge is sinking!" I repeated.

There was no answer for a while. Then Skill said, reassuringly, "Nah, everything's all right up here, Karneke. Go to work."

"Go to work, hell!" I yelled back. "Get me out of here! I tell you, this barge is sinking!"

Another silence followed. Finally Skill said, tightly, "Be calm now, Karneke. The barge isn't sinking, but—the tide's going out."

Now I remembered. In our cocksureness about the job, we hadn't bothered to check the tide before I went down. The support I had felt behind as I worked had not been my lifeline but the surge of the outgoing current. I was stung by a warning often heard at divers' school: The penalty for carelessness is death.

Skill's voice drilled back into my ears. "Don't get excited he said. "We're going to pull you up." After a moment, he added, "Stand by to come up!"

"Ready to come up," I said, making the standard response. I felt the lifeline tug at my breastplate.

"Can you feel us pulling?" Skill asked.

"Yes, but I'm not moving."

"You sure you're not moving?" Sometimes the diver can't tell because of the darkness or the slowness of the movement.

But I was sure. By now the 500-ton barge was resting on

my helmet and breastplate, pinning me against the bottom of the river. "Not an inch," I said.

Skill sounded a little plaintive. "Well, we can't pull any harder," he said. "We're afraid we'll part the lifeline."

This shook me. The lifeline could take a pull of 1,500 pounds. Now I knew I was in real trouble.

"What are you going to do?" I asked.

"Take it easy," Skill said. "We got a stand-by diver up here, you know."

A minute or so passed. When Skill spoke again, there was apology in his tone. "Karneke," he said, "the stand-by diver can't do you much good. He can't get to you. Wait a minute . . ." He broke off, as if listening to a new plan being discussed by the crew. "How do you feel?" he put in shortly, keeping in touch.

"Okay, but the only thing I can move now is my arms," I said. "You better do something fast." I tried a feeble joke. "This barge isn't getting any lighter," I said, not wanting them to get panicky topside.

Skill repeated my words so I would know he had heard right. There was a pause, then he said, "The chief wants to know if you'll be all right if we move the barge."

"Just a minute, I'll see," I said. I spread my arms, feeling the bottom. "Too many rocks in this mud," I said. "They'll grind me up. Don't move the barge."

"Got you—don't move the barge," Skill repeated.

Maybe I had only made a bad horse trade. The 500 tons were riding down harder by the minute.

"Take it easy," Skill called. "We're going to try to wash you out with the tunneling hose." The hose shoots a jet of water through a nozzle at pressures up to 750 pounds.

"How're you going to do it?" I asked, having in mind the piling on one side of the barge and our diving boat on the other.

"We'll move the diving boat and have the stand-by diver come in with the nozzle from the side," Skill explained.

This would take quite a while, I reflected. With the barge forty feet wide, a tunnel to where I lay under the middle would be twenty feet long. And it would need to be deep enough so that the tunneler could stand up in it. The job could hardly be done in less than an hour. Meanwhile, the tide would not be waiting. As it moved out, I would have a lot of ways to die. As the barge pressed me deeper into the ooze, the rocks could punch up through my mattress of mud and break my back. My helmet and breastplate, made of spun copper and brass, were not intended to support 500 tons. If they collapsed, I would be crushed and drowned at a stroke. Morbidly I wondered if I would feel my bones cracking before the water finished me off. Then too, it was getting time for the afternoon breeze to come up. This would make the water choppy, causing the barge to bobble, pounding me to a pulp. My air could be cut off as the sinking craft pinched the hose against a rock, causing my suit to fill with carbon dioxide from my breath, killing me in about twelve minutes.

There was a good chance, too, that the tunneler would miss me. Working in this darkness, he would have no sense of direction. How easy it was to miss had been impressed on me in an experience of my own a month earlier. I had tunneled under a pier to cut off an old piling, and was ready to start sawing when I discovered I had made a U-turn and was about to cut a piling near my starting point.

Out of these gloomy thoughts an idea sprang. I felt my life-line, making sure I could still reach it. Then I said, "Hey, Skill, how about tying the tunneling hose to the lifeline, dropping the nozzle down the middle well, and letting me pull it toward me?" That way the nozzle was sure not to go astray, and the digging would be done faster because the distance was shorter.

Skill repeated the suggestion. "Wait," he said. In a moment he was back. "The chief thinks that's a good idea," he said. "We'll let you know when to start pulling."

Minutes passed while the tunneling nozzle was being lashed

to my lifeline. As I lay waiting in the blackness, being mashed deeper into the mire, the steady whistle of the air coming into my hat was joined by a strangling sound at my exhaust valve. The vent, located toward the back of my helmet, at the neck, was being choked off by the encroaching mud. To give the exhaust air another way to get out, I reached for the hand-operated spit cock, at the lower left side of my face. It was jammed hard against the underside of the barge, its handle immovable. The vision of death by carbon dioxide poisoning came closer. So did death of another kind—my breastplate was beginning to sag against my chest. Any moment it could collapse like an eggshell.

Before me drifted scenes of the airy spaces of the farm at Cherry Valley. As a boy I had learned something from my father which helped me when I was scared. Meeting the first tractors in the neighborhood as he drove the team, my father would calm the horses by saying, "Steady, boy." When I was caught in the dark on my way home from an errand to the crossroads store, I called on the words as I passed the graveyard. "Steady, boy," I would breathe to myself. Now, lying spread-eagled on the bottom of a river with the weight of two locomotives on top of me, I said the words again, "Steady, boy."

Skill's voice broke in. "Okay, stand by," he called, "we're dropping the nozzle in the hole with full pressure. Start pulling."

I pulled. Nothing moved. I pulled again. Still no movement. "I can't seem to get any slack," I said.

"Just a minute," Skill answered. "The line is probably pinched under the edge of the well." He paused. "We'll try to wash some of the mud away at the bottom of the hole by swishing the nozzle around a little."

I held the line taut. Suddenly I felt it give. "It's moving!" I cried. Then it stopped. The line jumped again. It kept moving a few inches at a time, my hopes soaring and dying with the stops and starts.

In my mind's eye I could see the thundering nozzle at work somewhere in the murk beyond my feet—meeting rocks, blowing out the mud around them, then blasting away the loosened rocks themselves, and moving on. Would there be rocks pressed so hard by the sinking barge that they wouldn't move? The answer came as I began to feel the water being churned by the jet shooting from the nozzle. I heard pebbles bouncing off my helmet and felt them pelting my bare hands. Then, at a final heave from me, the nozzle burst through to my feet, wrapping me in a storm of swirling water, mud and stones. I groped through the boiling darkness and caught the nozzle by the neck. "Okay," I yelled, "I got the nozzle. I'm going to try to blast myself loose."

Skill called back, "Easy now. Can you untie the nozzle from the lifeline?" This was necessary so that the crew could haul back the accumulation of lifeline that had piled up by me as I pulled the nozzle toward me. It is always well to take up slack lifeline at once, before it fouls. This danger was especially strong here, because of the rock and debris.

"Wait," I said. I clawed at the rope binding the nozzle to the lifeline. "It's too tight," I said. My problems were not over.

"Can't you cut it?" Skill asked.

"If I can reach my knife," I said. By twisting my body to the left, and digging rock out of the way with an elbow, I managed to get my hand turned in to the knife at my belt. I gave the handle the three or four turns that unscrewed the knife from the sheath. "I got it," I said as I drew the blade out and eagerly started to cut.

"Be careful!" Skill warned. "Don't cut your lifeline." Where a diver can't see, this can happen. I slowed down.

"Okay," I called when I had finished. "Take up the lifeline!"

As the line began snaking away in the darkness, I freely maneuvered the watery tornado spewing from the nozzle, directing the stream toward my underside. Slowly, I sank away from the barge like a loosened stone. The lifeline went taut as the last of the slack was taken up, and I felt a slight pull on my body. "I'm moving!" I called.

"What'd you say?" Skill demanded.

"I'm moving—keep pulling!" I shouted.

Feet first, I slid along the trench blasted out by the nozzle, toward the center well and its promise of freedom. It was still only a promise, however, for the rocks in the trench banged against my helmet and raked at my suit as I passed. If they tore through or I was wedged among the rocks, I could drown.

"Okay, Karneke, we can feel your feet," Skill said presently. "We're going to pull you up."

One of the crew had gone down into the well to guide me home. I felt him pick up my heavily shod feet and direct them upward. Other hands grabbed them from above, and in a moment I stood on the deck, helmet off and squinting in the light.

Chief Lavesque tried hard to hide his feelings as he eyed me up and down. With mock rage, he roared, "Goddammit, Karneke, how many times I gotta tell you I don't want you coming up feet first?"

I only grinned and looked around, wondering how such a gray day could be so bright.

4. Pearl Harbor

When the fire and smoke were gone after the attack on Pearl Harbor, the hope slowly began to stir that maybe things weren't as bad as they looked. At Berth F-6, outboard of the battleship *Tennessee,* sat the *West Virginia.* She rested on the bottom, but except for listing a little to port, dipping her main deck into the water on that side, she looked normal. There was no damage to her superstructure. From a distance, if one didn't look too long, she gave the impression of merely riding a little low in the water. Perhaps the hole that let the water into her was small. This could be patched, and then all that would be necessary to get the *West Virginia* back afloat was to pump her out.

At the time of the attack, I was attached to the submarine escape training tower at Pearl Harbor, as instructor and deep-sea diver, and it fell to me to go down and have the first look at the *West Virginia*'s injuries. On the theory that the hole in the battleship was probably on her port side, since she listed in that direction, I made my dive on that side. All at once, as I slid down her steel skin amidships, there was no more side to her; I was dangling in space. Why, I couldn't see. I went on to the bottom, plumping into deep mud. In the darkness I held out my arms in the direction the ship should be. There was nothing. I took a few steps in the same direction—still nothing. When I had gone far past the point where the side of the ship would have to begin if it was there, I called topside, asking if I was headed the right way. "I can't find the ship," I explained, silly as it sounded to be saying that you couldn't find a 33,000-ton battleship that had been under your backside a moment before.

"You're headed all right," said the phone man. "Your bubbles disappeared inside the ship."

It dawned on me that there was a big hole in the side of the vessel, and that I had walked through it without knowing it. I kept going until I banged into something. "I finally feel some wreckage," I reported. "I'll back out, and while I'm doing it, you slowly pull up on the hose, so we can get some idea how far in I am."

This procedure showed that I had penetrated the ship by about thirty-five feet, meaning that everything in this area had been blown away. I began to grope my way up and down the side of the ship, trying to establish the dimensions of the opening. "Looks like this ship hasn't got any side," I said as I kept wandering in empty darkness.

"What do you mean—no side?" said the phone man skeptically.

"All I'm finding is a hole," I said. "There's no sides to it."

"Keep looking," said the phone man.

My hand swiped against the jagged edge of a torn steel plate. I felt it carefully, making sure that this marked one limit of the ship's wound. Then I turned and moved off in the opposite direction to find the other side of it. I kept going so long that when I finally came to it I was afraid I might have gone astray in the darkness, ending up where I started. If this was all hole, it was enormous—far bigger than the thirty feet or so ordinarily ripped out by a torpedo.

Next day two of us went down and measured it with a tapeline, one of us holding the tape at one side of the opening while the second man carried the line to the other side. The hole was 105 feet long. On the up and down, it was thirty-six feet. We repeated the measurements several times to make sure. How the Japanese had managed to open a gash of these dimensions we learned as we explored the cavity blasted inside the ship. They had done it with five torpedoes, as neatly spaced as stitches. We found the afterbody of one torpedo in the ship's hold. It showed that they had been driven by a reciprocating engine, unlike our own, which were propelled by a steam turbine. This was a jarring discovery. It was our first inkling that the Japanese weren't copying our torpedoes but were originating their own designs. That they also knew how to use them was mutely told by the evidence all over the harbor.

The discovery of what the Japs had done to the *West Virginia* banished the vision of a quick and easy job of getting her back afloat and spelled out the magnitude of the work ahead at Pearl Harbor. The *West Virginia* would need a whole new side before she could be refloated. This was a shipbuilding operation, something well beyond the scope of ordinary salvage work.

Grim as things were, the times were not without moments of humor. Some of the experts rushed out from the States were slow to accept the information we divers brought up and had us go down again. It wasn't always clear what, specifically, they wanted us to do—or easy to get them to tell us. A few days after we brought up the bad news about the *West Virginia*, we were called back to do some more diving on her. Arriving early, we had Tex Rutledge dressed and waiting to make the first dive when the experts came alongside our boat and busily jumped aboard.

"What are you waiting for?" demanded the head expert. "Why haven't you started diving?"

"We're waiting to find out what you want the diver to do," I explained.

He gave me a look of disdain and swept an arm over the

harbor. "When you look around you here," he began in a speech-making tone, "you see nearly the whole United States fleet sitting on the bottom—and you want to know what to do!" He paused dramatically. "It should be pretty obvious," he went on. "It's to get these ships up!"

I turned to the diver, still sitting on the stool. "Okay, Tex," I said, "you heard your instructions."

"Yeah, but what you want me to do?" Tex asked, keeping his seat.

"We'll put you in the water," I said. "Maybe when you get to the bottom somebody will think of something."

We tested his phones and put him over the side, where he quickly vanished in a froth of bubbles. "Okay, I'm on the bottom," he reported in a couple of minutes, his Texas accent floating out over the speaker. "What you-all want me to do?"

I turned to the visitors. "You heard what the diver said. What do you want him to do?"

"What does a diver normally do when he's down?" parried the chief expert.

"He works."

"Well, tell him to go to work."

I walked over to the phone booth and called down, "Tex, go to work."

"Doing what?" Tex persisted.

"The ship is sitting on the bottom," I pointed out. "We got to get it up. Go to work."

There was a short silence. "Okay, going to work," said Tex. Several moments passed, and then came a series of agonized grunts and groans from the bottom.

I called down with alarm, "Tex, are you all right?"

"Sure, I'm all right," he inserted between the sounds of labor.

"What are you doing?" I asked.

"What you-all think I'm doing?" Tex demanded. "I'm in under this battleship and I'm lifting." The straining noises went on. "Can you see if she's coming up any?" Tex panted.

Our experts looked at one another, then scrambled back aboard their own boat. As they pulled away, one called back, with a little grin, "You men just go ahead and do what you always do."

For us this marked the end of the don't-just-stand-there-do-something approach to the Pearl Harbor problem.

On the *Utah* our instructions were particularly explicit. When the attack came she had just arrived from the States with a load of ammunition for the fleet, tying up at Berth F-11 on the west side of Ford Island. She had caught three torpedoes in her port side, and turned turtle outboard. She lay with her belly to the sky like a huge dead fish. Our orders were to get the five-inch antiaircraft shells out of her as quickly as possible. The enemy was expected back any moment for another strike. Those ships that sat with their super-structures above water, like the *West Virginia,* could still shoot.

The job of recovering the *Utah*'s ammunition started out fast. Since her magazines were at the bottom of the ship, her upside-down position put them on top, just inside the ship's shell. We cut a hole in the shell, climbed through, and found ourselves in a trunk in the middle of the magazine area. At the first magazine we came to we cut the lock off the door, pushed it open, and within minutes were hoisting out the ammunition. We could send it up only a round at a time but each shell, weighing about a hundred pounds, could be the one that knocked down a returning Japanese plane.

The next day we ran into problems. The magazine area was laid out in a honeycomb pattern, with the doors arranged for maximum strength and use of space, and the door to the next magazine was on a different side, with the ammunition piled against it. The only way to get into this one was to cut a hole in the magazine bulkhead. This hole would be a lot harder to make than the one in the bottom of the ship, because now we would be working under water and in darkness.

We broke out an underwater cutting torch and started to

get it ready. "Wait a minute!" said a sharp-witted sailor. He pointed to the NO SMOKING signs all round. "If we can't smoke, how the hell can you light that thing?"

This was a good question and we gave it a great deal of thought. To put a torch through a bulkhead at a point where high explosives lay flush against the other side—and this amid several hundred tons of it—seemed one of the less attractive ways of proceeding. In place of the torch we decided to use an air drill, making a series of perforations around a circle and then knocking out the center. The air drill had worked well in cutting the opening in the bottom of the ship, but under water we found this method much too slow. In a half day of sweating and straining I managed to bore only two holes, and these, because I couldn't see, were hardly related to each other. As somebody remarked, "Christ, at this rate the war could be over before we got an opening big enough for a man to go through."

After much palaver, with an eye cocked to the sky for Japanese planes, the command agreed to take a calculated risk—to put us to work with the torch. After all, three thousand men already were dead. Many more could be killed in a return attack unless we were able to beat it off. The work force was cut to a minimum, with no more than two divers and three helpers on hand at a time. Everyone else—the twenty or thirty who normally stood by to receive the ammunition, plus advisers and assorted others—were cleared far out of the vicinity, and patrols were set up to keep it isolated.

Although nobody asked us, Tex Rutledge and I assumed we were the "volunteers" for the first turn at the torch. I went down first, Tex tending me from topside. The bubble formed at the tip of an underwater cutting torch explodes at irregular intervals, giving the effect of sporadic gunfire. At each pop, as I stood in the darkness holding white heat against a roomful of high explosives, I died a little. After an hour, I was happy to hear Tex on the phone, saying, "Why don't you come up and relax awhile, and let me take over?"

I thought Tex was being bighearted until I began to hear the popping of the torch as he went to work in my place. Then I realized that the suspense topside was even worse than below. Each pop could be the prelude to the big one—a shell exploding, which would set off the entire load of ammunition. After about the second bang, I couldn't help phoning Tex and asking if he was all right.

"Sure, I'm all right," he replied.

"With all that banging from the torch, I can see why you wanted to dive," I needled.

"What're you straining for up there?" Tex retorted. "You're sitting nice and safe topside, and you always said the diving was the dangerous part."

Tex got the hole finished and came up just before our nerves gave out. We counted it much in our favor that he had found heavy cork insulation lining the inside of the magazine, to help keep the room at an even temperature. The cork took up the heat from the torch before it could get to the explosives packed against it.

With the new magazine opened, we divers went prowling the black, water-filled interior of the *Utah,* preparing the way for further recovery of her explosive cargo. All went well for a couple of days, then a 1,000-pound armored hatch fell on me deep inside the ship, pinning me to the deck. As the vessel had turned over, many of the pins in the hinges of her doors and hatches had fallen out, leaving only the latches and dogs to hold them in place. As we removed these fastenings in our progress through the ship, doors slid from their upright positions; hatches, now on the bottom side of the decks instead of on top, fell away. Unfortunately, I was thinking about something else—possibly how good things were in the bright, sunlit world above—when I invited the accident.

The hatch was directly over my head, and I wanted to get into the compartment above. I ran my fingers around the edges and over the surface, determining that the hatch was big and that it was armored. Then I carelessly undogged this half-ton slab of steel, and a moment later I was lying pinned under it. My helmet was bent, and from the way it felt some of me was getting bent, too, if not broken. I gaspingly told the phone man what had happened.

"This is no time for comedy, Karneke," he scolded. "Get to work."

He couldn't know how truthfully he spoke. It was several minutes before my groaning and cussing finally persuaded him that I might be in some kind of minor trouble. He sent a man down to lift the hatch off, ignoring my protests that if one man could lift it I wouldn't need help. After my rescuer had failed, a heavy line was threaded down through the maze of passages that led to my entrapment, and made fast to the hatch. A big crew hauled on the line from above. Slowly the load lightened, and I squirmed free. I had been under the hatch for two hours, but aside from a few bruises I was none the worse for the experience.

"One of these days," said a philosopher after I was back in daylight, "you divers are going to tempt fate once too often."

I shook my head. "I don't think so," I said.

"How do you figure you keep having these narrow escapes and getting away with it?" he asked. "You must be a fatalist."

I denied it. I don't believe that the things which happen to one are predetermined. I was caught under the hatch because I was careless. For days we had been learning that the hinge pins were out of the doors and hatches, and yet I had acted as if I didn't know it. There are no fatalists among divers who have been at it awhile. They have learned that fate favors those who keep their guard up. The fatalists are soon buried.

The *Utah* continued to keep us occupied. Once we had opened the way to her ammunition cargo, we received word that she also carried $65,000 in unmarked money. We were asked if we would be interested in trying to find it and replied with inner stirrings that we would be glad to, trying to sound accommodating. While we waited for the paymaster to bring us the combination to the safe, we went on diving, but our minds were occupied with financial calculations. We wondered how much money from a safe containing $65,000, unmarked, a careful, competent diver would be able to bring up without a loss. Twenty-five thousand dollars? Certainly not more than $35,000.

Then, when the paymaster arrived, he asked if we could bring up the safe itself, unopened. We looked at one another. "It probably can be done," we agreed doubtfully. "But it's going to be tough."

"How can you know that so fast?" the paymaster demanded. "You don't even know where the safe is. You don't know the size—or anything about it. And still you know right away that you can't bring it up."

"We've had experience with safes before," we said darkly. "They're usually bolted to the bulkhead—there're a lot of problems."

The paymaster took a new tack. "I've been told," he said pointedly, "that when you divers open a safe on the bottom, very little of the money ever gets to the top."

We expressed indignant surprise, silently wondering what Judas he had been talking to.

"I understand you have a going rate of about ten cents on the dollar," the paymaster went on. He paused meaningfully, then produced a slip of paper. "This is your authority to bring up the safe," he said.

I leaned over and with a darting eye tried to rake a combination from it, but there was nothing—only the name of the salvage command and authorization to go to a new area of the ship and recover the safe.

Locating the safe was no problem. As for getting it out, we were easily able to make a plausible case for the impracticality of doing it. The safe weighed no less than a thousand pounds, we estimated, and it was bolted to the bulkhead with what we saw as unusual complexity and permanence. Finally, the safe stood below several decks and beyond a great labyrinth of passageways. All this we reported to the paymaster, our faces shadowed with doubt.

"Well, okay," he said disappointedly. "I'll inform them of your report."

That appeared to end the matter, and we went on to other work, cherishing the hope of coming back to the *Utah* on our own one day when the winds blew fair. A few weeks later, when the harbor had filled with all sorts of salvage crews from the States, we noted in passing near the *Utah* one morning that a diving boat sat alongside her. We went over and were further disquieted to find our old paymaster friend on hand, along with several officers. Mustering a tone of neighborly inquiry, we asked what was going on. They were making another attack on the safe, we were told. They had burned a hole in the side of the ship, and even as we watched they slid the safe through the opening and put it on their boat.

"I guess you old-timers aren't the experts you thought you were," commented some smart aleck in the new crew. "You see, we didn't have any trouble."

As we pulled away, Tex Rutledge mused sourly, "These guys may be pretty good divers, but they sure wouldn't look good in a crap game."

Actually, what Tex implied existed mostly in the diver's private dream world. We rarely found money, but the vision of finding a golden pile was always with us, and if it ever came true, we meant to be sensible about it.

Meanwhile, those less upright of character than ourselves spread the rumor that the divers were making a killing, giving away what they would do in our place. They said we were looting the lockers and even the dead as we prowled the sunken ships. This slander grew indirectly out of another rumor: that the government was reimbursing everybody for any losses in the attack on Pearl. It is accepted that a sailor is broke until his ship sinks, whereupon he turns out to have been rich, carrying most of his wealth aboard the ship that sank. But the prosperity that had prevailed in the Pearl Harbor fleet was remarkable. Never had so many sailors owned so much money. Lockers with $500 or a thousand dollars in them were the rule. When none of this wealth was found, the divers were blamed for it.

The complaints got so bad that we welcomed a new procedure, laid down by the salvage command. For each locker we were given a mailbag. Into this we packed all the locker's contents. Then we drew the drawstring tight, put a knot in it, and sent the bag up. Topside, a couple of officers of certified integrity opened the bag, took out everything of value and put it into an envelope marked with the identity of the owner as found in his effects, along with the name of the diver who had opened the locker. Later, when and if the owner was found, the contents of the envelope were checked with him. Typically, they consisted of a picture of the high school girl friend, a bill from a credit jeweler, and a letter from Mom.

If there was money, it never ran above ten or fifteen dollars. This the owner usually gave to the diver as a reward, in gratitude for getting back the picture of the girl friend, the bill from the jeweler and the letter from Mom. The money, water-soaked and stained with oil, had a beat-up look that plainly told where it came from. "Ah," the wise guys would say leeringly, "we know where you divers get your money." You couldn't win.

One day there was a recovery to make that involved no risk of honor. It was a brand-new kind of work for me, and eventually it would have an important effect on my career. The duty officer confronted me and said cheerily, "Well, Karneke, you're a gunner's mate. Here's a chance for you to work at your rating."

"Doing what?" I asked suspiciously.

"A destroyer over at 10-10 dock has lost a depth charge over the side. Can you go right over and take care of it?"

"Yes sir," I replied. I assumed that the destroyer had merely fumbled one while they were loading charges aboard, and that the job before us was a simple matter of going down and picking it up. When my crew and I arrived, though, we found the dock evacuated and a guard posted to keep everybody back. An atmosphere of suspense hung over the area. We pulled alongside the destroyer and I called up to her crew, anxiously gathered at the rail, "Where's the depth charge you dropped?"

"Right off the stern," someone answered. "We think it's armed."

That meant the charge hadn't been lost in loading. It had rolled off the rack on the stern, probably arming itself as it cleared the ship and fell into the water. Ordinarily, as the ship enters a harbor, the gunner puts a safety bar in place across the rack, so that if anyone presses the button to test the release mechanism—as had been done now—nothing happens; the charge rolls against the bar and stays where it is. This time the bar wasn't there. Somebody had goofed. If the charge had armed itself, the only thing keeping it from exploding was that the water apparently wasn't quite fifty feet deep, the point where depth charges are set off by pressure. How much less than fifty feet it measured wasn't known. A rising tide could make the difference.

"This should be simple for you, Karneke," hopefully said Buck Buckles, a new member of my crew, as I put on my gear. "After all, you're a gunner."

"Yeah," I said, "that's what makes it hairy—because I know if that pistol's cocked, it takes only a slight jar to set it off."

"Can't you just go down and disarm it?"

"I don't know," I muttered. "There may be a special safe procedure, but my job as a gunner's mate is to set 'em so they go off."

"What are you going to do?" Buckles asked, uneasily.

"I'll go down and tie a line to it—and hope nothing happens while I'm doing it," I replied. I jumped into the water, and in a few moments was running my hands over the surface of the charge. The two arming forks were wiped off, confirming the worst. I gingerly secured the line to a handling pad eye and returned to the boat. I called over to the destroyer that the line was in place, and that the charge was fully armed.

"We could have told you that," the destroyer men called back. "That's why we sent for you experts."

"Hear that?" said Buckles quietly. "They think we're experts."

"Just hand the line over to them," I directed, "and they'll never know the difference."

"Suppose it goes off when they start pulling?" said Buckles.

"Don't worry about it," I snapped.

The line was passed over to the destroyer crew. "Can we start pulling now?" they asked.

"Not yet," I said, holding up a hand. "We got to get the diving boat out of the way first." We moved a couple of hundred yards into the channel, and I gave the high sign to haul away.

After a minute or so, with all going well, Buckles took note of the distance between us and commented, "Now I know why you said not to worry. I'll bet these people think that depth charge was safe because you're an expert."

"Buckles, you're on your way to being an expert yourself," I said approvingly.

As I had promised, the destroyer men never knew the difference, for there was no explosion. But the experience made me decide to look into the chances of some day becoming what they thought I already was—an underwater ordnance disposal expert. Hereafter, I wanted to know what I was doing.

5. The Phantom Submarines of Pearl Harbor

During the attack on Pearl Harbor a single two-man submarine somehow got past the nets at the entrance and penetrated deep inside the anchorage. It was a neat accomplishment, undiminished by what happened to the intruder inside. As he rounded Ford Island, his conning tower cutting the water like a shark fin, the aircraft tender *Wright* put a shot through the tower. The submarine was then rammed by a destroyer, which was making a dash for the open sea. He was hit with depth charges and, completing his troubles, his two torpedoes blew up on him. The shapeless mass of metal that remained was buried in a fill.

The mystery of how the little submarine got into the harbor caused a lot of red-faced argument. There were three successive nets across the entrance: one for submarines, one for torpedoes, and third—a so-called indicator net—to give the alarm if the first two were breached. As a further precaution, no two nets were supposed to be opened at a time. When an incoming ship had passed the first net, that one was closed before the next was opened, which in turn was closed before the third was swung aside. How, then, had the submarine entered? The best answer seemed to be that it had followed a ship through the nets, hugging it close like a pilot fish with a shark.

Whatever its method, the exploit of the two-man submarine caused more jangled nerves than anything else in those jittery days after the attack, when repeat blows were expected. If one submarine could get into the harbor, it followed that more could do the same.

All that could be done, it seemed, was to intensify the vigil in the harbor itself and hope for the best. To this end, a civilian pleasure craft was hurriedly outfitted with all the latest underwater sound apparatus and assigned to a constant patrol of the harbor, keeping a technological ear to the water for any suspicious noises.

The sound boat heard little else. In fact, from the racket it picked up from the bottom, the harbor was never without two-man submarines. The sweating sound crew would make the contact as the invader bore to the right of Ford Island after entering. They would tensely follow him around the island, and as he was heading out again after having made a complete loop of the harbor, all hell would break loose as a covey of speedboats, alerted during the circuit, streaked out and hammered the water with depth charges.

When the last geyser had collapsed and some measure of calm returned, we divers went down to find the victim. We never found him. After a while this continuing failure to establish a corpus delicti began to be weighed against the disadvantages of these manic attacks on the quiet harbor waters. Each time it happened, salvage work was stopped all over the harbor, delaying by a few more hours the time when the fleet would be back afloat; and a lot of salvage divers were blown off the bottom with bleeding noses and sprained eardrums. The consensus was that these assaults were doing more harm than good. It could even be argued that the phantom submarines, in repeatedly holding up the restoration of the sunken fleet, were doing as much mischief as if they were real.

It was then decided to try alerting everybody before an attack was begun. Knowing when and where it was coming, many salvage crews would be able to keep working, and divers in exposed range on the bottom would have a chance to come up. This plan didn't work either, because it gave the "enemy" time to get away.

A third procedure was devised. This was to have the sound boat quietly mark the spot when it made a contact, then speedily round up a crew of divers and have one of them go down and tie a light line to the submarine. At the top, a buoy would be attached to the line, so that if the enemy got under way he could be followed.

For this work of belling the cat my group was selected. We had been doing harbor diving before the Pearl Harbor attack and therefore were considered to have the best knowledge of the bottom. In place of our regular diving gear, we used a shallow-water rig. This rude forerunner of today's SCUBA, or Self-Contained Underwater Breathing Apparatus, we made ourselves. Its main component was an ordinary gas mask. We removed the chemical canister and in its place attached an air hose, using standard quarter-inch pipe valve, fastened at the belt, to regulate the inflow of air. There was no need to bother about an exhaust valve. The one already in the mask worked fine under water. A lifeline to the belt completed the outfit.

This homemade rig allowed extra freedom of movement, and the mask, contoured to the face, was light and comfortable. There was only one drawback: when the air supply stopped flowing, the mask grabbed the face like a claw as the air rushed back up the hose. The suction tended to pull the eyeballs out. The countermeasure when the air quit was to rip the mask off, drop the belt and briskly head for the surface. After some of us had come up looking a little like Popeye a few times, we put a non-return valve in the hose, whereby the air could be blocked from escaping. We felt we were not overdoing the safety factor, though, in making it a rule that anyone wearing such a rig should be a good swimmer. For my own part, this I had been ever since, back on the farm, some older boys threw me into the creek, leaving me the easy choice of sinking or swimming.

Our gear was left on the sound boat, ready to throw on over our shorts or whatever else we were wearing as the boat picked us up and hurried to the scene of the contact. We wore sneakers and had it whispered into our ears up to the final moment before we went over the side to step lightly when we got down on the submarine. The Japanese were suicidal, we were knowingly reminded, and if they heard us, they were sure to blow themselves up.

Still, we found no two-man submarines. We would dive, find nothing, silently return aboard and stealthily cruise until there was another contact, dive again, and still be met only by the bare ocean floor. To us divers at least, the Japanese two-man submarine of Pearl Harbor was as mythical as the monster of Loch Ness.

Then one day the crew of the sound boat snatched us aboard with even more excitement than usual. This time there could be no mistake about it—the contact was the real thing. The sonarmen were so stirred that by the time we got to the scene, we divers were beginning to believe it ourselves, and I took special care to see that scarcely a ripple disturbed the surface as I was lowered into the water. When I was a few feet under, my line jerked in the emergency signal to come up, and I shot back to the top. "What happened?" I asked as I was mysteriously motioned back aboard.

The man in charge pressed a forefinger to his lips. "Sh-sh," he whispered. He pointed to a crewman hunched over the listening gear. "The submarine got under way. He's trying to pick him up again."

The man listening held up a hand, signaling to the helmsman to proceed slowly. We moved a few feet, and the listener signaled a stop. "Ah-ah," he breathed tensely, "they dropped a wrench."

"Shall we get the diver ready to go over again?" he was asked in a stage whisper.

He motioned for silence, then for more headway. The boat covered a half dozen lengths. Up went the hand to stop. He listened tautly a few moments, then snapped around to me. He stabbed a forefinger at the deck and commanded, as if to a Labrador retriever, "They're down there! Go get 'em!"

I slid into the water. Again, when I was a few feet down, there came the urgent jerking of the line to come up. I returned to the boat. There was more whispering, more stalking of our unseen prey to the imperious semaphoring of the man with the earphones. A third time I started down, and a third time I came back. A dozen times or more I plunged down and up.

By now the marauder below was well around Ford Island and heading back to sea. Extreme measures were in order. Harbor control was called, and in a few moments the speedboats were skittering across the area in an X pattern, flinging depth charges in all directions. Columns of dirty water, dead fish, and miscellaneous debris reared into the air, and thunder ricocheted around the cloud-ridden green hills beyond.

When peace returned, a diver remarked cynically, "There's another couple of holes for us divers to fall into." In these shallow waters, no more than ten fathoms deep, depth charges left craters on the bottom twenty to thirty feet deep. With all the blasting that had been going on, the bottom was like the pock-marked surface of the moon.

We divers were scarcely overcome with surprise when we went down to look for the remains of the victim and found no trace of him. But the crew of the sound boat was still convinced that two-man Japanese submarines were somehow getting into the harbor. The continuing contacts with the sonar gear proved it.

"How do you explain that they are able to keep getting out?" I asked.

"Simple," was the reply. "The same way they get in." What that was he didn't say.

The net tenders were being accused of laxity. "What about that submarine that got in?" they were asked each time we went through our pantomime.

"What submarine?" they would fire back. "Did you find one?"

The fixed answer to this was to throw up the December 7 attack to them. "What about Pearl Harbor?"

And the fixed comeback to this, generally spoken with out-thrust chin, was, "Yeah, what *about* Pearl Harbor?"

Things reached a climax after an urgent call one morning from the net people that something had hit the indicator net, setting off a great clanging of bells and other alarm devices. Even we divers thought we might finally have something. We instantly dropped what we were doing and hurried over on our diving boat.

"Are you sure the net isn't just fouled on the bottom?" I asked as we arrived. The net normally swept back and forth in the tide, and sometimes it caught on the rocks.

"If it's fouled on the bottom," they said, "why would it bounce up and down for about two hours?" They had tried to pull the net up but a lift of a thousand pounds hadn't begun to move it.

There seemed little doubt about it: a submarine at last. Although he was fast in the net, unable to get away, I decided to use my shallow-water gear in going down to look him over, so he wouldn't hear me. Knowing they were trapped, the two-man crew were probably ready to blow themselves up and were only waiting for a ship to come along so they could take the ship with them. I climbed warily down the net, straining to see past the ten-foot visibility limit. Soon I made out that the net had been gathered into folds and was tapering toward the bottom, with the folds enwrapping something at the base. I lowered myself a few more feet and saw that the fouled object was immense, whatever it was, reaching beyond my field of vision all around. A big chunk of scrap metal from the December 7 attack, I concluded from its grayish color. I relaxed and boldly dropped down to see if I could disentangle it, landing on the flat surface of the top. I bent over and took a handhold on a projection, only to have it slip from my grasp. Anything submerged for a time is covered with slime, so I tried again. But now, as I took hold of the object, it moved. The entire platform I was standing on felt live, twitching and shuddering underfoot. I bent close for a better look, and saw an eye the size of a mess bowl fixed on me.

I was back aboard the boat and standing among my crew mates almost before they knew what happened. I had no time for signals, emerging from the water like a wad from a pop-gun, unconcerned about relatively minor matters like the bends. "Why, Karneke, what are you doing here?" someone asked, blinking in surprise. "What happened?"

"I just saw a sea monster!" I said, breathing hard.

"Whaddaya mean, a sea monster?" he asked skeptically as the others crowded around us. "What'd he look like?"

I made a circle with my hands. "He had an eye that big," I said.

"What about the rest of him?"

"He was gray, and he covered the whole bottom," I went on.

"Cut the crap now! How could anything cover the whole bottom? How big again?"

"Well, I was standing on him and didn't know it—that's how big," I said irritably.

A school of infant hammerhead sharks filled the water alongside the boat, leading to the suggestion that what I had seen was the mother shark. This I strongly denied.

Chief Sugar Counts, in charge of the boat, took over. "Look, Karneke," he began in a troubled tone, "everybody thinks there's a two-man Japanese submarine down there. All of Pearl Harbor and maybe the whole Navy is waiting for this report. We can't just say there's a sea monster down there. We have to be a little more specific. Now stop and think— what did it look like?"

I started to repeat the description, beginning with the eye.

"Okay, so it had a big eye," Chief Counts interrupted. "What was the rest of him like?"

Again I told of standing on something gray and live, which reached out of sight all around. Chief Counts was still doubtful. "Do you want to go down and check again?" he asked.

"I don't need to," I said. "I'm already convinced there's something there, and it's not a two-man Japanese submarine."

Chief Counts turned to the rest of the crew. "Okay, who wants to make the next dive?" he asked, as if there was nothing unusual going on.

No volunteers were heard. The chief came back to me. "Well, Karneke," he appealed, "you know the conditions. Why don't you go down and take another quick look, and see if you see the same thing you saw the first time?"

I wavered. "If we send this report in the way it is," Counts pushed, "we'll be the laughingstock of the fleet."

"All right, I'll go," I said impulsively, right away wishing I hadn't. Before I could back out, the crew, with eager helpfulness, was already strapping my equipment back on. A knife was thrust into my hand.

"What's this for?" I asked.

"It's for that monster down there," they explained kiddingly.

"I don't think he'll need it," I said wryly.

On my reluctant way down, the vision of the thing I was going to meet loomed steadily in my mind. At the halfway point I decided that this trip wasn't necessary and I went back up.

"Did you see it?" Chief Counts asked as I came aboard.

"No," I said, "but it's there; I'm sure of it."

There was a conference. "Well, if that's the way it is," said Counts with resignation, "we'll just have to report that it's

some unknown object, but not a two-man Japanese submarine." He paused, looking around helplessly. "I hate to
send in this kind of report, but I guess it's the best we can
do."

Feste, a diver trainee who had been tending, stepped forward. "Say, chief," he said manfully, "would it be all right if
I went down?"

Feste couldn't have asked for promotion at a more oppor-
tune moment. "This is as good a time as any to start diving,"
said Counts, who was entitled to his opinion.

The new man was fitted with his equipment and reminded
of the emergency signal for coming up. "All set?" he was
asked.

Feste thought a moment. "I think I'd like to have a diving
knife," he said.

A diving knife is not normally carried with a shallow-water
outfit. With a saw blade on one side and a straight edge on the
other, it is not a weapon but a tool. The diver uses it
primarily to free himself when he gets fouled, and to cut
things loose sent down to him on the lifeline. Least of all is
it intended for killing sea monsters. By the time the diver got
it unscrewed from its sheath at his belt, which may take as
long as five minutes, it would be a little late, anyway.

But there was a feeling of indulgence toward Feste, and he
was handed what he wanted. He screwed the knife into its
sheath and started down. As he was disappearing from sight,
he suddenly reversed course and, without signaling, came
back up. He gestured that he wanted to be brought back
aboard.

"What's wrong?" Counts asked as he stepped onto the deck.

"I think it's better if I have the knife in my hand so it'll be
ready for instant use," he explained.

Willing hands unscrewed the knife and passed it to
him. Feste looked at the blade and made a few stab-
bing passes with it. "On second thought," he said, "how
about giving me another one, so I'll have two?"

Chief Counts hesitated. "It's going to be hard to signal with a knife in each hand," he pointed out.

"I know," said Feste, "but I think it would be better to have two."

No one was inclined to argue with him, but only to get him back into the water in a hurry before he had a change of heart. He was given the second knife and he started down once more. As he slowly sank toward the unknown enemy below, we kept track of his progress by measuring the hose being payed out. "He should be near the bottom now," somebody said after a minute or so.

The words were hardly out when Feste came blasting to the surface in a froth of bubbles. He jerked off his mask and babbled hysterically, "He's down there! He's down there!"

We dragged him aboard, and Chief Counts tried to calm him. "Steady now," he said soothingly. We patted him on the back. "Everything's okay—take it easy." He waited a little while. "Now tell us what you saw," he said.

"The biggest fish I ever saw!" Feste blurted.

"What did he look like?" Counts asked.

Feste threw up his hands, going to pieces again. "It's just the biggest—all over the bottom!" he cried.

Counts gave up. He reported that the object in the indicator net was a large fish, species unknown, and let it go at that. On our way back to the submarine base, Feste became garrulous as his fright wore off. After he had been over the ground about a dozen times, somebody asked what happened to his two knives, a point overlooked until now. "Oh, those things!" said Feste sheepishly. "I didn't get a chance to use them—so I guess I must have dropped them."

Next morning a crew with a floating crane pulled the net up. Entangled in it was a giant ray, weighing 1,800 pounds and spanning seventeen feet from tip to tip. The devilfish apparently had caught his tail in the net, then had become hopelessly fouled as he struggled to free himself, at the same time setting off the alarms that brought the submarine scare.

When I set foot on the ray's back, he was near death from exhaustion, with just enough life left to twitch a little. If I had come sooner, stepping on him while he was still strong, he very likely would have ensnarled me in the net along with him, knocking my mask off and otherwise putting me at a serious disadvantage.

. Slowly it now came to be realized that what the sound boat had been hearing in these early days of sonar was fish. The sounds they make were especially abundant in Pearl Harbor because these waters, being warm and sheltered, are a favorite spawning ground of sea life. And thus chasing phantom submarines came to an end.

6. The Shark Story

We ducked as the Beaufort swooped over us at mastheight, boring out to sea. "Looks like that fellow's trying to kill himself before he gets into the war," remarked the captain.

Our ship was the submarine rescue vessel *Chanticleer*. Launched in 1943, she was the first ship of the Navy built specifically for rescuing the crews of sunken submarines and salvaging the submarines themselves, all her predecessors having been conversions. For carrying out her primary mission, the *Chanticleer* was equipped with all the latest apparatus. Thus, we were rigged for diving at all depths, ready for anything.

Here in the peaceful waters of the Indian Ocean off west Australia, we were training with our Allies for the coming big push against the Japanese. The Beaufort, using our ship as a practice target, was making an attack run. The captain's words proved to be prophetic. As the bomber started to pull up at the end of the run, the nose suddenly snapped down and the plane dived into the sea, disappearing in a leaping curtain of water.

Port Control at Perth ordered the *Chanticleer* to make an immediate search for the lost plane and try to recover it. It was the fourth such disaster to befall the two-engine Beaufort in the past month. In each crash the pattern was the same, the plane abruptly diving to earth as the pilot pulled up after a low-level pass. The other three crashes had happened on land, the bombers exploding and burning so that there was no way of telling what caused them. Now that we had one in the water, smashed but at least not burned, maybe we could find the answer to the mystery.

As we headed for the crash area, we watched for an oil slick or some other clue to the exact spot the plane had hit. We found none. This raised a problem. We needed to know the position of the wreck within a few yards before we started diving. Looking for it after we got to the bottom wasn't practical, because of the short tether on the diver from his lifeline and air hose.

"How about putting a man part way down and towing him around on the diving stage?" I suggested. "It shouldn't take long to find it that way. The water's clear and he can see the bottom."

This procedure was not accepted practice. The diver could slip from the stage, getting a squeeze before he had time to adjust his air to the new pressure. His lines could foul on the ship's propellers. He could be snagged by a pinnacle thrusting up from the ocean floor, snapping his lines as the ship drifted on. Under the circumstances, though, it was decided to take these risks. Since they had been my idea, I was picked to take them.

I had been down about fifteen minutes, riding the stage about 100 feet below the surface, when I spotted the wreck, another thirty feet or so down. It lay scattered over a wide area, with the tail section more or less intact. Stretched out amid the pieces I could see the bodies of two of the plane's four crewmen. I reported my success topside, and a marker buoy was planted over the spot as the ship rode past. I was hauled aboard while the *Chanticleer* was quickly brought about and anchored fore and aft alongside the buoy. Then I plunged back into the water.

I slid down the line from the marker buoy, held to the bottom by a weight. Near the halfway point I resighted the wreck, some 300 feet offside from my line. I called for a recovery wire, the crew sliding it down by shackle loosely encircling my descending line. I caught the shackle in one hand and went on to the bottom. I landed behind a rise that cut off my view of the wreck, but I knew about where it was, and dragging the recovery wire with me, I backpedaled off in the general direction, casting an occasional glance over my shoulder as I went. I leaned backward to let the weight of my suit pull me along, and watched my tracks in the sandy floor to see that I kept on course. All at once the tail of the broken ship loomed over me. I passed this information up to the crew, panting from my exertions.

"Fine," came the answer. "Look for a good place to hook the wire—some place where it won't pull out."

"Just a minute," I protested. "How about letting me rest a little?"

"Okay, but we want to get hooked on as soon as we can," said the phone man grudgingly. "We don't have all day."

Suddenly, it was as if the day were already ending. A deep shadow swept over the scene, as from a cloud drifting across the sun. I leaned back and looked up through the port in my faceplate. Circling a few feet above were sharks—sharks in all directions, crowding on one another as more and more glided in from the surrounding shades. I had seen sharks before but always at a distance, and never this many at a time. They were not supposed to run in schools, but here was a whole college of them. And they were big, some the size of whales—twenty or thirty feet long. On their undersides I could see the crescent-shaped gash of their mouths, lazily opening and closing on rows of pointed teeth. These were man-eaters, the great white shark of the Indian Ocean I had heard about. When they were feeding they were said to strike at anything that moved. They had even been known to attack small boats.

I shrank down against the tail of the wrecked plane. More than at any time since I became a deep-sea diver I had that closed-in feeling. I had come a long way on that trip I wanted. Here I was, sitting on the bottom of the Indian Ocean, on the far side of the world, with an umbrella of killer sharks over my head. I sat still for a while, in the same immobile state as the time the blimp stared me in the eye in Gonaïves Bay. "Hey, there's a thousand sharks down here!" I finally managed to yell.

"Sharks—how many did you say?" asked the phone man. I repeated the figure. "You better count 'em again," he said.

"I'm not kidding!" I shouted. "There's sharks all over down here!"

"What're they doing?"

"They're swimming around." There isn't much else a shark can be doing.

"What are you doing?" was the next question.

"I'm just sitting here on the bottom."

"What are you going to do?"

"What do you think I should do?" I asked. I had never been more open to suggestions.

"If the sharks aren't bothering you, why not go ahead and hook the line to the tail section?"

I took a long look at the milling killers over me, and decided to take a chance. "Okay," I said. I stood up and warily passed the line over the fuselage just forward of the rudder. I reached under and brought the hook back, putting it over the top of the line, making it fast. The sharks kept circling, still growing in number. "What do I do next?" I asked.

"Come back to your descending line and stand by to come up," instructed the phone man.

Getting back to the surface was what I wanted most in life. But what would happen once I left the comparative shelter of the tail section, coming out in the open? On the theory that the closer I stayed to the ocean floor, like the flounder, the better, I got down on all fours and began crawling—not easy in a diving suit. If the sharks took any notice of me, I preferred not to know about it, and as I scrambled along, leaving a wake of flying sand behind, I was careful not to look over my shoulder. The three hundred feet to the descending line were the longest trip I ever made.

When I had been hauled high enough to see over the rise hiding the wreck, I saw why the sharks had left me alone. The lazy circling was over and they were attacking the dead crewmen of the plane. As the spilling blood tinctured the water they became frenzied. They whirled and dived like aircraft in a dogfight, shooting in and out of the wreck and sending shards of human flesh flying as they tore at the bodies entangled in the struts and braces. As their excitement grew, they attacked one another, the big ones devouring the little ones. Shark blood mingled with that of the dead men, turning the water red.

After a trancelike few moments, I told topside what was going on. "Okay, we're going to keep pulling you up," said the phone man. "Watch for the stage at your first decompression stop."

This was thirty feet from the surface, well away from the grim business at the bottom but still not far enough. I climbed aboard the stage, fervently wishing that I didn't have to spend about twenty minutes there to let the nitrogen bubble out of me.

"Can you still see the wreck?" called the phone man.

I squinted down into the murk and dimly made out the darting shadows of my late companions, still fiercely scrambling for the tidbits in the broken plane. "Yes, faintly," I said.

"Well, keep an eye on it," said the phone man. "It's getting late and we're going to start pulling the wreck up slowly. We'll move you up forward, so you'll be out of the way." Normally nothing is moved off the bottom so long as there is a man in the water, but this was not a normal time. "Watch the wreck as we start to pull," the phone man went on. "If it looks like the lines are going to foul you, let us know."

It wasn't fouled lines I was worried about as I was swung forward and watched the wreck dragged along the bottom to a position directly below the ship. Along with the wreck came the sharks. I sent word of this along.

"Do you think you're in danger?" asked the phone man.

"No—because the wreck is still on the bottom," I answered pointedly.

"Well, let us know when it leaves the bottom," said the phone man, reaching for something to say.

The wreck started up, and with it came the sharks, a few staying with the two bodies that had been lying clear of the plane. "The sharks are following," I said urgently. "Stop!"

"What's wrong?" asked the phone man innocently, as if I had introduced a whole new line of thought.

"The sharks are following the wreck!" I repeated. "Hold it!"

"Okay." The wreck and its swarming hangers-on stopped rising. After a few moments the phone man was back on the line. "We're going to bring you up to your twenty-foot stop," he said. I rode up the additional ten feet, where I would need to dangle another half hour. Then the phone man asked, "Is there any reason why we can't pull the wreck up now?"

"There's the same reason as before," I said testily. "The sharks are following it."

"Well, it's getting late and we want to get this wreck aboard as soon as possible," he replied.

"Yeah, but I'm worried about those sharks," I retorted, peering down at them.

There was a short delay. "We'll pull it up real slow," said the phone man. "The minute you think you're in danger from the sharks, let us know and we'll pull you out of the water."

"All right," I agreed reluctantly. "But if I holler, you better move fast." I sat down on the stage, measuring three feet by a foot and a half, and made myself as small as I could. I tucked my feet under me, my hands into my armpits, and bent my head forward. As the wreck came closer, it seemed as if the sharks had grown even wilder as the food ran out. Besides striking at the shreds of human flesh drifting like feathers in the eddying currents, they were now ferociously attacking the wreckage itself. They struck at pipes, wires—anything with blood on it. The smaller sharks were being wiped out.

Suddenly, when the wreck had reached a point about fifty feet below me, I could see that I would be caught in the sharks' traffic pattern. As they whirled around after each pass they were already coming within a few feet. In another couple of minutes the wreck would be even with me. I saw no reason to believe that the sharks then would continue to pass me up. "Better stop hoisting," I said into the phone, trying desperately to be matter-of-fact about it. I didn't want to alarm them topside by screaming, for fear they might jerk me off the stage, presenting me to the sharks like a dangling grasshopper to hungry trout. There were sharks in this outfit that could take me that easy, helmet and all. "They're getting pretty close now," I added.

"What did you say?" asked the phone man, who had had no trouble hearing me before. The wreck kept coming.

"Stop hoisting!" I yelled, giving up the pretense of calmness.

"What's wrong? What's wrong?" came the response with seeming surprise, the wreck and its orbiting sharks coming steadily closer.

I screamed into the phone. "Stop the goddamned hoisting! You want the sharks to get me?"

The wreck hung still in the water. "Well, we stopped," said the phone man blandly. "What's wrong?"

Speech had left me. The wreck was hanging nearly level

with me, and I could feel the grating rasp of live sharkskin on my suit as the sharks brushed past, threatening to knock me off my perch. I didn't dare expose my hands to hold on. Dimly I heard the phone man repeating, "Karneke, can you hear me? What's wrong? Are the sharks getting close to you?"

I made no effort to answer. Two- and three-ton sharks would be easily visible twenty feet down in this water, and I knew topside could see for themselves what was happening. All at once my paralysis passed. Finding I was still alive, I began to think I might stay alive. "Just pull the wreck the hell out of the water—all the way up," I called disgustedly. I spoke from the strength of one who knows things can't get any worse; and it struck me that once the wreck was out of the water, the sharks might go away.

After I had satisfied the phone man that he had heard right, the wreck was quickly hauled clear and swung aboard the *Chanticleer*. The sharks streaked back to the bottom, re-joining those that had stayed with what was left of the plane and the two bodies on the ocean floor. I was brought up to my ten-foot stop, and after forty-five minutes there, mostly de-voted to concentrating on the idea that the sharks would not be back when they were through on the bottom, I finished the dive.

As I sat on the diving stool being undressed the tender com-mented, "Your suit is sure wet inside. You must have been sweating quite a bit."

"Yeah, it was pretty warm," I said.

"Boy, I'm sure glad I wasn't down there!" exclaimed an eager sailor. "I'd sure be scared."

After an appropriate interval, I replied casually, "Those sharks can really be mean sometimes."

How mean was further attested next day when an-other diver, going down to recover what might be left of the late bomber crew, brought back a leg-filled boot.

But sharks were no meaner than an airplane improperly

put together. With the tail section of the Beaufort recovered for examination, the mystery of the crashing bombers was soon cleared up. A control cable to the elevator was found to have been rubbing against an adjacent structure, gradually wearing thin. Finally, under the extra strain put on the cable at the pull-up, it let go and the ship dived out of control to its doom. The Australian Government was pleased about the help we had been and sent the *Chanticleer* a letter of recommendation.

So it had been a good dive. It would help to save lives, and by affording me an intimate field study of the subject, had made us unusual authorities on the feeding habits of sharks.

7. Australian Days

Up at Exmouth Gulf, several hundred miles farther north, we made a recovery of another kind. An Australian PT-boat had caught fire and sunk a few miles offshore. Like everything else we needed to start the war rolling back the other way, PT-boats were scarce. This one in particular was valuable because it carried special equipment for use in testing torpedoes. The old torpedoes had proved embarrassingly unreliable. They ran erratic courses or thudded harmlessly against the side of the target without going off, only serving to alert the enemy. The new torpedoes being tested were retrieved by the PT-boat, which ran alongside to the end of the run, then with its special equipment reached over and fished the torpedo out of the water.

The *Chanticleer* was rigged to lift as much as forty tons, well over the weight of a submerged PT-boat, with the water helping to lift it. Since the sunken boat was sitting in only sixty feet, we decided to use our homemade shallow-water diving rigs in going down to put the lift straps under the craft.

After we had finished this job and raised the boat a few feet off the bottom, I went down to see that the straps were still securely in place; tide action, for one thing, could cause them to shift. Something seemed to be amiss. Either the boat hadn't been raised as much as we thought, or it was settling back into the sand. When I had examined the near side, I walked around the stern to the other side, trailing my air hose behind. I could find nothing wrong, and prepared to go up. I checked my air hose and saw that it had worked its way under the boat as I came around the end. I tried to whip the hose free, but it seemed to be caught on something, and there wasn't enough free hose on my side to allow me to pass around either end of the boat. I bent down to see if I could crawl underneath. This couldn't be done either, for the hose wouldn't move: the boat was practically resting on the bottom, fortunately not yet hard enough to pinch off my air. I was tethered on the ocean floor with no way to let them know topside that I was in trouble. We had arranged no hand signals for emergencies. Our only signal was the standard four pulls to come up.

I had escaped from shallow-water rigs at Pearl Harbor. I would now do it again. I gave the hose four sharp pulls that I was coming up. As the crew started to haul on the line, pulling me toward the point where the line passed under the bottom of the boat, I released my belt. I took a final deep breath, slipped off the mask and headed for the top. As I rose I was careful to exhale to prevent air embolism, or exploding lungs, as the pressure from the water eased off. I popped to the surface about fifty feet off the rail. I called to the ship, but at that moment everyone mysteriously dashed over to the far side. A few fast strokes brought me to the sea ladder and I climbed aboard, crossing the deck to see what the excitement was about. As I approached, I saw my dripping belt and mask being examined as if they were some new curiosity of the deep. "What the heck do you s'pose happened to him?" I heard the tender asking helplessly.

To the first man I came to, not yet grasping the situation, I said, "What's the trouble?"

"I guess something's happened to Karneke," he said. "They

just pulled his outfit up, and he wasn't in it." He did a double take. "Why, you're Karneke!" he exclaimed. He yelled to the crowd at the rail, "Hey, Karneke's here!"

The others turned startled faces toward me. Now they had a new mystery. If I was here, who was the man in the water? While half the group kept staring at me, the rest went back to looking at the water, as if they half expected to see somebody else come to the surface. The light came slowly as I told what had happened. Now they understood why the lines holding the sunken boat in suspension had gone slack: the tide had gone out, letting the boat down again. But Pitman was being careful. "Karneke," he said, looking me over narrowly, "if this is one of your grandstanding stunts, we ought to tie a diving weight on you and throw you back over."

Good old Pitman. We got the PT-boat up without further adventure, and it was soon back in action.

During our two years in Australia, the Aussies kept accounts well in balance with a lusty, deadpan humor that brought many laughs where there wasn't much to laugh about. In the harbor of Darwin, a fleet of eighteen or twenty Allied ships, assembled to meet an expected attack on the East Indies island of Timor, lying across the Timor Sea to the northwest, had been surprised and sent to the bottom by the Japanese. It had been a major calamity about which little was said at the time, for security reasons, although the Japanese must have known how well they had done. Working in separate sections of the big harbor of Darwin, we and the Australians both were diving on these ships. We wanted to find out exactly what happened to them, thereby hoping to learn something of value in preventing the same kind of disaster in the future. Also, the sunken ships were a hazard to harbor traffic, and there was possible salvage to think about.

It was rough work. The tides at Darwin are as great as the more famous tides at the Bay of Fundy, rising and falling fifty feet. The surging water, racing a dozen miles an hour as the sea came and went, swept us back and forth and kept the water silted up so that it was nearly as dark as night. But something else worried us, too. This was the giant jewfish, the outsize member of the grouper family. The fish lay sluggishly against the sunken wrecks, hardly bothering to move out of our way. Once, as I came down in the darkness, I landed on top of one. He took off, upending me in a tangle of lines and leaving me badly shaken. It is a poor feeling to have the bottom of the ocean move under your feet. These big fellows were supposed to be harmless, but it was felt that nothing that big, with a mouth you could walk into with your hat on, could be harmless.

A new diver who joined us, nervous to begin with because these waters were the home of man-eating sharks, sensed our uneasiness over the jewfish, suffering further damage to his morale. It got so all he talked about was the big jewfish, hoping to find out the truth about them. After a week he thought he saw his chance one evening when a crew of Aussie divers came to visit us aboard the *Chanticleer*. The shop talk hadn't gone far when the new diver asked the visitors if they had noticed the groupers.

"Yes," replied one. "They sure are big blokes, aren't they?" Not much help in that.

"Do they ever attack anybody?" our man asked.

The visitor pondered a moment, then said carelessly, "It's not known for sure that they attack divers—but there's a rumor going about that a fisherman caught one the other day with two diving helmets in 'im."

Our man was shaken. "Diving helmets!" he exclaimed. "What was he doing with diving helmets in him?"

"I don't know," said the Aussie. "I s'pose the bloomin' bloke couldn't pawse them."

In the howling laughter that followed, our man fell silent. He asked no more questions about the big fish.

Christmas of 1944 our Australian Allies took us into their confidence for a combined operation which truly tested the strength of the alliance. About a week before the holiday we tied up at a Darwin pier to burn off some steel plates which were sticking up from a nearby sunken ship. The place we occupied, forward of a supply ship just arrived, belonged to an Australian diving boat which, unequipped for the job, moved to the other side of the harbor channel. We hadn't been working long when I noticed a diver from the displaced Aussie boat standing on the pier intently watching us work. He had a wistful look about him, and after he had been there all morning, I got the feeling he wanted to say something. We exchanged shop talk, but there obviously was something else on his mind.

"What are you Yanks going to do for your holiday dinner?" he blurted finally, shifting to the other foot.

"I guess we'll have the same old thing—turkey and trimmings," I said.

"You going to have any spirits?"

I said no, but added that maybe we could get some beer at the quonset ashore where we drew occasional rations. The Aussie began to come around. "It is a bit inconvenient and stupid, isn't it?" he said. After a moment he added, "I guess your chaps could do with a bit of Scotch?"

I straightened up. "These divers," I replied, looking him in the eye, "would do anything for Scotch."

"They wouldn't consider diving for it, would they?"

"You're kidding!"

"No, I'm not pulling your leg, Yank," he said earnestly. He motioned me over toward the rail, away from earshot of the others. He pointed to the supply ship astern and in a low tone said, "They're bringing in Christmas provisions for the troops in the area. And of course there's some Scotch in the cargo. The dock workers get a bit careless at times and spill things overboard, you know. After a ship pulls out, we divers usually go in and recover it for them. They in turn show their appreciation by giving us part of it. Last Christmas we did quite well.

"Seeing you Yanks have our place at the dock, we won't have an opportunity to dive this year." He sighed heavily. "Our chaps out on the diving boat will be very disappointed."

I knew there was no liquor to be had closer than Perth, 2,000 miles away. We were in an area under strict military control, with all civilian activity at a dead standstill. "We'll be glad to help," I assured him warmly, having visions of the rewards.

His face relaxed. "Good," he said. "There'll be a dock worker around to see you."

I confided the development to Pitman and Krassic, who agreed we should keep it from the others until we had made an actual recovery. This would give us a chance to spring it on them as a surprise—besides satisfying our natural bent for secrecy. I kept an eye out for the dock worker who was to call on me, but the rest of the day passed with no sign of the emissary.

Next day the supply ship pulled out, and still no word from any of the men who had unloaded her. As the three of us who were in the know sank into melancholy, Pitman expressed all our thoughts. "Maybe the Aussies changed their minds and plan to slip in with their own diving boat in a day or two and do it themselves during the night," he said. "Why don't we cross them up as soon as it gets dark and search the whole pier area? We don't need anybody to tell us where the stuff is. We're bound to find it."

"We're bound to find it, sure," I answered. "But don't you think that's a pretty sneaky thing to do?"

"Yes," agreed Pitman soberly, "but remember, this is Scotch. It's not just buried treasure."

"You convinced me," I said, virtue going down at the first turn. Besides, if word leaked out that we had passed up such an opportunity, we would be the laughingstocks of the diving fleet. It must be done for the honor of all divers. "When it's dark, we'll get the rest of the divers down to the locker and make plans to go after it," I went on. I started top-side.

Halfway up the ladder I met the gangway watch. "There's a guy at the gangway that wants to see you," he said.

I scrambled past him and confronted the visitor, giving my name. "I'm Clarence, the dock worker," he said. "Are you the master diver?"

"Yes," I said.

He spoke into my ear. "Ned told me to get in touch with you," he muttered. "He said you'd help us out with some of the stuff that dropped overboard while we were unloading the ship."

"When do you want us to start diving?" I asked, rushing to the point.

He cast a cautious look around. "I think it would be more convenient if we waited till it got a bit darker," he said. He jerked his head in the direction of the dock. "If you'll follow me, I'll show you where I think most of the stuff fell over," he invited. He led the way down the gangplank to a point about three hundred feet astern of the *Chanticleer*. He nodded toward the water. "There should be four kyses of King George V," he said. "This would be a three-wye go—between you chaps, our own divers, and us dockers. One kyse and four bottles for each." Talking about it seemed to excite him. "How soon could you have it up?" he asked.

"I'll have to make a few arrangements," I replied slowly. We couldn't just put a diver down without a reason. We would need a cover story in case the captain got wind of the goings-on and came to investigate. "How can I get in touch with you when we're ready?" I asked.

"Have no fear—we'll be watching you, old boy," he replied pointedly.

Back in the locker room of the *Chanticleer* the secret had somehow leaked out, and the place was buzzing with talk of how to get our hands on the prize. Wisniewski had the best idea—to wait until the movie started, getting everybody back on the fantail. Then we would slip a diver over the side in a shallow-water outfit, and have the men on the pier drop him a line for the goods. For emergency there would also be a line over the rail on the far side of the *Chanticleer,* to tie the cases to, as insurance against losing them should it be necessary to interrupt the operation. At the gangway would be one of our own men, allowing the regular watch to go to the movie—the value of this being carefully weighed against the possible suspicion such an unusual kindness toward the watch might arouse. The cover story would be that the diver was looking for a lost tool.

Since the plan was Wisniewski's, he drew the glory dive. When deep night had settled and the movie had emptied the decks, he climbed silently down the ship's rope ladder and disappeared into the water. Reaching bottom, he felt his way to the pilings and by counting these as he went, knowing the distance between them, measured off the 300 feet he needed to go.

Meanwhile, to oversee the proceedings and let the Aussies know that the operation was under way, I walked along the dock to find them. As I approached, Clarence fairly leaped at me from behind a little shed. He and his friends dropped their line into the water, and in a few moments hauled up the first case. They lowered the line a second and a third time, scoring cases two and three, but at the fourth lowering of the line, it hung idly in the water. In the dim light I saw a trail of bubbles moving back toward the *Chanticleer,* indicating that Wisniewski had completed his work. I went back aboard the ship, arriving as Wisniewski popped to the surface alongside.

"What happened?" I muttered. "Didn't you find the fourth case?"

"I got it," he croaked. "It's tied on the emergency line. I thought if those Aussies tried anything funny, at least we'd have a case."

A moment after we had brought it up, an Aussie appeared

at the gangway happily perching one of the three cases from the pier on his shoulder. "Your chap seems to have missed the fourth kyse," he said. "So here's yours. One kyse even."

I quickly handed over the eight bottles which the Aussies had coming from the case in our possession, mumbling some thin excuse for having it in our hands, and trying to act as if we had meant to do this all along. He received the bottles with polite surprise—and no doubt with inner thoughts of how right Clarence had been about these sticky-fingered Yanks.

We carried our treasure down to the diving locker and there tenderly put it away in our diving suits, the diver's favorite hiding place. We wrapped the bottles in rags and slipped them one by one into the legs of the suits where they hung from the rack. Few things in their purpose come so close to perfection.

As the Aussies and ourselves had combined forces to recover the Scotch, it was decided to do the same for Christmas dinner, again with the idea that in alliance we could do better than alone. The Aussies provided the boat and the beverage, and we the turkey and trimmings, thus bringing together some of the best features of the occasion from each of our two cultures. At five o'clock, catching us with song and story at full tide, our boat arrived by prearrangement from the *Chanticleer* to take us home. Our hosts generously offered to see that those of us who wanted to stay a while longer got back, provided we agreed to do the rowing. But when we next gave thought to leaving, the tide had trapped us. If we ventured across the harbor now, the current would sweep our small boat to sea like a canoe in a rapids.

The next thing I knew, having been swept away on a sea of a different kind, I was being shaken awake by an Aussie. "I say, digger, the tide has slowed and if you're ready, we'll take you back to your ship," he was saying. The others had signaled the *Chanticleer* for a boat and gone home hours ago, he added, leaving me the only visitor left aboard. The Aussies steadied me into a skiff in the care of the man who seemed in the best condition to handle the responsibility, and we set out for the *Chanticleer*. Dimly remembering the bargain made early in the evening, I tried to give the boatman a hand with the rowing, but my co-ordination wasn't too good, and he rather sharply recommended that I use the oar only to help steer.

Coming at last to the *Chanticleer*, I caught the sea ladder and started up the side, the boatman heading about for the return trip. Halfway up the ladder, I missed my hold and fell back into the water with a noisy splash that brought the gangway watch running from the other side of the ship. It was two o'clock in the morning, and he seemed to fight the idea that someone could be threshing around in the drink at this hour. It was quite a while before he realized that in my flailings I was trying to catch the ladder and he lowered it all the way to the water. As I presently stepped over the side, he asked, his mouth sagging open, "What happened to you?"

"I slipped off the ladder—what the hell do you think!" I snapped peevishly, letting it go at that.

Next day the story ran around the ship that I had swum home from the Aussie diving boat, besting one of the strongest tides in the world. Nonbelievers were converted by the gangway watch, who told how he had lowered the ladder to me as I completed the feat. For a long time after that, at all discussions about the Darwin tide and the fate that was sure to overtake any man who tried to swim it, there would come a head-shaking silence as someone recalled, "That master diver did it."

"Not only that," it would be added with desperation, "but he did it when he was drunk!" Then would follow a rehash of the events of Christmas night. Legends alone may not make heroes, but they help.

An officer, hearing about the "swim," observed seriously, "It's time we got Karneke out of Australia. He's trying to kill himself." He spoke of my encounter with the shark circus in diving on the crashed Beaufort.

For quite different reasons, there were those who felt that it was also in the captain's interest to move on. The things he had been up to were hardly more believable than my tidal swim. The skipper was a dignified, mild-mannered, respected Southerner who seemed to have none of the usual frailties. Then it came out that while we were in Perth, he had been loose on a sheep ranch and allegedly had dallied with three women in the same family. Looking back on the affair, a fellow Southerner whose protégé the skipper had been, commented sadly, "Lawrence was such a nice fellow but he went hog-wild. He was a disgrace to the South."

When we stopped in at Darwin for supplies on our way to the Philippines, we found that our skipper's reputation had preceded him all the way from Western Australia. We held a going-away party on board for our Aussie friends, and next morning as we were pulling out, none too sharp from the night before, port control signaled us by blinker, "What is your hoist?"

This was a curious thing to ask. We had been cleared to leave—and we had been around long enough to know all about clearance flags. There was a different one for every hour, identifying the ship and indicating permission to go.

"What is your hoist?" the blinker repeated.

We blinked back, "We're flying the proper clearance flag for the day and hour of sailing." The blinking continued. The duty quartermaster was checking with the code book to make sure, when the blinker commanded, "Lay to!" Next would be a shot across the bow. Somebody then had the bright idea simply to look up and see what the flag was. What he saw was no flag at all. In its place the mischievous Aussies had bribed the crew to put up a symbolic tribute to the captain, still peacefully asleep in his emergency cabin off the bridge. The symbol was that well-known item of the nursery—a bassinet.

8. Death in a Recompression Chamber

Heavy work awaited us when we reached the Philippines. Our job: to recover the anchors and chains from some of the ships sunk in Subic Bay during the reinvasion at this point a couple of months before. Anchors and chains were scarce in the area, and while there were plenty in the States, the time of shipment presented an insurmountable problem. A ship's anchor weighs five to ten tons; a single link of the chain that goes with it, up to 150 pounds. That kind of load couldn't be put aboard airplanes, but had to be sent by ship. So we went about our work little suspecting that for the first time our group was marked for tragedy. The first ship we dived on, about a half mile offshore, was a former British freighter. The Japanese had captured her at Singapore, indicating the new management by simply inverting the name plate and putting on their own, *Yama Buki Maru*. In a preliminary look at the sunken vessel, Pitman discovered some strange white material lying loose in the hold. He sent up a sample in a mailbag, thereby causing a delay in getting after the anchors as the amateur chemists aboard the *Chanticleer* gathered to speculate on the nature of the stuff. It was granular to the touch and had a strong fishy smell. Decomposed rice? Artificial rice? Processed seaweed? The more pessimistic suspected it was some kind of explosive.

The captain ended the confab by ordering the sample sent off to Naval Intelligence for analysis (which in due course showed it to be ground fish meal). "Okay, Karneke," he said briskly, "let's get these divers over the side and get these anchors off. They're screaming for them."

I wanted to put Padgett down. Since he was a bosun's mate, the rating that specializes in rigging, cables, anchors, and the like, he was the logical choice. But we had a new diver with us and he was straining to go. I hesitated to send him, because he had never worked under these conditions. The deck of the ship below was a tangle of rigging, lines, and cables, all waiting to foul the diver's lines as he crossed to the chain locker.

The new man, though, had other notions about my motives. "What're you running, a clique?" he asked sourly. "Nobody dives except the fairhaired boys?"

"No," I said, "but getting these anchors off is going to be a touchy business, and I want to send somebody who knows ground tackle."

"Look, I'm a diver," he said, projecting toward the captain. "You tell me what you want done, and I'll do it."

As intended, the captain heard. He stepped over to me and said anxiously, "I hope you're diving all the divers."

I got the message. "All right, get him dressed," I directed the tenders. To the new man I said, "You'll be Red diver." We used color designations for divers on the bottom to prevent confusion, painting their equipment to match.

Somehow he got the notion that this would make him the Number Two man of the pair that was going down. "Well," he said critically, "I guess I'll get the tending diver job. The way you run things, you'll have a first-class diver tending a second-class diver working."

Although the tending diver is as important as the working diver—in fact, more so, because he has the responsibility of keeping the working diver out of trouble—it is the working diver who has the glory. This is one reason why colors instead of numbers are used to distinguish the divers. There is no known way to shake the doctrine that numbers, as they go up, mean progressive inferiority. I shook my head. "I'm going to disappoint you," I said. I turned to the phone man. "Put Red diver down as working diver, and Black diver as tending diver," I directed. Black diver was Krassic, one of my best men.

Standing together on the double stage, the two disappeared under the surface. As the tending diver, Krassic would be first to leave the stage after they arrived below. In a few moments, the phone man routinely called out, "Black diver on the wreck, standing clear of the descending line."

"Okay, tell Red diver to get on the descending line," I said. We were moored slightly offside, rather than directly over the sunken ship, so that the descending line, tied over to the wreck, went down at an angle. When word came that the new man was off the stage and on the line, I said, "Tell Red diver the descending line has quite an angle to it, and to be sure he's over on the wreck before he turns loose of it." Otherwise, he would drop short, going on to the bottom.

The phone man passed on this instruction, presently relaying to me, "Red diver says he's not making his first dive." Then the phone man added, "Red diver says he's on the wreck, and he thinks he's solved the mystery of what's in the hold."

I walked over to the phone booth where I could hear more clearly for myself what was coming over the speaker from the man on the bottom. "Have Red diver say what he thinks the stuff is," I said to the phone man.

The answer that came up rang with scorn that the rest of us could be so dumb. "I'm standing waist-deep in this gooey material," said the authority. "I've eaten enough of this stuff on pancakes to know what it is. It's molasses!"

I pulled my head out of the booth and walked over to Pitman, leaning on the rail. "Where did you say you got that sample you sent up?" I asked.

"I scooped it off one of the beams on the side of the hold," said Pitman.

"You sure you were in the hold?" I asked.

"Yeah, hell, I was standing in it."

"Did the stuff seem gooey to you?" I pursued, a theory forming in my mind.

"Wasn't gooey at all," said Pitman. "It was real hard, like wet sand."

I turned back to the phone man. "Ask Black diver where is Red diver," I said.

Krassic responded, "I saw him coming down the descending line, and as he got close to the wreck, he let go. He must have gone on to the bottom. I can't see him."

The new diver appeared to have done the very thing I had cautioned him against: he had let go of the line too soon. I went back to the phone booth and pressed the button for direct communication with Krassic. "Frank, this is Karneke," I said. "What was that about Red diver?"

Krassic repeated what he had told the phone man.

"Why didn't you say something?" I asked.

"I did, but nobody answered," Krassic replied. "So I figured you were talking to him." This was plausible, since the phone system carried only one conversation at a time.

"Can you see him?" I asked.

"No," answered Krassic. "All I see is bubbles coming up—and a lot of silt. I guess the bottom must be muddy."

"Okay," I said. I was now sure that the new diver had missed the wreck and gone on to the bottom. The goo he was standing in was not anything he had ever eaten on pancakes. It was the mud of Subic Bay. To the phone man I said, "Tell Red diver to stand by to come up."

The phone man passed this along, and received a question in return. "Red diver wants to know if you want a sample of the stuff he's standing in," he said.

"Tell him we won't need it," I replied. "Just let us know when he's ready to come up."

In a little while came the message I expected. "Red diver says he can't find the descending line," said the phone man. Naturally he couldn't find it. Being tied over to the superstructure of the wreck rather than anchored on the bottom in the usual way, the line was far above where Red diver stood, down alongside the ship. "He wants to know if it's all right to come up heavy," relayed the phone man.

This meant coming up by the lifeline and air hose. With no descending line to use, there was no other way. "Tell him to keep himself heavy," I cautioned. Without the descending line to hang onto, he could easily float up too fast from overbuoyancy, risking the bends. I told the tenders to carry his lines forward while they brought him up by the decompression table, making room to put another diver down. During the hour or so Red diver spent on the stage coming up, he was more or less given the silence treatment. By the time he was back on deck, he was spoiling to know why he had been brought up so soon.

"Did you have enough information?" he asked.

"Yes, we had enough information," I answered noncommittally.

He lingered, wanting to make conversation. "You know, what's got me puzzled," he said, scratching his chin, "is what the hell those Japs were doing with all that molasses."

"I couldn't tell you," I said briefly, and walked away.

By evening, after he had heard himself called "Molasses" all day, the new diver had seen the light and was a subdued and wiser man. He went on to become one of our better divers.

Meanwhile, the work of getting up the anchors and chains had progressed fast and smoothly, as if we were old-timers at it rather than rank beginners. The first anchor had been released and was on the bottom. Wisniewski, who went down as Red diver in the new man's place, dropped over the side of the ship, put a cable around the hook, and it was hauled up by winch. To free the chain, he cut it with a torch where it came out of the chain locker, losing only what little was in the locker.

The second anchor was still housed, and to get at this one it was first tripped, exactly the same as in a normal anchoring of a ship. The clanking rumble of the chain as it payed out, picked up on the phones of the men below and flooding out over the fantail from the speaker, was eerie to hear when there was no ship visible.

But now was to come the great shock in our fortunes. A couple of guest divers came aboard, one of whom, Lieutenant R. W. Cook, was eager to make a dive. We were always glad to have help, but I knew nothing about Cook. He had never dived for me; we had never worked together. So it was with much apprehension that I finally agreed to let him go down. Nothing out of the way happened while Cook was below, but late in the evening, after he had gone back to his ship, the submarine tender *Howard Gilmore,* we received a blinker message that he had the bends and was being sent over for treatment in one of our recompression chambers. When he was brought aboard a few minutes later, Cook was barely able to move, although still on his feet. Weakly and in great pain, he told how the symptoms had first appeared in his arms and legs, spreading through his whole body.

The symptoms of bends show themselves in various ways, striking from the time the victim is still in the water up to twelve hours later. They range from a deep-red skin rash, caused by microscopic bubbles blocking the capillary ends in the skin, to a coma and total paralysis. If the victim has turned blue, it means his circulation has been stopped by the bubbles in his blood, and he must be placed in a recompression chamber at once. The bubbles may rupture nerves and blood vessels, leaving the victim crippled, and there may be lasting injury to the brain tissue. Brain injury, however, is rare—one theory being that divers don't have enough brains to injure.

In all forms and stages of the ailment there is intense pain.

No sedative may be given because pain is the chief guide to the victim's condition. The only other tip-off to what's wrong with him is the knowledge that he has been exposed to pressure. This is why divers carry cards that tell of such exposure. Some forms of the bends make the victim seem drunk, and the card can make the difference between landing in jail or getting the care he needs to save his life. This is not to suggest that divers are unknown to take a drink, but anyone seeing a diver behave erratically should call the nearest diving activity as soon as possible. He may not be drunk.

As we hurried Cook to the recompression chamber, we gave instructions to signal his ship and have them send over a doctor, since the *Chanticleer* had none. We got the stricken man into the chamber at 7:17 o'clock, Wisniewski and Padgett going in with him. Sometimes the pain as the pressure is raised in the chamber is worse than it was to begin with, among other things making the victim feel as if ice picks are being stuck into his head at the ears. The victim may go out of his mind, becoming violent.

But things went well for Cook, no complications developing as the pressure in the chamber was built up to match the pressure he had been under in the water. In using a recompression chamber the same terms are used as in actual diving, and at 125 feet, reached at 7:19, or in two minutes, Cook already felt better. For margin, we sent him down to 165 feet. With all going well, Wisniewski now left the chamber, pressure in the outer lock being brought up to that of the inner chamber while the door between was opened for his exit. After the required thirty minutes at 165 feet, we brought the patient up to his first stop, at ninety feet, leaving him there for seven minutes.

At 7:52 Lieutenant Commander J. J. Kane, the *Howard Gilmore*'s doctor, arrived and entered the chamber. We watched through the port as Dr. Kane, trained in submarine medicine, checked the pulse and blood pressure of the patient lying quietly on a mattress. Then the doctor sat down on a bench to watch and wait. On the other bench lay Padgett, idly snoozing away his boredom. Ordinarily, the master diver draws such duty, but Padgett hadn't dived that day, so he had drawn the assignment. Besides, to give the ship the normal complement of two master divers, he had been given the status of acting master.

At eight o'clock Cook was brought up to eighty feet, his second stage. At the same moment came an air raid alert. The only worse time to be threatened with attack is when a diver is in the water. This is why, during dives, the ship's entire attention is directed toward keeping watch for trouble. Lookouts are posted on the bridge. All sonar is kept going, listening for suspicious sounds in the water. The radar sweeps around the horizon, a cocked ear for hostile approach by air. If anything unusual is detected, up comes the diver, with no delay to find out what it is.

With the threat of attack catching three men in the recompression chamber, the same suspense gripped the ship as if they had been on the bottom. If anything happened to cut off the power, letting the pressure down, they would suffer the equivalent of being popped to the surface in the water. The *Chanticleer* lay in the midst of the concentration of ships that was inviting the attack. Except for the heat-lightning effect of the guns from the direction of Manila, not a light glimmered anywhere, and with the blackness of a tropical night hiding us all, one from another, there could be no thought of maneuvering out of the area. We were trapped in the bull's-eye of the target.

While all hands scurried to battle stations, I stayed by the chamber, ready to act if anything went wrong inside. Every few moments I checked my three charges through the little port in the side. Except for Dr. Kane, who sat alertly upright, keeping his shirt on despite the heat, it was a scene of restful unconcern. Padgett and the lieutenant remained stretched out on the bench and mattress, stripped to the waist. There was no reason to worry them with word about the emergency.

At 8:23, after twenty-two minutes at eighty feet, the pressure was eased off for seventy feet, and after twenty-four minutes at this level it was eased again, to sixty feet. At this point I began giving the men in the chamber pure oxygen. This speeds up decompression, helping to chase the nitrogen bubbles out of the victim's system. Unfortunately, pure oxygen can't be used below sixty feet, because the concentration caused by the pressure of the water makes it toxic to the diver. Rather than being pumped into the chamber, the oxygen is given through a regular airman's mask, conserving it and reducing the danger of explosion. As a further precaution, to prevent the oxygen from accumulating in the chamber, I kept valving it off.

I carefully logged twenty-two minutes at sixty feet, a half hour at fifty feet, and finally thirty-four minutes at forty feet. At two or three minutes before time to surface, I looked through the port for a final check of the occupants before phoning them to stand by to come all the way up. It was now about 9:50, or two and a half hours since the procedure began. Although the air strike still hadn't developed, it would be a relief to get the men out of the chamber. At the instant I looked in, my eye caught Dr. Kane half rising from his seat and gesturing with both hands toward the reclining Cook, as if something had gone wrong. There, in mid-action, the doctor was photographed on my mind, as a camera stops high-speed motion, for I saw no more as a brilliant flash filled the chamber, followed by an obscuring fog of smoke. From the loudspeaker at the side of the chamber came a low, agonized "Help! Help!"

I snapped off the oxygen and spun open the valve to start venting the chamber. The escaping air was so hot that it blistered the paint on the vent pipes. I phoned in, urgently asking if they were all right. There was no answer. I called for help from the two men at battle stations in the chamber room, but there was nothing we could do until the venting slowly brought the pressure down. Until then, pushing open the door to the inner lock, which swung inward, would be like pushing over a building. To get the door open in the usual way, by first pressurizing the outer lock, would take as long as the venting, and there was no way to speed up the process. We couldn't smash the ports; they were made of several layers of quartz, easily standing up to a fire ax. Three men were trapped in a pressure cooker, and all we could do was to stand and wait.

When we finally got the door open and rushed in, we were met by a blast of searing heat and the pungent smell of cooked flesh. Doctor Kane was slumped back against the side of the chamber. The other two lay as before, Cook on the mattress and Padgett on the bench. All three were unconscious, breathing as if in a deep sleep. Their skin was blistered and peeling. We caught them by the wrists to drag them out, only to lose our grip as the flesh came off in our hands. We then slipped our arms under their shoulders from behind and half carried them to the open air. I took Padgett, thinking how he had had my place in the chamber only because I had dived that day and he hadn't.

Out on the ship's deck, a corpsman shot morphine into the three victims and gave such first aid as he could while an appeal for medical help was blinked to Cook's ship. As we waited, the three faintly revived and with swollen tongues pressing against roasted lips, pleaded for water. We were giving it to them when a doctor arrived and they were removed to the sub tender, where there were hospital facilities. About two hours later the message was blinked back that Lieutenant Cook had died.

I spent the rest of the night trying to persuade myself that Padgett would pull through, and thinking about the big hole it would leave among us if he didn't. Together we had fought the twin hazards of Australian sharks and Australian beer. He was a shipmate's shipmate. If there was a tough job to do, Padgett was the good right hand you could always count on to help see it through. If you needed five dollars, and he didn't have it, he would get it for you somehow. When the sweat, toil and tedium bore down hard, Padgett was the one who would come up with a well-timed practical joke to bring a badly needed laugh.

Padgett's favorite subjects for his pranks were the self-important and the fussy who complained about the way they were being dressed. For a long time he had wanted to get at Hollingsworth, known to all as Hollywood, the assistant engineer officer. In his prior life Hollywood seemed to have known only people who were important, or people who knew someone important or were related to someone important. He was always dropping names, and as he moved loftily among us he gave the impression that he felt he was slumming.

One day came the opportunity which Padgett had been longing for. There was something wrong with the ship's screws, preventing us from making proper headway, and the chief engineer spoke to Hollywood about the need to go down and have a look at them. "Let me make the dive," said Hollywood eagerly, explaining that he had once been a diver.

The engineer hadn't known this about his assistant. "Are you sure you can do it?" he asked doubtfully.

Hollywood argued that not only was he qualified to make the dive, but as an engineer he had the advantage over us ordinary divers that he could evaluate the trouble. The engineer yielded, and Hollywood was placed on the diving stool to get dressed. "Let me dress this guy," muttered Padgett evilly.

We all knew what this meant, and we couldn't have been more agreeable. We watched in silent admiration as Padgett's deviltry this time took the form of hitching up one shoulder strap shorter than the other. The shoulder straps led from the belt to the helmet at the back, crossing each other. They are chiefly what holds the helmet in place against the upward push of the air.

When he got down into the water with this uneven hitch,

and the air began to push up on his helmet, Hollywood found himself in an embarrassing position. "I can't see," was the best he could offer concerning the propeller. "My helmet is on crooked. The port is way over on the side."

To the engineer this confirmed his misgivings about letting Hollywood make the dive in the first place. It also cast a cloud on the things Hollywood finally did report about the screw. One could hardly trust the engineering diagnosis of a diver who would claim his helmet was on crooked. He was brought up, and his work taken over by one of us peasants.

There were more reverses for Hollywood. While he was below, Padgett placed his shoes in position by the diving stool and nailed them to the deck. The plan in this worked out with such perfection that it looked staged. At the exact moment Hollywood leaned over to tie his shoes as he sat on the stool, the captain appeared, as if on cue. Here was a chance to report about the propeller directly to the top authority, and Hollywood was not one to miss it. "Captain," he began, taking off toward him from his bent-over position. With his feet failing to follow, he crashed face down at the captain's feet like a pilgrim prostrating himself at the gates of Mecca.

"This man has the bends!" cried the captain, looking down in startlement at the flattened form before him. "Get him into the recompression chamber at once!"

We couldn't tell the captain the truth. Neither could Hollywood, who by now knew very well what had happened. He could only go along with the play to its natural end, and he said nothing as we carried him off to the chamber, where we gave him the minimum table for one hour. This bonus result of Padgett's horseplay, everyone agreed, made it one of his finest successes.

The joke on Hollywood that nearly got out of hand stood tall among the memories of Padgett that passed before me as the hot night wore away after the explosion in the chamber. I was drifting off to sleep at daybreak when another message came from the *Howard Gilmore*.

Padgett was dead.

As we glumly went about our work in the following days, we brooded on the mystery of what had caused the explosion. We had been using the chamber every day. Under combat conditions it was safer to bring the divers up and let them decompress in the chambers than to leave them in the water, decompressing on the way up.

A board of inquiry decided after long investigation that the likeliest explanation of the accident was that the fan in the chamber had arced, setting off the oxygen. Also, the mattress might have had oil on it, blotted from a diver's suit. Or the varnish in the wooden deck could have had something to do with it. What meaning was given to Dr. Kane's half-risen posture and his gesturing toward Lieutenant Cook at the instant of the blast, I never found out. The doctor, afforded some slight protection by his shirt and apparently exhaling at the moment of the explosion, finally pulled through.

In the chamber the smell of cooked flesh hung on, seemingly impregnated in the metal. We aired it out for days and then thoroughly covered the inside with new paint, but the aura of death was ineffaceable. The newer divers didn't seem to notice, but we who were there never used the chamber again.

Ever since then, all Navy recompression chambers have had nothing in them that could touch off an explosion or support combustion. Many times I have heard divers ask as they looked around in the heat inside a chamber, "What's the matter with having a fan in here, to cool things off?"

Now they know.

9. War Plans from the Sea

It was a bright, tropical morning, and the sun drove its rays deep into the smooth, clear water, dimly outlining the big wreck sitting on the bottom, just off Corregidor. Who she was we didn't know. There were hundreds of such wrecks around, sunk by bombs, mines, torpedoes, and gunfire in the Battle of the Philippines. Several times more ships rested on the bottom of Manila Bay than on the surface. With the guns still harrumphing beyond the horizon, we took them as they came, going down to see what information we could get that might help to shorten the war. We Navy divers were, in effect, underwater intelligence agents.

As the master diver in charge, I drew the first dive of the day. I landed on the mast, and there paused to get a fish's-eye view of the dead hulk under me. Like all the other sunken vessels I had dived on, she sat nearly upright, listing some twenty degrees to starboard. I could see with mounting interest that she was a combat ship, apparently a cruiser. We didn't get many of these. I asked for slack on my lifeline and air hose, trimmed my buoyancy and drifted like a flying squirrel down to the bridge, feeling good because only seldom were we favored with such clear visibility.

My elation vanished as I came to rest next to a gun tub. The piece was still manned! Swaying lifelike in the gentle currents, each man of the crew was exactly in his place: the gun pointer and trainer on their seats, the gun captain leaning over them as if checking the loading of the gun, the two ammunition passers at the ammunition locker, one reaching into the box for a shell, the other sitting by ready to receive the projectile and pass it on to the man at the breech. In the weird twilight of the subsea, still wearing their helmets, life preservers, and coveralls against gun blast, they looked as live as when they had been shooting at their enemies—except that they seemed to be posed in their positions, reminding me of the dummies I had often seen giving realism to exhibits at county fairs.

I walked over to the gun captain for a better look, half expecting that he and his crew would turn around in surprise as I approached, and got a new shock. His face was missing. The features had been eaten away by crabs, the clean-picked bones showing white under his helmet. I looked one by one into the faces of the others and under each helmet found the same death's-head, staring spectrally from hollow eye sockets.

"Think you found anything important?" came a voice in my phone from the living world above.

"No," I replied with restraint, "just a bunch of dead guys."

It was the first time I had found dead men in exposed deck positions. The gun crew hadn't been carried away by the sea, our ship's doctor later explained, because in all probability the men had been hit by blast, either from a gun or a bomb. This had instantly ruptured their stomachs, keeping them from being bloated by the gases that normally form in the decomposition of stomach contents, and leaving the bodies neatly balanced between buoyancy and gravity.

I left the gun tub with its ghostly crew and headed for the chart house, little suspecting that aboard this ship we were soon to find far more meaningful novelties than the dead gunners. Conveniently spread out before me on the chart table were stacks of charts, lying just as they had lain in use when disaster struck. I gathered them in, along with a welter of other documents in easy reach in drawers and on shelves. Then I called for a mailbag, ideal for this use because of the drawstring at the top and weights in the bottom. I put the papers into the bag and had it hauled up, in a little while coming up myself.

When I reached the top, I found the Naval Intelligence officer excitedly leafing through one of the booklets I had sent up. "What're you doing, Lieutenant?" I asked as my helmet was lifted off. "Reading some Japanese version of *Lady Chatterley's Lover?*"

He gave me an intent look. "I'm afraid it's a little more important than that," he said tautly. "Where did you find these papers?"

I told him.

"You mean to say you found all this stuff out in the open—not locked up?" he demanded. In our own Navy, important papers are securely locked away, subject to automatic destruction if the ship is sunk or captured.

"That's right," I replied. I eyed him narrowly. A big show of enthusiasm over the documents we divers brought up was often used as a trick to spur us on. "Did I send you something really important, Lieutenant?" I asked cynically.

"You certainly did," he said. He turned to the captain. "I'd like permission to send a classified message to Washington immediately," he said. The captain nodded, and the pair hurried off together.

When the captain came back a little while later, he led me aside and said confidentially, "The Navy Intelligence officer thinks we got something very important. He wants us to bring up every scrap of paper we can find down there."

This was somthing new. Ordinarily the only papers we paid any attention to were those found on the bridge. Now we were to comb the ship from bow to stern, picking up anything with writing on it. This became our top priority mission, rather than, as usual, identifying the vessel and assessing the damage.

As to the identity of the ship, this alone was cause for excitement. She was the heavy cruiser *Nachi*, fabled terror of the Japanese Navy. All through the war we had heard stories of how the *Nachi* blew her enemies out of the water while remaining strangely immune to injury herself. Five-hundred-pound bombs dropped on her decks apparently had no more effect than BB shot on an elephant. Many times she had been reported sunk, only to show up again. Once, a submarine "sank" her, the crew proving it with pictures they had lingered to take as the cruiser was going down. The pictures showed the ship's decks awash, with only the superstructure still above water. In a few weeks, she reappeared, showing no signs of having been in trouble.

When at last the *Nachi*'s time had come, we found out later, she took a clobbering that would have sunk several ordinary ships. It happened on November 5, 1944, when Admiral Halsey's Third Fleet airmen from the carriers *Essex, Lexington,* and *Ticonderoga* jumped her as she was trying to escape from Manila Bay during the reinvasion of the Philippines. According to Navy historian Samuel Eliot Morison, they hit her with nine torpedoes, thirteen 1,000-pound bombs, six 250-pound bombs, and sixteen rockets before it was enough.

During a month of diving on her we discovered the secret of the *Nachi*'s amazing constitution. All unnecessary openings aboard had been welded shut, turning the compartments into watertight cells, and thus tending to localize any damage. In one place, deep inside the ship, a 1,000-pound armor-piercing bomb had exploded after crashing down through four decks, producing no results except slightly sprung walls. The usual doors and hatches would have been blown out. How the crew had come and gone from the compartment we never learned. We got into it only by following the bomb hole down from the top. That the bomb had penetrated this deep was itself remarkable, for the decks had been covered with extra layers of heavy steel plating. The watertight integrity of the *Nachi* probably made her as close to unsinkable as any ship ever built.

But far more than the *Nachi*'s structural curiosities, what continued to interest the Intelligence officer were the papers we kept sending up. There must have been twenty bagfuls in all, containing books, letters, post cards, magazines, newspapers—and diaries. In the U. S. Navy, keeping a diary is a court-martial offense. The reasons for this were well demonstrated by the important information that came into our hands from the diaries kept by the Japanese. They told, in the candid language of one setting something down for his own eyes alone, how our side looked to the enemy and how we had performed in different actions.

It was from the diary of some Japanese Samuel Pepys aboard the *Nachi* that we learned the fate of the cruiser *Houston,* until then missing with all hands. The diarist, who had seen the fight with the *Houston* from another ship before coming aboard the *Nachi,* recorded that some 300 survivors had been taken prisoner.

All we could get out of the Intelligence officer, though, was an occasional crumb from the diaries. We tried needling him for more. "Is that stuff really that juicy, Lieutenant?" we would ask as he tensed over some new document from the bottom. But most of the time he said nothing. Every few days, as he apparently ran across something of fresh significance, he rushed out another batch of the papers by the Catalina Flying Boat that had been brought in for the purpose. Whatever was in the papers, the sight of the big seaplane storming off across the water with them certainly made it look as if it was something important. This made us feel good—although we knew that to some Intelligence officers everything was important.

When we found Vice-Admiral Kiyoshide Shima's flag, still secured to its halyard on the signal bridge, our spirits soared. More than documents, this fallen chieftain's symbol, marking the *Nachi* as a flagship, told us our side was making progress. The men on the bottom now became harder to control, wandering off on souvenir hunts. This problem one day came up with its own solution, luckily at no serious cost. The usual two men at a time were down. Black diver working, Red diver standing guard outside the compartment, tending the other's lines. All at once from the loudspeaker there pealed the wild, chilling scream of a man scared crazy. Word flew around the ship that a diver was trapped, bringing everybody from the messboy to the captain crowding to the fantail.

At first I thought it was the working diver who was in trouble. I unplugged his phone connection to the speaker to block the noise while I talked to his tender outside the door. But the screaming went on, indicating that it came from the tender. I blocked him off and called to the man in the compartment. "Black diver, what's wrong?"

"Nothing wrong here," he replied calmly. "I'm busy loading up this mailbag with books and things."

"What's the tending diver doing?" I asked.

"He's tending me outside the door, I guess," said the man in the compartment.

"Something seems to have happened to him," I said. "He's screaming his head off. Better go out and see what's happened."

After a few moments, the working diver reported, "I'm outside the door now. He's nowhere around here."

"Can you see his hose and lifeline?" I asked.

"Wait a minute—yes, it's going down a passageway."

"Okay, follow it. But be careful—he's panicked. We can't get conversation to him so he'll know you're coming." A diver in panic is more dangerous than a man drowning—there are more ways he can kill you.

"All right," said the working diver after a minute or so, "his lifeline and air hose are going into a compartment, and the door's closed."

I knew what had happened. With the ship listing, the door

had slowly swung shut behind the diver after he entered the compartment, blocking out what little light had been coming through the opening and leaving him in darkness. Then, as he moved around, he stirred up the silt in the water, making it blacker still. When he couldn't find the door after he decided to leave, he lost his head, forgetting that all he had to do to get out was to follow his lifeline and air hose.

I said to the rescuing diver, "Open the door and pull on his lifeline and air hose—but be careful he doesn't come out and grab you." To a diver in trouble on the bottom, anything that moves is an enemy.

I plugged the phone lead to the trapped man back into the loudspeaker. "Help, something's pulling on me!" he cried in a despairing wail. Before we could answer, he was heard again, saying sheepishly, "I see the door now. I'm okay." The opening of the door by the other diver had brought him abruptly back to his senses. When the two were safely joined up, I asked, "Red diver, what happened?"

"I guess I must have fallen down and slid into this compartment and got trapped," he explained lamely.

What Red diver had been up to, as he realized we all knew, was souvenir hunting. He hunted them no more. Next day he turned in his diving suit and went back to his regular rating, working in the engine room. He never again spoke of diving, nor was he ever again seen to hang out with divers. And there was no more souvenir hunting, by anybody. Few things are as good for discipline as to hear a man scream on the bottom.

In making a systematic deck-to-deck, room-to-room search of the *Nachi*, a big help was a book of blueprints showing the construction layout of the ship, which we found in the literature we recovered. With the book to go by, we could pick our spots, saving time and trouble. One of the first was a compartment on the main deck, marked on the blueprints as the communications control center. This would be filled with such important items as coding machines, code books, and logs with the latest messages concerning the state of the fleet. The blueprints showed the compartment to have a watertight door, opening off the deck.

But when I got down to the compartment, I found the door welded shut. This posed a dilemma: I could try to find the new entrance to the compartment, which probably lay up through the deck from inside the ship, entailing a hazardous and time-consuming search by feel, or I could try to make a hole where I was. I decided this was best, and I proposed to do it with explosives.

This idea was not well received topside. "You seem to forget that the whole ship might be loaded with explosives," the phone man objected sarcastically. "You want to blow us all up?"

I answered in the same vein. "You don't suggest I chisel my way in, do you?"

"What's the matter with using a cutting torch?" the phone man asked.

"An excellent idea," I said, "But what if there's ammunition on the other side of the bulkhead? A torch would set it off, too, you know, just the same as a charge."

I lost the argument and received a torch, which sustains a a white-hot flame under water by burning hydrogen and oxygen sealed in an air bubble formed at the tip. For a half hour I applied the flame to the steel siding, cutting more or less in a circle. "I almost got it," I said finally. "The plate should fall any time."

"Well, don't get carried away. Just burn a hole big enough to get through." Topside liked to rub it in a little when the master was down.

There was a flash, seemingly right at my head. When I came to, I was lying on the deck, the phone man's voice frantically flooding my helmet. "Karneke, are you all right? Are you all right?" More than anyone else in the crew, the phone man is the keeper of the man on the bottom. Perched on the diving stool in front of the speaker, he leans close and listens to his breathing, the air exhausting from his helmet

—all the other sounds of a diver at work, each telling something of how he is doing.

"Yeah, I guess so," I said slowly. "What happened?"

"Whaddaya mean, what happened! You tell us! We heard a big bang over the phone, and then nothing."

"I don't know what happened," I answered. "There was an explosion. That's the last I remember till I woke up stretched out here on the deck."

"Is everything okay?" the phone man insisted.

"I still got my arms and legs," I said, sitting up and checking them. "But my telephone has been knocked loose in my helmet, and either I'm sweating like hell or I'm bleeding. There's something running into my eyes."

"Can't you tell which it is?"

"I got no mirror down here."

"Can you see if you burned a hole in the compartment?"

I rose to my feet and gropingly found where I had been working. The dim twilight was gone, turned to full darkness by the sediment churned up in the commotion. I ran a hand around an irregular cut in the bulkhead. "I think I got enough to get through," I said.

"Be careful and go through feet first," the phone man warned.

"Yeah, I know, feet first!" I echoed irritably. I wished I knew what the stuff pouring into my eyes was. For sweat it felt funny—there was no sting to it.

I stuck my left foot through the hole, swinging it around a little to probe the darkness inside. As I put weight on it, something clamped around my shoe. I tried to pull loose. Nothing doing. I could neither go forward into the hole nor pull out of it. The phone man heard me struggling. "What seems to be the trouble?" he asked.

I described my predicament. "Think you can use some help?" he offered.

"Yeah," I admitted, and soon Krassic was with me. Bending over at my side, he laid hold of the heavy folds of my suit below the knee and heaved upward. We huffed and pulled for about twenty minutes. Then, all at once, I was free. We sent the glad news topside simultaneously, each in his own phone. "You want me to check and see what was holding me?" I asked. The man on the bottom makes no moves on his own.

The answer was fast and curiously urgent. "No! We're bringing you up immediately. You're hurt." Unknown to me, Krassic had reported that I was "bleeding to death."

"There's nothing wrong with me," I said.

"Don't argue!" the phone man snapped. "Stand by to come up!"

Krassic put an arm around my middle and we started up. As we slowly rose, standing together on the diving stage, I kept motioning to him that I was all right. Through the side port of his helmet I could see Krassic shaking his head. By the time we reached the surface, he had me pretty well convinced that I wasn't much longer for this world. The others thought so, too, as they took off my helmet and saw that my face was solidly smeared with blood. They rushed me off to sick bay, where it was found that things were not as bad as they looked. My only injury was a break in the skin at my temple, made by the telephone as it was blown in against me from its well in the helmet.

As for what had caused the blast, we at first assumed it was a booby trap, always on our minds. But as we thought about it, we realized that we had provided the makings of the explosion ourselves. Unburned gas from my cutting tool had leaked into the compartment as I worked, building up and finally being set off by sparks from the torch.

With the excitement over, somebody remembered that the compartment I had been cutting into was now open and ready for inspection. Wisniewski was picked for the honor of making the first dive to recover the top secrets certain to be found there. Patched up with Band-Aids and back directing the work, I cautioned him to look out for the thing that had caught my foot.

He hadn't been down long when he loudly reported back for all to hear, "Tell Karneke that thing he had his foot caught in was a Japanese toilet!" He chortled gleefully. "Tell him he's probably the only master diver in history that ever got stuck in one of those things!"

Far from being the ship's communications center, the vision of which had filled us with such great expectations, the compartment was an officers' bathroom. This day had not been one of my best.

Still making sounds of merriment over the joke on me, Wisniewski asked for another diver to tend him. "I found a watertight door, and I want to go through it," he explained.

I sent a man down to post himself outside at the hole I had cut, and in a few moments Wisniewski called up from the new area he was in. "I just came on a door with a big padlock on it," he said. "Send me a hammer and I'll bust it off and see what's here."

Our letdown at the prosaic yield of the "communications center" disappeared in a new flight of hope. A lock meant important things stored behind it. We sent Wisniewski the hammer, and soon we heard the *klunk-klunk* as he smashed away at the lock. Meanwhile, we waited suspensefully for word of what lay within. Finally it came. "Nothing in here but rice bowls," said Wisniewski, sounding as if he had been betrayed. The dishes had been securely locked away while top secret documents were left out in the open!

Excitement flared again when Krassic, going down to relieve Wisniewski, sent up the electrifying news that he had located a safe.

"How do you know it's a safe?" countered the phone man warily as everybody cocked an ear toward the loudspeaker. We had had enough disappointment for one day.

"Well, it's got a dial on it and it's got a big handle," said Krassic. These were thrilling words. To us divers a safe meant only one thing—money.

"Can we bring it up?" asked the phone man.

"Naw, it's secured to the bulkhead," Krassic answered.

"Do you think you can open it?"

"Send me a hammer and I'll see," said Krassic. With the hammer he succeeded only in knocking the dial off. Successively, we sent him a hacksaw, a chisel, and a crowbar. No luck. "From what little damage I can feel," he said disgustedly as his time on the bottom ran out, "all I'm doing is knock the paint off."

With the suspense over the safe unbroken at day's end, it was all we talked about at chow and far into the night. There was much guessing about the contents—not on whether there was money in it, but how much. It seemed unsporting to intrude the thought that the safe held secret papers, though in view of the exposed condition we had found all the other papers in, this appeared unlikely. The salvage laws came in for discussion. There was talk about who properly should own the money.

"I'd like to see Intelligence try to claim *money* as secret and classified," somebody said stoutly.

"Looks like the first diver opening the safe should have first claim on it," it was offered.

With a hard glance at me, a third man said, pessimistically, "The master's been hogging the glory all along, so he'll probably get this, too."

I fooled this prophet of gloom next morning. In a tone of mock injury, I took stock of "the slurring comments" that had been made about me, and quietly had Krassic make the opening dive of the day.

Krassic first tried to punch out the shaft that the dial turned on, hoping to get a hole he could reach through and trip the locking mechanism. This failed. We then considered sending him a torch, but dropped the idea: the flame might burn the safe's contents. It would be the final tragedy to stand this close to wealth, only to destroy it by our own hand. We decided to use explosives.

For this, a man of experience was to be desired. "Anybody here ever blow a safe?" the captain queried, looking sharply from one to another of us. If anyone had, he wasn't telling. Somebody looked at me and said, "Old Qualified there used to work in a coal mine, so he ought to know about dynamite." My rating as a gunner's mate was mentioned, and I myself put in that as a boy on the farm I had helped to blow tree stumps.

Adding all this up, the captain said, "Then you should know quite a bit about explosives."

"That's right, Captain," I agreed, "but I never cracked any safes." I wanted to make that clear.

The question of who should draw the blasting assignment was set aside for the moment, and we concentrated on the problem of the kind of explosive to use. Like all ships, we carried an assortment for demolition purposes. After long discussion, it was decided to use Composition C. This is a putty-like material, twice as powerful as TNT, which can be molded into shape and stuck in place by adhesion.

As the gunner's mate, a former coal miner and stump blower, I drew the ticklish job of making up the charge. While the crew stood respectfully back, I formed a pound of the explosive into the shape of a cup, with the detonator buried inside, to fit over what was left of the safe's lock mechanism. The captain then ruled that because I had made up the charge, I was the logical choice to take it down and plant it.

It was a nervous bunch of railbirds I left behind as I went over the side. They knew that the *Nachi,* as a combat ship, carried ammunition—probably hundreds of tons of it—and that it would be a good trick to blow the safe without setting off a chain reaction of explosions, maybe ending with a blast that sent us all to kingdom come. For that matter, I had known more relaxed times myself. The charge I carried in my hand, having had to be prepared in advance, was live and ready to go. And many things could make it go: a simple jarring, a radar beam, a static charge generated in the firing cable as I dragged the cable into the water.

I eagerly disposed of the charge against the lock. It had seldom been so good to get back up to the *Chanticleer*.

Now came a new debate—whether to detonate the charge where we lay, or to back off a bit. We compromised by veering the *Chanticleer* as far as we could without breaking the moorings, putting some 500 yards between us and the sunken *Nachi*. Tensely we waited as the plunger on the blasting machine was pushed down, sending an electrical impulse down to our Composition C on the safe. Nothing happened. After two more tries, the ship's electrician suggested helpfully, "If you want some juice, why don't you unhook that damn hellbox and stick the cord in one of these sockets?" He pointed to a handy deck outlet from the ship's electrical system.

This was done, and in a moment there came a low, muffled thud from the bottom, followed by a slight boiling of the sea just above the explosion. A moment before, we had expected the sea to rise towering above us, possibly carrying the *Nachi* up with it. Now, at the little *poof* we got instead, we speculated that the safe was probably still intact.

We pulled the *Chanticleer* back over to the wreck, and Posey went down to see the results. He sent up word that both doors of the safe had been laid open, and the safe itself blown loose from the bulkhead. There he broke off, leaving us hung on the overriding subject of what was in the safe, if anything, after the blast. "Damn silt—I can't see," we heard him mutter. After a couple of minutes he tantalizingly reported, "Hey, I think this thing's loaded with money!"

A reverent hush fell on the fantail crowd as these tidings floated out of the speaker. "How do you know it's money?" asked the phone man, guardedly.

"Well, it's stacked up like cordwood, and it's got bands around it," replied Posey excitedly.

The Intelligence officer pressed forward. "Have him check and see if there's anything besides money down there," he instructed the phone man. The Intelligence officer was down-grading the money, we suspected, because he knew he couldn't have any of it.

When he had received this instruction, Posey shot back, "Tell him not to worry. There's nothing here but money, and lots of it."

"Okay, fill the mailbag and let us know when it's ready to come up," said the phone man, his voice fluttering.

The first bagful came over the side and we spilled it out on the deck. Money it was—Japanese money, in bundles of 10-yen notes. We stood looking at it in abashed silence. Finally somebody roared, "Well, what the hell did you expect to find on a Japanese ship—dollars?"

Well, no—but not yen, either—just "money." That was as far as the thinking had gone. Now that it had been rudely made to go further, the shock passed as it was realized that even Japanese money had value and there was a swing to the sunny outlook of the man who cried, "Boy, this dough'll be terrific for our first night in Tokyo!"

The Intelligence officer heard our talk quietly, saying nothing of the reasons for his own happiness over the money. Authentic enemy currency, rather than counterfeit, was highly useful in spy operations. Phony money found on a spy is a dead giveaway.

Posey kept the money coming until, with the safe empty, we had about two million yen aboard, or half a million dollars. Besides all her other functions, the *Nachi* had also carried the payroll for the fleet. When Posey was told to stand by to come up, he said, "Just a minute, I think I'm fouled."

This was odd: he had said nothing before about being fouled. We offered to send help but this he was quick to turn down. "I think I can clear myself," he said. "Just give me a few minutes." He was strangely vague about his trouble. We all guessed what he was up to. Poor fellow, he couldn't see that it was Japanese money he was dealing with, and no one had told him.

"Okay, I'm ready now," Posey called. When he broke surface, bundles of money were sticking from his belt, the tops of his shoes, his cuffs—wherever he had been able to fasten it. Seeing how it looked as his helmet was lifted off, he pretended surprise. "Jeez, how'd all this stuff get stuck to me?" he remarked comically. Then Posey joined the rest of us in disenchantment.

The money was dried out, then put aboard the Catalina as the Intelligence officer was getting ready to fly out with the final batch of documents. "Don't feel too bad about this money," said the officer as we wistfully watched the boxes being loaded. "It wasn't too important."

"What's more important than money?" somebody demanded belligerently.

"Those papers you brought up back at the beginning," he said cryptically. "Don't be surprised if this war ends in three or four months—that's how important those papers are." Leaving us with our mouths hanging open, he boarded the plane. There would be no reason to kid us now that the job was done.

In three months, just as the Intelligence officer had said, the war was over. At a Navy League victory dinner at the Waldorf Astoria Hotel, Secretary of the Navy James Forrestal told for the first time about the papers we had found on the *Nachi*, and what was in them. The "*Nachi* Papers" contained Japan's entire war plans and orders against the West, along with details of her defenses and preparations for meeting the coming invasion. Not often, if ever, had so much critical military intelligence turned up in one place.

10. The Mystery of the Moro Maru

The captain was a real-life version of a Hollywood ship's master. He was handsome, quiet, self-assured, and he seemed to be in a perpetual struggle to hold back a grin, without ever quite succeeding. This morning, though, he was doing pretty well at it. "We got orders to check a hospital ship," he said grimly as I arrived on the bridge in answer to his summons. "Our guys are supposed to have sunk it." He shook his head. "I can't believe it," he mused. "There's something phony somewhere."

We had finished diving on the *Nachi*, our next job after Subic Bay, and were back to our more regular work of salvage and routine underwater intelligence. To find out why a hospital ship had been sunk was something brand-new again. In the shoot-'em-up confusion of the reinvasion, some shots were bound to have gone where they shouldn't, but to sink a ship takes deliberate, sustained attention. As the captain said, something was haywire.

We weighed anchor and hurried out to the area where the sinking was supposed to have taken place, in shallow water about fifteen miles at sea from Manila Bay. There she was, exactly where the Japanese had said she was in their com-

plaint. Even in its sunken state, the ship offered little excuse
for mistaken identity. The white mast with its red cross near
the tip thrust high out of the water like a bleeding finger held
aloft. Looking down into the shadowy depths from the fantail of the *Chanticleer,* we could also make out the red crosses
on the deck. Nor could there be any doubt that the vessel had
been correctly lighted. There were the fixtures, each in its
proper place. Along with these marks of innocence were those
of attack. Bullets had pocked the mast and ripped splinters
from it, clear evidence of strafing. It looked like an open-and-
shut case of blundering by our side. But how had it been possible? We hoped to find the answer as the *Chanticleer* anchored alongside fore and aft.

As usual, being the diver in charge, I went down first.
Landing on the wing of the bridge, I secured my descending
line to the structure and took a look around. The water was
moderately murky, giving the effect of looking through
a thick fog. All around me for several feet objects were dis-
tinctly visible, with the fore and after ends of the ship lost in
the gloom.

I moved into the chart house. The charts, customarily
thumbtacked to the chart table, were missing. This was highly
unusual. Ordinarily, on a ship sunk in battle, there isn't time
to save the charts. I pulled out a desk drawer. It was empty.
I opened the rest of them. All were empty. The books from
the shelves were gone. Clearly, there had been no fast scramble over the side to get off the ship, as in an emergency. I
reported my findings topside for the ears of two experts from
the beach who were with us as an official investigating board.
"S.O.B.'s from out of town" we called such visitors, because
they were full of authority, telling us what to do.

I went into the captain's emergency cabin, and there found
something which seemed to contradict the evidence of lei-
urely departure found in the charthouse. Laid out on the
captain's bunk, all ready to put on, was the Japanese skipper's
full-dress uniform. Certainly this seemed to say that the cap-

tain had left in a hurry. I sent up word of this eerie discovery. Back over the phone came the voice of some fantail comedian, asking, "Is the captain in the uniform?"

Except for the uniform on the bunk, I found nothing in two hours of inspection, on and around the bridge, to break a strange pattern of orderliness for a ship supposed to have been sunk suddenly. We had a first-class mystery on our hands.

We began a systematic check of the ship from bow to stern, looking for possible military reasons why the ship might have been sunk. These reasons could include the presence of armament and contraband—that is, materials not used in the running of a hospital ship. We also looked for damage, hoping to find out what had made the ship sink.

Things were going along quietly, with Pitman on the bottom, when suddenly out of the loudspeaker came the exclamation, "Holy mackerel!"

"What's wrong?" the phone man asked alertly.

"I just opened a door and the place is full of shoes!" Pitman replied.

"Ask him what's so unusual about finding a bunch of shoes," I said to the phone man.

"Listen, wise guy," Pitman shot back when he got the question, "did you ever go into a compartment and find it full of shoes with no feet in 'em?"

I turned to our two experts and passed on the intelligence about the shoes. This formality was not strictly necessary, since they had heard the information on the speaker the same as the rest of us, but my relay made it official. They reacted with curiously strong interest. "Have the diver check out the compartment thoroughly," one of them directed. "Find out if the shoes are boxed, what type they are, and so forth."

I pressed the intercom button and gave these directions to Pitman directly. "What the hell did you think I was going to do?" he growled back. We heard him rummaging among the shoes, cussing to himself. After a while, he reported, "You can tell 'em up there that there's nothing down here but shoes, shoes and shoes!"

As our two guests made full note of this, I called down to Pitman. "Stand by to come up," I said. "Bring some shoes with you."

When he broke surface, Pitman was nearly hidden by shoes slung from his neck by their laces. Our duet from the beach examined the footwear intently, again making copious notes. Why they were so interested in the shoes they never condescended to tell us. If the shoes had been new, it could have meant that they were contraband, but they were all used, probably cast off by patients as they were brought aboard for treatment.

The mystery of the sunken ship deepened as the day passed. There was no sign of mortal damage to the vessel. We found no guns to justify attack on her and, strangest of all, we found no bodies. How a hospital ship, filled with wounded men, could be sent down in battle with no one left aboard seemed far beyond reason.

But our visitors from the beach were determined to get the answers to the riddle. "Are you sure there's no damage?" they kept asking. "Are you sure there are no holes—no ordnance?" When the diver each time said he was sure, he next was asked, "What do you think sank the ship?" By evening this prodding was bringing muttered comments like, "The way these experts are acting, you would think the divers kicked holes in the bottom of the ship."

Next morning we started off the day with a dive by myself onto the after part of the vessel. It came near being my last. Visibility had fallen off because of a shift in the current, and as I walked along the deck I abruptly stepped into space. I let out a yell and down I went, hitting with a loud thud in the darkness somewhere far below. Wearing an outfit that weighed 200 pounds—thirty-four of them in my shoes alone —I got no breaks from gravity. Luckily, I had been keeping a lot of air in my suit as insurance against such mishaps, so that I had a good cushion around me to hold off the extra pressure from the deeper water. The worst I got was a terrific bear hug. It knocked the wind out of me and left me feeling as if I had been kicked in the stomach, the one part of the body that has no internal bracing.

"What happened? What happened?" the phone man called excitedly as I shakily picked myself up.

"I fell down a hole," I panted.

"Are you all right?"

"I'm okay," I said, not too sure.

"How do you feel?" the phone man pursued.

"I'm fine—but my guts sure hurt."

"You want us to bring you up?"

"No, no, I'm fine," I insisted.

"Okay," he said, making a vulgar suggestion to lighten things. "That hole you fell through—does it look like a bomb hole?" he asked. If it was a bomb hole, we at last would have something positive for our two guests, getting them off our necks.

"Just a minute," I answered. "Let me feel around, I can't see a thing." Getting down on all fours, I found an edge to whatever I was standing on. I followed the edge with my hands to a right-angle corner and made out that I was on a platform, maybe ten feet square. I felt cables running up from it. "Looks like I'm on an elevator," I said.

"Maybe it's a platform for a disappearing gun," the phone man offered hopefully. "Check and see."

In the floor I found pad eyes, used for making fastenings. I told of this. "Then it would be possible to mount a gun on the platform?"

"Yes—possible," I said. I had in mind that an ordinary elevator, too, might have pad-eye fittings. I crawled around the platform some more, making sure of my findings. Then I was ready to come up. After a fall of what proved to be four decks, I had had my bellyful for the day. It was reluctantly agreed that the elevator was just that—nothing more. We still had learned nothing.

Our hopes flared again when, on the third day, a diver sent up word from three decks down in the sunken ship that he was in an area with a lot of strange objects in it. Weapons, maybe? The prodding we had been getting from our visiting investigators to find some ordnance aboard, incriminating the vessel, had made us suggestible. The man below said the objects felt like knives. "Bayonets?" he was asked.

"Yeah, bayonets," he replied. This seemed to be confirmed by the news the next minute that he had cut his hand. We pulled him up and prepared to send down a replacement. The presiding expert was happy for the first time since he came on board. "I feel that we've finally located where they are keeping all their weapons and explosives," he said to me. "So we would like you to go down." He huddled with the captain, who seconded the idea.

To protect my diving suit against cuts and punctures, I pulled on a pair of chafing pants—overalls of heavy canvas, with a bib and side pockets—as well as leather gloves; and I took along a flashlight, wrapping it with tape for extra waterproofing. A light isn't much good in murky water, which stops the beam like a wall, but I thought that by bringing things I wanted to examine up close to my faceplate and then shining the light on them, it might be of some use.

I hadn't been down long when I found a locker door. I opened it and carefully running my hands over the shelves behind it, I felt an ogival object, maybe four inches long and three inches in diameter. "I think I've got something here," I said into the phone. "It feels like a fuse."

"Be careful," came the response. "It probably is a fuse and it may go off and blow us all up."

Such fantail wisdom is one of the things a diver has to put up with. "Okay," I said, "I'm going to bring it close to my face and see if I can identify it." I cupped the object in both

hands and gently pulled it from the shelf. With my left hand
I held it gingerly against my chest while with the other hand
I reached into my leg pocket for the flashlight. As I did so,
the object slipped away from me. I threw my right hand under it, catching it at my knees. At the same instant the water
around this point lit up with a light glow. I promptly lost
all voluntary functions. As I waited helplessly for the explosion, my ears slowly began to register the sound of words
pounding into my helmet from topside. "Karneke, are you
all right? Are you all right? Answer us!"

"Yes, I'm okay," I finally managed to say.

"Did something go wrong?"

"I don't know, but I think I may have set this fuse off,"
I replied shakily.

I could hardly have said anything more disquieting.
"What's happening—what's it doing?" the phone man demanded excitedly.

"It's glowing," I said, still grappling to get my wits back.

"What are you doing?"

"I'm just standing here holding it." If this sounded less
than bright, it was no worse than the advice that now came
down to me.

"Well, whatever you do, don't drop it," said the phone
man.

As my brain began to recover, it occurred to me to give the
glowing object a closer look. There was nothing to lose, I rea-
soned. I brought it up to my faceplate. I noticed that the glow
didn't rise with it but stayed in place below. Then I realized
that the glow did not come from the fuse but from the flashlight, still in the pocket at my leg. The light had shorted out
in the water and turned itself on. I sent this news up, so full
of relief that there wasn't room to feel foolish.

"Damn it, Karneke," protested the phone man after a long
moment, "quit scaring people!" Topside became outright
happy when I confirmed that the object was a fuse, all right.
Even the two experts now conceded that divers were some

good. The fuse meant there was ordnance aboard--whole stores of it, somewhere, justifying the sinking.

But we found no more explosives, nor any other military items. For days we dived, turning up not even a pistol. We decided that the lone fuse must have been a souvenir, stored in the locker by a patient. And the big area where the fuse was found, we concluded, had been the operating room. The "bayonet" on which the other diver had cut himself must have been a surgical instrument. We were back where we started.

After three more days of vainly prowling the inside of the sunken ship, we dived to check the hull from the outside, working from the ocean floor. Again, nothing. The ship appeared to be as sound as the day she was launched.

Now we were asked to do the thing that all divers dread. This was to go into the engine room and look for the sea valves, to see if they were open. A ship's engine room is a jungle of pipes, cables and sharp edges, waiting to cut and tear the diver's suit and foul his lines. Another hazard is oil, which usually spills all over the engine room from crippled machinery and ruptured fuel and lubricating tanks. Unable to see for the oil on his faceplate, as slippery as a greased pig from the oil covering him, and scarcely able to stand for the tricky footing, the diver in the engine room is prey to all kinds of accidents.

We held a conference on the deck, and I asked for volunteers. When no one spoke up, I nodded toward the next man in line due to go down. "Pitman," I said, "I guess the next dive is yours."

"Yeah, I just volunteered," he said ironically.

Besides being next in line, Pitman was also one of my most experienced men. Just the same, as he was being made ready, I cautioned him about things he already knew. "Look out for valves and levers," I said. "Don't get yourself snagged. And remember, the hatches and watertight doors in Jap ships are small. Be sure you go through them feet first. Don't stick your head in where your broad end won't follow. I'll have Krassic posted outside the engine room, to tend your lifeline and air hose."

No diver likes to think of one dive as being more dangerous than another, and Pitman remarked sarcastically, "I know you used to be a diving instructor, Karneke, but do you always have to sound like one?"

We put Pitman over the side and in a few moments he reported from the bottom, "I'm in the engine room now." Bubbles of oil came boiling to the surface, underscoring his words. Pitman continued, "I'm going down the ladder to the lower level and try to find the sea cocks." We heard him muttering as he started down, "This place sure is full of oil."

At the phone, Wisniewski made conversation for the lonely man below as he proceeded on his way into growing danger.

"Whoa!" Pitman yelled suddenly. There was a thud, followed by a groan.

"What happened?" Wisniewski called anxiously.

"I slipped off the ladder," said Pitman.

"Are you all right?"

Pitman's answer was lost in a high hissing sound, as if his exhaust valve was standing wide open. "Cut your air down," said Wisniewski. "We can hardly hear you."

"Jeez, I'm trying to!" Pitman protested, grunting heavily.

"What's wrong?"

"I'm floating. I'm spread-eagled and I can't reach my control valve." said Pitman. "I'm fouled."

In our mind's eye we could see what had happened. With the air in his suit at high pressure, Pitman was floating like an inflated pillow, unable to bend his arm against the pressure to reach his control valve at the lower left side of his chest.

"Take it easy," said Wisniewski calmly. "We'll cut your air down from up here."

When we had done this, reducing the air in Pitman's suit, he reported, "Okay, I'm starting to sink."

"Fine," said Wisniewski. "Let us know when you get control of your air."

There were sounds of struggle and then Pitman said, with irritation, "I can't close my control valve. This damn oil is making everything so slippery I can't work it."

"All right, we'll keep controlling your air from topside," Wisniewski assured him. "Is everything else all right?"

"No!" Pitman retorted. "I seem to be hung up on something."

"How do you know?"

"I can't touch the deck." In the total darkness of his surroundings, Pitman would have no notion of his orientation—whether he was upright or horizontal.

"What's holding you up?" asked Wisniewski.

"I can't tell. Everything is so black . . . I'm feeling around." There was a pause. "I got it," he said. "I'm hanging from one of these engine-room valves."

"Do you think you can clear yourself?" Wisniewski asked.

"What the hell do you think I'm trying to do?" Pitman flared. "It doesn't feel any goddamned good hanging here like a side of beef!"

"Could Krassic help you if I sent him in?"

"I don't know," said Pitman in a discouraged tone.

"Well, stay there. Take it easy," said Wisniewski, trying to keep his spirits up.

"Don't worry, I'm not going any place," said Pitman bitterly.

I pressed the intercom button and spoke to Krassic, posted at the door to the engine room. "Pitman's fouled," I said. "He's hanging from a valve."

"Okay, I got that," Krassic came back alertly. "What do you want me to do?"

"Take a good strain on his lifeline and air hose, and see if he gets the signal," I directed. Then I informed Pitman of what Krassic was going to do. "Let me know if you get it," I said.

In a few seconds Pitman reported, "I can feel him jerking, so my hose seems to be clear, but somehow my dress is fouled on the ship's valve."

I called to Krassic, "All right, stop pulling and stand fast." Then to Pitman I said, "Can you tell me just how your dress is fouled?"

"It seems like the ship's valve is jammed under my belt, between my hose and breastplate," he answered.

"Do you think another diver could get in there and help you?" I asked.

"I don't see how," he said unhappily.

"What do you suggest?"

"I'd like to come up," Pitman snapped.

"No wisecracks," I said, glad he still had some humor in him. "Do you think cutting your belt loose would help?"

"No, because I'd lose my balance and probably end up standing on my head."

"Isn't the belt fouled on the valve?"

"Yes, but that's not the only place. My control valve seems to be hooked through the ship's valve some way."

"Okay, wait," I said, wondering what to do next.

"Okay, wait—yeah!" Pitman mocked.

"If we sent you the tools, do you think you could get the valve off?" I asked.

"Look," Pitman cried, "if I could get the damn valve off, I could get out of here!" He swore feelingly. "Just let me be for a minute—let me take a blow," he said wearily.

"Okay, take your time," I said. Pitman was not one to panic, but I didn't want to press him too much.

The voice of the captain came over my shoulder. "How're things going?" he asked. From his manner he wasn't simply passing the time of day.

"Not good," I said. "I got one of the divers fouled on the bottom."

"Fouled!" the captain exclaimed. He frowned deeply. "What're you doing about it?" he demanded.

"The way it looks right now, there isn't much we can do for him from up here," I said.

"Well, what's happening down there?" he went on impatiently, pointing at the water. "What's the man doing?"

"He's taking a blow."

"Taking a what?"

"He's resting."

"That's a hell of a place to be resting!" I had seldom seen the captain so agitated.

"I think once he gets a little blow, he'll probably be able to clear himself," I said coolly.

The captain's next words were chilling. "Well, he better rest fast. I just got word the Japs are going to counterattack. We got to get out of here—right now. If you can't get him up at once, he may be down there for good, and the *Chanticleer* may be down there with him!"

I pressed the button and talked to Krassic, at the engine-room door. "Look, Frankie," I said with quiet urgency, "I want you to pull as hard as you can on Pitman's hose."

"But if I jerk the hose too hard, I may cut it on something," Krassic objected.

I didn't want to tell him that this was a risk we had to take —that against it was balanced the certainty that unless we got Pitman freed very soon, it would be the end of him. "Jerk the line as hard as you can," I ordered sharply. "And keep doing it!"

With the captain standing anxiously by, I said to the trapped man, as calmly as I could, "Pitman, you got to get out of there."

"How about letting me rest a little longer?" he protested. "What's the rush?"

"Frankie is pulling on your lifeline and air hose," I said, ignoring his question. "He's going to pull as hard as he can."

There was a *clunk*, followed by Pitman crying happily, "I'm okay now! I just fell to the deck!" Krassic at the same moment confirmed that the hose was free.

"Okay, hold it," I said. Before I could say more, Pitman came in again. "Do you want me to go looking for the sea cocks?" he asked.

"No! Clown!" I shouted. "Follow your lifeline and air hose. Frankie is going to pull you out. And check your control valve because we're going to give you control of your air."

Pitman replied presently, "I can't operate it. It's bent."

"All right, just follow your lifeline and air hose." To Krassic I said, "Start pulling him slowly toward the hatch."

"Slowly is the only way I can pull him," Krassic replied. "His hose is covered with oil and slicker than owl—" In a moment he added, "Okay, I can see Pitman now." He broke into laughter.

"What's so funny?" I asked.

"Pitman looks like a tar baby."

I turned the phone over to the phone man, saying, "Tell the divers to stand by to come up." Matters were now back to routine. As the men came over the side, the captain turned to his messenger and said, "Tell the exec to get this ship out of here before it's too late—if it isn't too late already!" To me the skipper remarked desperately, "You know, you damned divers are going to get us all killed someday!"

As we raced farther to sea, the rumble of guns coming closer, our two guests from the beach repeated the question they had been asking all week, "What do you think made the ship sink?"

Pitman replied, with a knowing grin, "I guess these Japs thought their ship was a submarine and tried to submerge."

This put into words what we had been thinking for days: that the hospital ship *Moro Maru* had been scuttled.

Or had it?

11. Unlocking the Golden Gate

"All right, you men," said Chief Dugan, facing us in the diving instructors' classroom, "you've been telling everybody how easy it is. Here's your chance to prove it."

The war was over. We had been closing out the Navy's net depot and diving school at Tiburon, on San Francisco Bay. Everybody was gone except Dugan and the instructors. Making full allowance for Dugan's skill at finding things for us to do, we wondered what mischief he could have found for us at this late stage.

"We got orders from Washington to clean those nets off the bottom in the Golden Gate," Dugan went on aggressively, as if it was all our fault. "They're lousing up shipping."

His words hardly filled us with joy, for we had been looking forward to a change of scenery. This job would take months—if it could be done at all. The nets had accumulated during the war. Intended to keep out enemy submarines and torpedoes, they had been hung like an underwater fence all the way across the mile-wide opening to San Francisco Bay from the ocean. The nets were suspended by a giant buoy at each end, with a series of smaller buoys in between. At the bottom, to prevent them from standing out like a skirt in the wind as the Golden Gate's tremendous tides came and went through the narrow throat of the bay entrance, the nets were anchored at each corner by a ten-ton pyramid of concrete, or "clump." These clumps, in turn, were moored by anchors arranged in a radial pattern around their bases. When a ship wanted to pass through the channel, a section of the net was swung aside and then quickly closed again, before an intruder could slip into the bay along with the ship.

The nets called for constant attention, keeping a fleet of specially equipped tugs busy. The nearly ceaseless surge of the tide, first in one direction then the other as the 420 square miles of San Francisco Bay emptied and filled, would "walk" the clumps out of position, so that they continually had to be re-established. The pull of the sea as it poured through the nets, made of interlinked steel rings up to three feet in diameter, caused the sections to become twisted and fouled. If the tangle was too hopeless—and it usually was—the solution was to cut the sections loose and let them fall to the bottom, to be replaced with new sections. There wasn't time to fool around with more economic procedures.

The same was done when a ship's propeller caught the net. Only then it was less simple: A man had to go down with a torch and cut the mess free from the blades. This was a slow, hazardous business that sent many a diver to the hospital. The steel links, under tension from entwining the screw, would fly apart as the torch cut through them, clobbering the diver and ripping his suit.

Gradually, as section after section of net was cut away and dropped to the bottom through the years, the floor of the Golden Gate came to be heaped with nets. Ships dropping an anchor into these piles of steel spaghetti saw the anchor no more. And a ship without an anchor is no good either to itself or to other ships. Many vessels simply didn't come in, for lack of a safe place to drop their hooks. It was said that the Navy had closed the Golden Gate so tight that no one could use it.

What to do to get the Gate open again was a new kind of problem, outside the normal scope of Tiburon's activities. Besides the storage of nets these included operation of a boom and net school, with both training and experimentation going on. We diving instructors would first lower a simulated ship's propeller fouled with a net. Then we sent the trainee down to cut the net free. Very often he ended up needing to get himself cut loose. As he concentrated on the cutting, he would forget to look out for his lines, getting them entangled with the screw and the big steel rings of the net. The trapped man seldom got loose on his own because, in the darkness, he couldn't see what was holding him. We averaged two or three rescues a day, taking nearly as much time for this as for actual training.

About one man in four came up from one of these experiences saying, "I don't think I'll be diving again for a while. I don't feel so good." And that would be the end of him as a diver. He would have come to the point which nearly every diver seems to reach sooner or later, usually involving a big scare, when he remarks grimly as he comes out of the suit for the last time, "There are easier ways to kill yourself."

The tricky task of underwater cutting required a great deal of concentration. To begin with, the torch was a deadly weapon. Once I absently laid a torch against my breastplate while I talked into the phone. By the time I woke up, the breastplate had scorched a mark on me nearly as lasting as a brand burned on a steer. The worst problem came from facing into the white glow of the torch, which temporarily blinded the diver, completely taking away what little vision was left to him by the water. In his blindness he found it almost impossible to keep a cut lined up as he was hauled this way and that by the shifting currents, or broke off to hear something on the phone over the popping of the torch. So the diver kept making new cuts, using up time which for a man in the water is always limited.

To ease this problem, I suggested a system that had worked

well in the Philippines and other places around the tropics. That was to put the free hand behind the spot where the flame was being applied. By the heat coming through to the hand, one kept track of his progress and the position of the cut. The idea of putting the hand into a flame that melted steel was not well received, though. So I took a man down to show that all he had to do to keep his hand from getting burned when he felt the heat was to lift it away an inch or so. In water as cold as this, I pointed out, the procedure should work even better than in the warm water of the tropics.

I came up from the demonstration with the satisfied feeling that I had accomplished something—a feeling soon confirmed. As I sat on the stool being undressed, hands clenched from the cold, the tender asked with alarm, "What happened to your hand?"

"What do you mean, what happened to my hand?" I demanded.

"Your left hand, there—where's your fingers?"

The hand was a shapeless mass of blood, the fingers apparently missing. I flipped it over and with relief found the fingers clenched against the palm, but with all the flesh burned off the tips. The hand had been so numbed by the water that I hadn't felt the heat. It was still anesthetized by the cold, keeping me from feeling the injury. That I hadn't burned the hand off was sheer luck. They speeded up my undressing and hustled me off to sick bay just as I went into shock. I was off diving for a month.

"It's a good thing the school's closing," somebody commented loudly next day, with a look in my direction. "Any more of the master's handy hints, and he'd end up with his arms off to his elbows."

The assignment to clear the nets off the bottom of the Golden Gate gave me a chance to redeem myself. First, we tried the obvious. We dived down and into the tangle of hooked cables leading from the barges used in hanging the

Master Diver Joseph Sidney Karneke on board the submarine rescue vessel U.S.S. *Coucal* off Lanai, Hawaii. Karneke has just completed a dive using helium instead of ordinary air. Helium diving permits descents to greater depths but also confronts the diver with many new hazards.

On board the *Coucal* the helium tube is tightened to the diver's suit just prior to his descent. OFFICIAL U.S. NAVY PHOTO

In training, the Navy diver learns under carefully simulated conditions. Above, two students, one wearing the Navy's standard shallow water outfit, the other the standard deep sea rig, prepare to bolt pipe flanges in a mock of a pipeline. OFFICIAL U.S. NAVY PHOTOS

At a depth of 200 feet in the clear waters off Nassau, Bahamas, a Navy diver (*above*) squares away his air hose and lifeline, then (*right*) prepares to surface, his training salvage operation complete.

The Navy diver at work. OFFICIAL U.S. NAVY PHOTOS

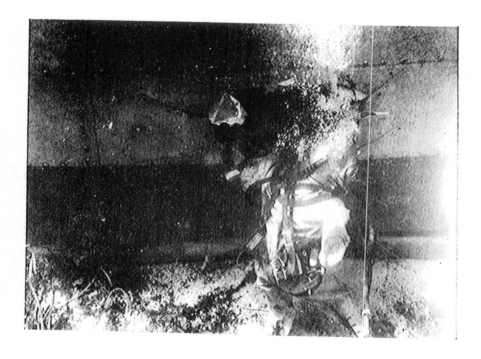

Navy divers wait out decompression on the platform after a
200-foot dive off Key West, Florida. OFFICIAL U.S. NAVY PHOTOS

Mine disposal is one of the Navy diver's most important assignments. Above, a mine disposal diver places an explosive cutting charge on a mine in Pearl Harbor waters. Below is a Soviet horned contact mine of the type frequently encountered during the Korean war. OFFICIAL U.S. NAVY PHOTOS

In Wonsan Harbor, Korea, Master Diver Joe Karneke has just rendered harmless a Russian mine developed to blow up harbor and river boats whose shallow draft rendered regular mines ineffective. Oil drums mark the safe path through a land mine field.

nets. The barges heaved up on the cables, reeling them in over the ends of the booms standing out from their bows. The load would rise so far, and then, with the barge dipping forward into the water from the strain, the load would break away and sink back to the bottom. It was no use. Locked together like coat hangers, and with the big concrete clumps ensnarled among them, the nets were far beyond the forty-ton limit the barges could handle.

The only solution was to go down with our torches and cut the clumps out, which we calculated would make the big difference. But this gave us the tide to contend with. The period of slack water, when the tide was neither coming nor going, lasted only about an hour. Allowing for the time it took to make the trip down and up, this left little time for work on each dive. At this rate, the job would go on indefinitely.

There were many reasons why the diver could not work in the tide. The rushing sea, reaching a peak flow in the Gate seven times the volume of the Mississippi at New Orleans, would sweep him off his feet, swinging him toward the surface by his lines. This would threaten him with the bends from the quick change of pressure. There would also be danger of air embolism. This is an air bubble in the blood stream, affecting the victim in the same way as a blood clot or thrombosis. Being a bubble, it tends to rise. When it reaches a place too small for it to pass through, it stops, blocking the blood flow. Unless the victim is rushed to a recompression chamber, where the pressure of the water can be duplicated and then eased off gradually, he will shortly be dead.

If the diver became fouled as the current carried him away —always a danger when there is movement through the water—his air hose could be torn loose. He would then be crushed by the implosion of the sea and drowned at a stroke. Nor, if he was fouled, could he hope for help from the boat crew. It probably would be having its own troubles with the current; and, anyway, in this plunging sea nobody would be able to dive down to give him a hand. He would be strictly on his own.

The interval of slack water was measured by the surface current. How long it lasted on the bottom, where the pattern of movement was not necessarily the same as on top, nobody knew for sure. No one had ever stayed down long enough to find out.

For several days we carried on in the usual way, bringing the diver up as soon as we saw the current begin to move. Most of the time we seemed to be sitting in the diving boat, watching the water and boring one another with our sea stories, telling the same yarns over and over. We groused about the extra pay we were missing, belaboring the point that there was no diving pay in sitting on the diving stool.

One morning when it was my turn to go down, someone mused as we waited for the tide to slacken that if a diver could stay on the bottom during the tide, he could get a lot of work done.

"Has anybody ever tried it?" I asked.

"No, and I don't think anybody wants to," he replied, giving me a look that meant he had me in mind.

Dugan took up the thought. "Since you're so interested in finding out," he said, "do you want to try?" This showed some faith on his part that it could be done, since he was in charge of the operation and would have the responsibility if things went wrong.

I wasn't aware that I had shown the interest he spoke of, but I replied, "If you're willing to take a chance, so am I."

There was a cackle of laughter, fading when I stood up and said, "Get me out of this Number Three suit and bring me a Size Two." This size was a little small for me, but what it lacked in comfort it made up in giving me better control of my buoyancy.

"Get him a Number Two," directed the tender as he peeled me out of the one I was wearing. "He means it."

The smaller suit was brought, and as I was getting into it

there were witticisms like, "Is there anything of value in your clothes that you want us to hold for you—like money?"

"Thanks," I said. "But I intend to get back."

"Yeah, we know you'll be back—but on which side of the Golden Gate?"

At the last moment, Dugan seemed worried. "Look," he said, "I know how you feel in that Number Two suit, but for my sake how about us putting an extra belt on you?"

I wasn't happy about the extra one hundred pounds this would give me—ten lead weights of ten pounds each—but it was reassuring to know that Dugan was concerned about his job. I accepted the extra load; like the sinker on a fishline, it would help to hold me against the current.

In a few minutes I was in the midnight world of the bottom. I landed next to a clump looming like a miniature pyramid in the darkness, and prepared to go right to work cutting the entangled net away from it. Whatever was in store for me, I planned to make hay while I could. I swung my torch into position and reported my arrival topside.

"Are you ready for gas?" the phone man asked.

"Ready for gas," I replied. The gas was a mixture of air, oxygen and hydrogen, each flowing down in its own hose, with the three tied together. Hydrogen rather than acetylene gas made up the third component because it safely withstands pressure, which has to be above the pressure of the water. Acetylene gas, in contrast, is highly unstable under pressure, tending to explode.

The gas was turned on. I adjusted the valves to the right settings. "Gas adjusted," I said. "Turn on igniter."

With the current on, I flipped the two carbons together, closing the circuit and drawing an arc as I pulled them apart to the proper separation. The loud bang made by the torch as it lights up, sending a shock wave against the diver that sometimes jars his head in the helmet and is heard topside, made my next call superfluous. "Igniter off."

"Igniter off," topside echoed. "Go to work."

I attacked the net from the landward side of the clump, and as I worked I cast frequent glances over my shoulder in the direction the tide would come from. What I would see I didn't know. I knew only that it would be along within an hour. Meanwhile, I kept alert for the signs I knew from experience: a gentle tugging at the hose and lifeline, as when topside is taking in slack; silt slithering along the bottom; seaweed drifting by. Every few minutes, too, I scuffed the bottom with my foot, to see which way the mud and silt were moving, in the diver's version of the farmer throwing a handful of dirt into the air to tell the direction of the wind. Things were as peaceful as a pond.

A half hour or so had passed when word came from topside that the tide had started to run. "Can you feel anything down there?" asked the phone man.

I gave the bottom another kick and looked around at the murkiness enclosing me. "Nothing unusual down here," I said.

"Better check your lifeline and air hose and make sure they're clear," the phone man cautioned. "We're going to tend you closer." I felt a pull as they took up on the lines. The close haul on them cut down on my movements and added to my discomfort, but this was offset by the reassurance it gave me that Dugan was on the ball. I felt a mounting sense of impending danger.

"Are you all right?" asked the phone man. He repeated the question every few minutes; a diver's telephone is notorious for its habit of failing at crucial moments. The repetition of the question, to which the diver must keep responding, becomes irritating because it carries an accumulating suggestion to the diver that he might not be all right. After a while he nervously begins to wonder if there are things going on that he doesn't know about.

Keeping up my reassurances that all was well, I went steadily on with my work, every now and then giving the bottom a kick for signs of motion by the water. My plan was to stay down as long as I could, instead of running at the first hint that the tide was moving. As I squinted into the white flame of my torch, with the minutes continuing to pass un-eventfully, I fell to reflecting that maybe the famous Golden Gate tide was overrated—another of those things overdram-atized for lack of knowledge. Here I was, at the bottom, and nothing could be more peaceful. Not a grain of sand moved; not a sliver of seaweed drifted by.

All at once, it was darker. The opaque walls of my twilight room pulled in around me. I shot a glance over my shoulder and saw a towering wall of solid black sweeping toward me. I had the fleeting impression of a line-squall thunderstorm. I called into the phone, "Is there something going by up there?" Passing ships sometimes throw a shadow on the bot-tom, or stir up the sediment with their propellers.

"No—why?" the phone man came back suspiciously.

"There's a big black—" That was as far as I got. The light went out and I was slammed toward the clump as if I had been hit by a truck. I threw up my hands to brace myself just as I crashed with a loud grunt against the side. As I hung there, spread-eagled and helpless as a bug caught on a wind-shield, it went through my mind that I now had firsthand in-formation that must be exclusive on what it was like to be hit by San Francisco Bay on its way out to sea. The darkness was caused by the mud and sand rolled before the onrushing cur-rent like the dust at the expanding base of an atomic blast. Where I would have been if I had been caught on a different side of the clump I would think about some other time.

The phone man's voice was crowding the helmet. "Are you all right, Chief?" he was asking anxiously.

"Yeah, I'm all right," I gasped, struggling to get my wind back. "But I can't move," I added, describing the situation.

"There's a heavy pull on your hose," the phone man ad-vised.

"Better get some slack on it," I replied. I wanted to get the strain off it, knowing that if it parted I would be instantly dead.

A few moments went by. "Do you feel any easing of the strain?" asked the phone man.

"No," I said.

"We got an extra 200 feet out now," said the phone man. "We only got fifty feet left on deck."

The plunging current was snatching the hose taut again as fast as the slack was payed out. "Better not let out any more," I said. We were only increasing the danger of snagging the hose without gaining anything in return. "How's the boat?" I asked. We were anchored dead in the middle of the Golden Gate, and it seemed reasonable that the boat might join the rush to sea.

"The boat's okay, Chief," the phone man answered confidently. "It's not going anywhere." After a pause, he added hopefully that the pull on the hose at least wasn't getting any worse. "How do you feel?" he asked.

"I never felt better—extra belt and all," I replied with a jauntiness born of knowing I was probably going to survive. I was glad I had the extra belt. It would come in handy to hold me in place on the way up.

The tide would make that two or three hours away, however, and the prospect of being idly pasted against the clump for that long, doing nothing except drawing my extra five dollars an hour, promised to get pretty dull. Maybe I could put the time to some use. Little by little I managed to inch my arms down. I screwed my body sideways, taking care not to get my stern stuck out past the edge of the clump. Laboriously I bent down and retrieved my torch, which I had dropped when the storm hit. That it was still there to retrieve was because I had a line to it from my belt. The torch had gone out.

"Turn on the igniter," I called. "I'm going to try to do some work."

"Be careful—don't get swept out," said the phone man uneasily.

The juice was sent down, and with the torch going again, I found that I enjoyed an advantage over normal conditions as I experimentally applied the flame to a steel ring. With the water holding me rigidly against the clump, I had no trouble keeping the torch steady and burning through a link without losing the cut and having to start over. When I had done all there was to do on that side of the clump, the tide had slowed enough so I could safely venture past the corners and cut elsewhere. By the time I called it a day, this clump was free and ready to be pulled up.

When I finally arrived back at the surface, I had been down three and a half hours, compared to a previous diving time of less than one hour. Dugan concealed his satisfaction behind a dour comment. "It was about time some bubble-head came up with an idea to do a job faster but at the same time make more money."

Having discovered that we could stay down during the tidal run, with due attention to being on the right side of the clumps at the right time, we all began working through the tide. The extra belt gave added safety, going and coming, and as one man came up at the tail end of the tide, another arrived at the bottom to work through the next one. In weeks instead of months the job was finished—the lock was off the Golden Gate.

12. The Balloons of Monterey Bay

There was one more job for us before we left Tiburon. In Monterey Bay an abortive experiment in storing aviation gasoline in underwater balloons, for the convenience of seaplanes at advanced bases, had been carried on. Made of neoprene, the balloons were held in place by a canopy of wire mesh stretched over the top and gathered to a point underneath, where the net was secured by cable to a concrete clump like those we had worked with in the Golden Gate. From the submerged top of the balloon, a small hose led up through the water to a fueling nozzle fastened to a buoy, which also served to mark the location. The pressure of the sea on the sides of the balloon forced the contents up through the hose as the nozzle was opened for service. It was the squeeze-bottle technique used in a big way, with the ocean supplying the squeeze.

An interesting idea, but it hadn't worked out. The currents pounding against the sides of the balloon caused the clumps at the bottom to "walk." One clump, it was to be found, had made a good start toward the open sea, moving several hundred feet. Also, passing boat operators had discovered that high-test aviation gasoline mixed with kerosene made fine boat fuel, and had helped themselves until only one balloon was left with gasoline in it. The other three of the original four presumably lay collapsed somewhere on the bottom of the bay.

Our job was to retrieve the lone survivor while there was still time, and try to locate the others. We were to find the assignment unexpectedly exciting, though not altogether for reasons directly related to the work itself.

We loaded our gear aboard a Coast Guard buoy-tending ship tied up at Treasure Island, sailed out through the Golden Gate, and headed down the California coast. It was an unusually hot day, and by the time we moored alongside our balloon, with the ship's steel deck flinging back the sun's heat, the temperature aboard was like July in Death Valley. It was a great time to don the suit and go over the side.

But the cooling water of a hundred feet down soon lost its effect as I fought to mount the six-foot clump and put a hook through the pad eye on top. The clump was bucking like a bronco from the tides boxing it, adding the danger of snagging my air hose under a corner to the problem of scaling the sides. These were slippery with slime and I kept sliding back, my diver's stiff, lead-soled shoes hardly being suited to this kind of thing. The sweat rolled from me in showers, squishing up around my feet.

Hearing my struggles, the phone man asked, "What's the matter down there, Chief?"

"What's the matter!" I repeated. "Did you ever try to get aboard a greased hobbyhorse in a diving dress at the bottom of the sea?"

I decided to try a little science, moving around to another side where I could make use of the tide. As it surged with me, I gave myself a shot of air and, presto, I was on top. I slid the hook into place, and soon was back on the boat.

Noting my heated condition as my helmet was lifted off, the captain remarked hospitably, "You look like you could stand a cold one."

"I sure could," I agreed, brightening.

"Go back to the galley and the cook will take care of you."

The cook met me in the doorway, sweating as hard as I was. "How are you, diver man?" he greeted me, grinning widely. He handed me a tall glass of ice tea. "This'll fix you right up," he said.

Tea wasn't exactly what I had in mind, but it would do. As I sat sipping it at the table, the cook flipped the sweat from his forehead with a forefinger and made a memorable observation. "It sho' ain't no country for a white man," he said.

Out on deck, meanwhile, the crew was hoisting the balloon with its load of gasoline from the water. I joined them just as the big bag was swung over the side. There was a loud poof, and in a moment the deck was running with high-test aviation fuel. It spilled into the water all around, leaving the ships sitting in a sea of potential fire. A tense couple of hours passed before we got the gasoline hosed off the decks and the tide carried away the threat on the water. Not often had I seen a crew so disciplined about not smoking.

"These divers are trying to make it hotter for us," one of the Coast Guard men remarked when it was over. This brought things back to normal. There is always someone who thinks the divers are trying to make trouble.

At the end of an unusually perverse day, the captain came up to me and said, as if to make amends, "We have a boat, Chief. If you and the divers are interested, we'll be glad to take you ashore for a little relaxation."

Rarely can a man be as sure that he speaks for all as I was when I replied on the spot, "That sounds good, Captain. We'll be ready by the time you get a boat crew together."

When the four of us in my crew leaped ashore a little while later, we thought the captain must have been kidding. If there was "relaxation" to be had, it didn't show in this rickety little village that seemed from the deserted streets to have lost even the few people who lived there. We shuffled along the waterfront street, thinking we had probably made a mistake to let the boat go back to the ship before we checked the place. It looked like a dull several hours before the boat returned to pick us up.

Then we came to a weathered door with painted-out windows on each side. From within came the jangling of a jukebox and the clink of glasses. Spirits leaping, we pushed through the door and found ourselves in a well-populated gin mill, which must have been the town's social center. We found seats at the bar and as we looked around with a drink in hand, we noted that the clientele had one highly interesting peculiarity: it was *all* female. Except for the bartender, there wasn't a man in the place. Whatever the reason for this pleasing mystery, we silently toasted the United States Coast Guard, and particularly the captain of a certain buoy tender lying out in Monterey Bay.

On our reluctant way back to the ship late in the night, we all had abundant reason to agree with Ski, the lady-killer among us, when he remarked with a happy sigh, "Gee, this diving job is sure turning out a lot nicer than we expected. I could go on diving for these balloons for months."

Next evening as we eagerly prepared to go back ashore, the captain said genially, "Well, how did you find the fishermen last night?"

"Fishermen?" Ski asked with surprise. "All we found was gals."

"I see," said the captain, smiling strangely.

So that was it—this was a fishing village, and all the fishermen were out fishing, leaving the girls to make the most of their loneliness while they were gone. In this we continued to give them our co-operation each evening—and then came the sad reminder that all good things must come to an end. After four days, with all but one of the balloons found, the captain decided to secure the operation and return to San Francisco. We divers stoutly assured him that, with a little more time, we certainly would find the other balloon. We expressed pain at leaving a job unfinished, but the captain's decision stood.

We went ashore looking forward to a big time on our final night. As we lightheartedly walked through the door where we had been greeted with such warmth on other evenings, we sensed that things had changed. The girls were gone, and in their place was a crowd of large, unneighborly-looking men. They stopped talking, fixing us with hard, malevolent stares. An ominous quiet came down all over the place. Even the jukebox was silent. These, we knew, were the fishermen.

For an instant the survival instinct checked our steps, but Navy tradition prevailed and we pressed resolutely forward, heading for the bar. Dugan laid a heavy fist on the mahogany and, with the same convivial tone of other evenings, said, "How about a round of cold ones, barkeep?"

The barkeep didn't know us tonight. Dugan repeated his request.

"Take it easy," said the barkeep impersonally. "I'll get to you in a minute."

The drinks came, and as we lifted them, the man next to Dugan bumped his elbow, spilling the drink on Dugan's sleeve and over the bar. Dugan silently contemplated his glass for a moment. Then he turned to me and in a conservative statement that took our first spoken notice of the situation, muttered, "I think these guys are looking for trouble."

I turned my head slightly and out of the corner of my eye saw that we were solidly hemmed in behind. They stood over us in quiet menace, blocking the way to the door. I leaned close to Dugan. "I think we better get out of here," I whispered. There are times when one retreats without dishonor.

"Do you think we can make it?" Dugan muttered, accepting the idea.

I turned to Ski, at my other elbow. "We're going to make a break for it out of here," I said. I nodded toward our fourth member, seated next to Ski. "Tell Ed," I said.

With everybody alerted to the plan, the problem was how to see it through. If we all got up and started out together, we were sure to be jumped. I stole a look around the room. The only way out was the same way we came in, by the front door. Next to the door I noticed the telephone booth. I mentioned this to Dugan, and was encouraged to find that he was thinking the same thing I was. We agreed that one of us, moving alone, could probably make it to the booth without attracting too much attention.

"I'll go and get in it," Dugan volunteered. "Then I'll turn around and say something to distract these characters. When they come at me, I'll slam the door, and you guys make a break for it while I'm holding 'em off from inside the booth. I'll get out some way."

Dugan was well endowed with fighting Irish spirit, generally preferring to settle issues by peaceful means only as a last resort. If any among us could bring off what he proposed to do, it was Dugan.

With a signal to us to be ready, he got up and casually moved off through our hard-eyed friends, remarking so they could hear that he had to make a phone call. When he was inside the booth, he turned around and from the open door bellowed to the house at the top of his lungs, his face twisted in a snarl, "Are there any slimy fishermen in this place?"

Dugan's calculations that this would be effective were immediately confirmed. As one, the horde exploded toward the booth.

"Let's get out of here!" I yelled.

We passed the booth just as Dugan opened his defense, smashing a fist into the nose of the first man to reach him. But as he closed the door of the booth, an unforeseen complication arrived. The two largest members of the opposition tore the booth from its moorings. They brought it down to horizontal and, one at either end, began to jounce it around, Dugan meanwhile issuing colorful condemnations of the proceedings from inside.

I stopped the flight of the three of us. "We better stick around and help him," I said. We went after the pair with the booth, and the fight was on. It ranged up and down and across the room, attended by sounds of splintering glass and collapsing furniture, the thudding of fists and the crash of things being thrown. The door burst open and the battle spilled into the street. There, some citizens, sensitive to the sight of blood and strife, called the police. They sirened up just in time to save the Navy from disaster. We had made a good showing but we were badly outnumbered. As Ski said, wiping blood from his mouth, "I never knew there were so many fishermen in the whole world."

Dugan, who had left the booth early in the action, shook his head with the sad air of a man not used to losing. "I never saw so many knuckles in my life," he said. He looked accusingly at Ski. "This is what I get for coming ashore with a lover type," he added bitterly.

On the ship next morning, the captain saw the marks of conflict. "I guess the place wasn't so friendly after all," he observed, as if he had secretly known all along it would come to this.

Back at Tiburon, the officer in charge greeted us with, "It looks like you had a pretty rough operation."

"Yeah," I said offhandedly. "We had some unforeseen things come up." The officer said no more, for that made it routine. On a diving operation unforeseen things were always coming up.

13. The Treasure of the Nickajack Trail

"You know anything about explosives?" asked the assignment officer.

With the Golden Gate cleared, the diving school at Tiburon at last was closed out and I was at 12th District Naval Headquarters in San Francisco for reassignment. "A little—based on experience," I replied.

"Good," said the officer. "How would you like to go on the A-bomb tests at Bikini?"

I assured him that my experience didn't reach to A-bombs. "That doesn't matter," he said. "There'll be a lot of conventional blasting to do first."

"When do I leave?"

"How long will it take you to pack?"

"A couple of hours."

"Fine." He glanced at his watch. "We got a plane leaving for Pearl at 1600. You'll be assigned as master aboard the *Conserver*."

I had heard of the *Conserver*. She was an ARS—a rescue and salvage vessel. The same size as the *Chanticleer*, her primary concern was ships, not subs—ships grounded, beached, or sunk. Since such operations are in relatively shallow water,

143

she was rigged for diving at depths not over a hundred feet. When I arrived at Pearl Harbor, though, I found the *Conserver* being fitted with much of the special paraphernalia of the submarine rescue vessel. Among many other things, extra air compressors and recompression chambers were being loaded aboard, and her diving equipment was being modified for diving at two hundred feet, the maximum depth of the lagoon at Bikini. Heavy stress was placed on fire-fighting equipment, a strong hint of one way salvage would be different in the atomic age.

Nobody knew for sure what we were getting into as we headed for the Marshall Islands, 2,000 miles southwest of Hawaii. Scuttlebutt and speculation took up most of the conversation. This would be the first underwater atomic shot ever fired, and there had been a lot of discussion in the newspapers and over the radio of what would happen. A few thought the explosion would destroy gravity, causing everything hereafter to fall upward. Some were afraid that the water of the ocean would be turned to gas, dropping ships to the bottom. Others expected the blast to blow a hole through the ocean floor, letting all the water drain out—presumably into that same big space where Columbus was supposed to fall as he sailed off the edge of the earth in 1492.

In a different version of much the same eventuality, H. S. Uhler, professor emeritus of physics at Yale University, worried that the explosion would cause a crack to form in the bottom. The sea, rushing into the opening and coming into contact with molten rock at the earth's core, would turn to steam and set off a series of titanic explosions like those of 1883 in the Straits of Sunda, when Krakatoa volcano blew its 18-square-mile island off the map. Professor Uhler foresaw a tidal wave a mile high, rushing at express-train speed across the seas, swamping islands and continents in its path. He also warned of a possible upset to the gyroscopic balance of the earth, causing quakes and shudderings on this "sorely stricken human carousel."

We heard that a shipload of newsmen on their way to the tests nearly panicked at the news a few days out that a tidal wave would roll over all ships, leaving no survivors. This prediction came from one Anatol J. Schneiderov, at Johns Hopkins University. The school was quick to make it known that Schneiderov was not a faculty member but only a student, of "Russian origin," and calm returned to the news ship.

That there would be tidal waves there wasn't much doubt. The only question was how high and how far they would travel. People living inland in the United States felt sorry for those living along the West Coast. In Los Angeles, thousands picked the day of the shot as a good time to be in the mountains picnicking. The same thing was happening in Hawaii, people on the flats heading for high ground. Fortune-tellers were doing a brisk business at their crystal balls, finding out for their customers where it would be safe.

Even Admiral W. H. P. Blandy, in charge of Operation Crossroads, wasn't laying any bets on what would happen. He spoke darkly of 1,000-mile-an-hour winds, and heat of 100,000,000 degrees, which would instantly fuse the steel plates of the ships.

But those of us aboard the *Conserver* weren't losing any sleep. Too many experts who ought to be pretty sure of what to expect were going to Bikini. And my own philosophy had long been, if the fellow in the know is going to be there, you haven't much to worry about.

The big lament as we sailed into the Bikini lagoon was not that we might be at the scene of our last adventure but that no Dorothy Lamours in sarongs appeared among the palm trees swaying in the breeze at either side of the passage. Chief Juda and his 150-odd subjects, of mixed Melanesian-Polynesian stock, had already been moved to Rongerik, an island about 130 miles to the east. Most of the crew had volunteered to extend their enlistments for these tests but now, with the vision of dusky island beauties faded, there were irreverent remarks about sacrifices above and beyond the call of duty.

The floor of the lagoon was studded with coral heads thrusting up from the bottom like inverted cones, and where the water was shallow we were put right to work blasting out these obstructions, so that the target ships could be brought in and anchored. To go down and plant the charges, working in teams of two, we donned our shallow-water outfits, a refinement of the homemade rigs we had used in Australia early in the war.

The explosive was a high-velocity TNT, prepared especially for this job—fat sticks five inches in diameter and eighteen inches long, packed in crates. To make sure they sank, the crew ripped a couple of slats off to let the water in, then heaved the crates overboard from a landing craft drifting overhead, dumping them in wherever they saw our bubbles rising. Having been briefed that the stuff was highly unstable, the crew was a little slow to handle it in this carefree manner until we explained the cushioning effect of the water. It also took them a little while to get used to the idea of heaving these goods down on our heads; they never could understand how we missed getting hit. But with our shallow-water rigs, allowing free movement, this was no problem. We ducked and dodged like prize fighters, alternately getting out of the way and coming back to guide the crates into place against the coral as they peppered down through the clear water.

Each shot required from twenty to one hundred crates, weighing about fifty pounds each—or 1,000 to 5,000 pounds all told. Around one stick in every other crate we laced primacord. This is the equivalent of the old-time powder train, except that in place of slow-burning black powder, the core is loaded with TNT-type high explosive, through which the fire explodes at 21,000 feet a second, or almost simultaneously. The shock from this sets off the charge at the other end without the need of percussion caps. Wrapped around a medium-sized tree, primacord can knock the tree down.

While being powder monkeys with extra-touchy TNT on

the bottom of the ocean wasn't the safest thing to be doing, the one close call we had came from something else. I was hurrying to intercept a sinking crate and jockey it into place when I felt something grab me by the shorts from behind. I spun around and there was my partner, Doc Schmidt, urgently pointing down at something just in front of me. I looked, and jumped back even with Doc. One more step and I would have put my sneaker-covered foot into the mouth of a Tridacna, or giant clam. I had never seen one before but Doc, fortunately, had noticed several in his area and was on the lookout for them.

The clam was buried upright in the coral so that only the mouth showed. The mouth was fully a yard long and yawned open ten inches or more. What we could have done about it if I had stuck my foot into this trap—between those rows of interlocking teeth—I don't know, but from the tales I had heard about these oversized chowder makers, the outlook wouldn't have been good.

I made sure we would never face the problem with this one. I jammed a stick of dynamite in where my foot was supposed to have gone, and as the closing jaws crushed the stick flat, I put a couple of extra loops of primacord around it, hoping what the clam was doing to the stick didn't set it off prematurely.

When we got back topside I said to Schmidt, a pharmacist's mate trained as a diving technician, "Thanks, Doc. You probably didn't want me as a patient anyway."

"My job is to look after you guys on top," he replied in mock complaint. "Now it looks like I got to play nurse to you on the bottom, too."

We pulled the boat back to the beach, and as the handle on the hellbox was about to be pushed down to set off the ton or so of TNT Doc and I had planted down on the reef, someone observed, reflecting the group's keen appreciation of the historic implications of the Bikini tests, "Boy, I betcha that clam'll have a headache."

In the sheet of water that leaped two hundred feet into the air, we made out fish and other solid objects but nothing that looked like a giant clam. "Probably blown to powder," it was theorized.

After lunch, when the water had cleared, we dived back to the bottom to see what had happened to the clam—and, incidentally, the coral head. Rolled up on the ocean floor we found a great blob of bloody white flesh. About a hundred feet away lay the empty shell. It was still intact except for the scalloped edges. These had been blown off, revealing a thickness of four inches in the shell.

Since nobody would believe how big the shell was, or that it had withstood a blast that would sink a ship, we wound a line around it and, back topside, assigned the two strongest nonbelievers to haul it up. "Get yourself a nice ash tray," we said.

They braced themselves against the side of the ship and pulled, getting nowhere. "What are you wise guys trying to do?" they protested. "Did you tie his line to an anchor or something?"

We gave them a hand, and when we finally got the shell aboard—harder work than anything we were being paid for —the scoffers were well cured; the shell weighed 600 pounds. It was dragged to one side and left on the fantail, where in its pale green translucence it was boastfully shown to visiting sailors from other ships, becoming the subject of tall tales that grew taller with the telling. From having their master diver nearly put his foot into the clam's mouth to having him actually do so and then fighting himself free in a dramatic battle on the ocean floor—well, this was but a short step in a natural progression, and the crew of the *Conserver* was not prone to avoid short steps of that nature.

It wasn't that anyone wanted to make a hero out of me; the idea was to cast glory on the ship. To cast it on the master diver would have been unthinkable. Far from honoring anybody, especially rank, the crew looks for ways to get laughs at his expense. One day while we were laying buoys to moor the target ships to, the *Conserver* accidentally got hung up on the cable connecting two of them. With an underwater cutting torch in hand, I climbed down onto the starboard buoy. It had been pulled under the surface by the weight of the ship on the cable, so that water washed over my backside as I draped myself over the top and reached down to start cutting.

Working in this awkward position was bad enough in itself, but as I burned through each strand, releasing the tension on it, the strand sprang outward, knocking my torch aside and further irritating me. Besides all this, there was a hearty laughter coming from the railbirds, for reasons not apparent to me. "What's so damned funny?" I finally demanded, twisting a sweaty face up at my audience.

"Keep going, Karneke," somebody answered merrily. "You're doing great."

I went back to my work with some muttered references to their origins, still not suspecting the thing everyone but myself could see coming. The last strands of the cable let go and the freed buoy popped to the surface, pitching me out into space on a long arc that landed me with a loud belly-smacker fifty feet away. Even as I flew I could hear them howling on the ship. "There goes the old master—grandstanding again!"

They threw me a line and helped me back aboard, but I stayed in a surly mood for a while. This prompted the remark, "I notice the old master doesn't seem to see anything funny about it."

"Hell no," said another, "this is no joke to him. He's going to log it as a pay dive, and he's probably figuring how to get flight pay for it, too."

Our work in the Bikini lagoon was interrupted by a call for help from a fleet oil tanker, the *Nickajack Trail*. She had been on her way with fuel for the ships of the atom test fleet, but had run aground on Japtan Island as she put into the harbor at Eniwetok, about a hundred miles away. Disaster had come, so the story went, after she swung aside to avoid an out-bound vessel. We were sent to try to pull her back into the water.

When we reached the tanker, we found considerably more than a routine grounding to deal with, not to mention other unusual circumstances. The tanker's engines were burned out, caused by racing the propellers in a desperate effort to free her. This meant that the ship was dead, unable to give us a hand in the effort to refloat her.

Such work is done with beaching gear. Off the stern of the stranded ship, a spread of spring buoys is anchored in a fan-shaped pattern at right angles to the ship. From the buoys cables are strung to the vessel, where they are linked into block and tackle, by which the cables are then drawn taut until the buoys are pulled under water. The buoyancy of the buoys causes them to push upward against the cables, caus-ing the cables in turn to put a pull on the ship—a steady pull of twenty tons. Hence the name, "spring" buoys. From time to time, as the waves and the shifting tides act on the ship, tending to loosen the pull on the cables, they are taken up with the block and tackle. This, if it works, keeps the stranded ship inching seaward.

The first problem was to get our equipment aboard the *Nickajack Trail*. There were tons of it, probably a million dollars' worth. The air compressors alone weighed several tons each. Since there was no power aboard the tanker to turn her steam-driven winches, the job was complicated. After some pondering, we thought of a clever solution. With our work boat moored alongside the tanker, we ran an air hose from one of the compressors in our boat up to a winch on the tanker. Then, with the air from our compressor turning the winch, we used the winch to lift the compressors aboard. From there on the work was downhill. We glowed with pride at our genius.

While a crew laid the buoys, I went aboard the *Nickajack Trail* with ten men to rig the block and tackle. It was hard, dirty work, and at the end of the day, after supper, my crew and I gathered on the fantail to take the breeze. In a little while someone of the tanker crew, who hadn't been much in evidence during the day, joined us with a bottle. More tanker men drifted up, and I noticed that they all seemed to be afflicted with third-degree hangover—the kind that can be built only on the installment plan. The supporting evidence downwind was overpowering.

As they laid the groundwork for a new installment from the bottle being passed around, they grew talkative. They complained about the tough luck that had hit them. There was a lot more to it than the grounding alone, for which they blamed the captain. There was grievous personal calamity involved as well. After leaving the States, they confided, they had stopped at a Mexican port and picked up a large cargo of whiskey, at seventy cents a fifth. This merchandise they had planned to sell at black-market prices to the crews of the Bikini ships they were going to refuel—making it, so to speak, a kind of double refueling. They had visions of returning home as rich men. Now these dreams were gone, shattered on the rocks of Japtan Island.

In their disappointment, they had drunk up a good part of the secondary cargo. Then, in a flash of alcoholic hopefulness, they had decided to carry the balance ashore and bury it, keeping back a reasonable inventory for current needs. On some brighter tomorrow, then, they would come back and recover the treasure. This hope had waned until we arrived, but now, with their spirits soaring as those in the community bottle declined, they were sure that we had brought them salvation. There even was talk that maybe they should dig up the liquor and bring it back aboard.

But when we checked the holds next day, things did not look good. The ship seemed to be impaled on a coral head, the rock thrusting up through the bottom. What damage hadn't been done in the beginning had been accomplished later in the struggle to get free, and by the coming and going of the tide. The constant grinding of the ship against the rocks had made the first holes bigger and punched out new ones. It looked as if the *Nickajack Trail* had completed her final voyage.

But it would be a while before we found out for sure, for the *Conserver* was now called away to help the tugs towing the Japanese battlewagon *Nagato* to the Bikini target area from Japan. The tugs were in trouble from a storm, about three hundred miles to the northwest. My beaching crew and I were left behind aboard the *Nickajack Trail* to await the *Conserver*'s return. We settled down to make the most of what we expected to be a dull time, but we could hardly have been more wrong.

Having seen us rescuers shake our heads over the damage we found in the hold of the tanker, and heard our negative comments about the prospects of freeing her, the tankermen had lapsed back into melancholy. The first night after the *Conserver* pulled away, two of them stole ashore on a raft to look for the buried liquor, having in mind to consume their share on the spot. We saw them next morning, standing on the beach looking like end men in a minstrel show from the oil covering them. They were waving their arms and screaming hysterically.

Brought aboard, they shakily told of a night of terror. "There's no whiskey buried over there!" they cried emotionally. "There's nothing buried over there except dead men!" They looked accusingly at their shipmates. "Why didn't somebody tell us?" they asked.

What they hadn't been told was that Japtan Island, besides being the gravesite of the liquor, was a burial ground for those killed in the invasion of the Marshalls two years before. The pair hadn't seen the cemetery from the ship because of the palm trees fringing the island. The white crosses in the darkness, the ghostly creaking and groaning of the vessel on the rocks—the two had badly needed the drink they couldn't find.

Whoever knew the whereabouts of the buried whiskey still wasn't telling, and as the stocks that had been kept behind began to dwindle with the passing days, the tanker crew resourcefully took to making raisin jack. This was something new to us of the Navy and, ever eager to improve our minds with new knowledge, we were quick to learn the recipe for it. All that was needed was fruit and sugar, mixed and set in a warm place. This cheering friend of the parched sailor originally was made with raisins, accounting for the name, but any fruit will do.

As the days dragged idly by, with nothing further happening to break the monotony or to encourage the hope of getting them out of their troubles, the tanker crew took to hitting the raisin jack hard. There were fights and threats of mutiny. The captain, near nervous collapse, locked himself in his cabin and stayed there. I instructed my men to keep away from the tanker crew, but they were nipping raisin jack themselves now, and this made for camaraderie.

I was prepared for anything—until one of my crew came up to me one day as I worked at a winch. "You know, Chief," he said with the enthusiasm of discovery, "that guy Romeo can hypnotize people!"

Romeo Jones, a tall, handsome fellow with dark features, was a seaman with us on the *Conserver*. This was the first I had heard that he possessed special talents.

"You're crazy," I said. "You've been hitting the raisin jack again. I told you men I don't want you drinking that stuff!"

"I'll admit I've been drinking," he said, "but Romeo's down in the crew's recreation room right now, and he's actually got a couple of guys hypnotized."

I looked at him closely. I had never believed in hypnotism. "How do you know they're hypnotized?" I asked skeptically. "How can you tell?"

"Well, he's got 'em doing all sorts of crazy things—pretending they're taking a shower, thinking they're seasick—things like that."

"I don't believe it," I said. "What you need is some work to do." I pointed toward a set of block and tackle. "Go over there and tighten up that Number Three set of beaching gear!" I ordered.

The word that there was a hypnotist aboard was all over the ship, however, and after supper I went down to the recreation room to see for myself what was going on. Romeo was sitting at a table, being modestly reluctant to perform as a big crowd pressed in on him. A couple of ship's officers, including the purser, came in.

"It's all a fake," declared the purser, pushing forward. "There's no such thing as hypnotism."

Romeo turned and looked up at him disdainfully. "Well, Purser," he said slowly, "I guess you don't mind if I hypnotize you, do you?"

"Go ahead and try," replied the purser confidently. "It can't be done." He took a seat across the table from Romeo.

"All right," said Romeo with sudden authority, surveying the crowd. "Turn some of these lights out—and everybody be quiet!"

The room darkened, and in a low tone Romeo began talking to the purser. After a few moments, he commanded. "Stand up!"

The purser stood, his face blank.

"Now see all these ash trays," Romeo went on, indicating the half dozen on the table, spilling over with cigarette butts. "They're all filled with money. Don't let anybody see you— look right and left—then take this money and put it in your pockets."

The crowd strained forward without a sound as the purser obediently checked right and left, then surreptitiously picked up the ash trays one by one and emptied their contents into his pockets.

"That's fine," said Romeo approvingly. "Now sit down and count your money."

The purser resumed his seat and started to reach into his

pockets. "That's good," Romeo interrupted. "You got it counted." The purser's hands fell back by his side. Romeo looked at his audience. "What else you want me to have him do?" he asked. It took them a few moments to recover from their trancelike fascination. "Make him go up and have the captain open his cabin," somebody suggested with sudden inspiration.

"Okay," said Romeo. He turned back to the purser, still sitting expressionless across from him. "Go up and show your money to the captain," he directed, getting up to lead the way. The purser joined him and together they walked the hundred feet along the catwalk to the captain's cabin, forward. Prompted by Romeo, the purser rapped sharply on the door.

"Who is it?" the captain's voice was heard from inside.

Romeo prodded the purser, whispering hoarsely, "Tell him who you are."

"This is the purser," said the purser.

"Get away from here!" the captain yelled.

"Tell him what you want," Romeo urged fiendishly.

"Captain, I want to show you my money," called the purser.

"If you don't get away from that door," screamed the captain, "I'll shoot! I'll put a bullet right through it! Get out!"

Romeo got the message even if the purser didn't, and he discreetly led his subject back along the catwalk to the recreation room. He returned him to his chair, then said, "You're going to want a smoke after a bit, real bad. Now I'm going to count to five. When I say five, you'll feel real good." He made the count. "How do you feel?" he asked.

"I feel real good," said the purser as the lights came back on. "I thought you were going to hypnotize me."

"I did," said Romeo, watching him closely.

"Oh, no, you didn't," argued the purser. He added suddenly. "How about somebody giving me a cigarette?"

Nobody moved. The purser slapped his pockets and began

searching them. "What the hell is all this?" he demanded as he discovered the butts and ashes. "Who planted these butts on me?" He paused, grinning foolishly. "I was hypnotized, wasn't I?" he conceded.

Afterward, somebody mused that in learning his lesson the purser could have been shot by the captain. "If that happened," he went on, "the captain would have been tried for murder."

"That," said another uncharitably, "would be the nicest thing that could happen to both of them."

In a few more days the *Conserver* returned. We waited for the next extreme high tide, then gave it the old college try to get the tanker off the rocks. Three tugs from the area gave us a boost as we took up on the cables. It was no use. The crew was removed, and so far as I know the tanker is still there on Japtan Island. So, too, I suppose, is the buried liquor—the treasure of the *Nickajack Trail*—liquid spirits resting among the spirits of the honored dead.

As for us of the *Conserver,* while we had failed in our mission, we did not come away entirely without accomplishment. We had learned the secret of making raisin jack.

14. Bikini

When we returned to Bikini from the attempt to refloat the grounded *Nickajack Trail,* the work of anchoring the target array of nearly a hundred ships was almost finished. The ships were spotted all over the lagoon, separated by roughly the same distances as in a normal fleet dispersal. In the center of the formation, painted a brilliant orange and now known as *Scarlet Fever,* sat the old battleship *Nevada.* She would be the bull's-eye for Able-Shot, a Nagasaki-type bomb, to be dropped from the air.

But getting the ships anchored wasn't the end of it. They had to be herded like cattle. They rolled and swayed at their buoys and kept breaking loose, wandering off toward Enyu Passage, the lagoon's main gateway, as if they knew the fate awaiting them and were trying to escape. The herdsmen were the salvage ships, each assigned a certain number to look after. Besides dashing here and there to head off the strays, we also had to keep an eye on the ships with heavy battle wounds, like the *Nagato.* We checked these every day for leaks, to see that they didn't give up and sink before they could die for science.

The rare times when we weren't on duty, the captain found other ways to keep us busy. The Warden, as we soon called him, was a martinet who took Navy tradition to heart. He was always correctly dressed, permitting no heat to drive him to the sartorial informality of the rest of us. He carried his tall, thin figure rigidly straight, wore his cap square with the horizon and kept his chin out, as if in perpetual challenge.

But we had to hand it to the Warden for one thing: As men of the sea we were supposed to hate all captains. The Warden made it easy for us. Not a day passed but his voice came crackling over the squawk box, "Now hear this: Light off all equipment! We're going through the array!"

Then we would head through the target flotilla at full speed, our hoses spewing long trajectories of water from either side, and the foam generators laying down a heavy blanket on the waves. "We got to let 'em know we're here," the captain was once heard to say grimly.

There was no glamour about salvage ships. They had no guns, no planes, and they were small—among the smallest seagoing craft in the Navy. No one knew they were there— until the *Conserver* came along. Her daily performance came to be the highlight of each day. Photographers watched for it, running alongside in their boats at a safe distance and taking pictures as we got under way. When it was over, the Warden was relieved for several hours of the need to think up something else for us to do. It took that long to clean up the foam that covered the ship.

As the time for the first shot neared we were more than ready for it. On the target ships the night before, things were put in final order. Hatches were closed—or opened, as the case might be. The thousands of instruments fixed aboard were set and given a final check. The animals were moved into exposed positions. The crews who had been staying aboard some of the ships to keep them afloat and under control, were taken off—this as the very last thing at dawn. No human life was left behind.

With the shot set for eight o'clock, we were out of the lagoon by six, pointing for the open sea and ambitiously putting distance behind us. Nobody was worried—but we could have done without the news from Honolulu, carried in the ship's newspaper, that Hawaii was preparing for a tidal wave. The conversation died out, each man seemingly preoccupied with watching the palm trees behind us slowly draw into the sea. When at last we stopped, after two hours, the suspense was pretty high. Tidal wave or not in Hawaii, any explosion that required such a distance for safety was a big one. The ship came about, and we were instructed over the intercom to face away from Bikini, put our heads down and put our arms over our eyes. We were no sooner in position than we realized the countdown was on: ". . . six, five, four, three" came the words on the intercom, as leisurely as for the start of a sack race. "Two, one. Fire! Bomb away!"

The seconds ticked by. There was no flash, no sound. We listened for the all clear. We heard none. For an event that had people heading for the hills in Hawaii, thousands of miles away, there was certainly little commotion here. Somebody uncovered and sneaked a look to the north. "There's a cloud up there," he said, more hope than excitement in his voice. There had been no fleck of cloud anywhere before.

We all uncovered and surveyed the sky toward Bikini. Hanging a little above the horizon was a small white mass with the rounded, domelike shape of cumulus, rising higher as we watched. The shot had been no dud.

But as we steamed back toward the atoll, meeting neither hot wind nor high wave on the way, it was agreed with the garrulousness of release from tension that the big show had been a bust. "Hell," said one critic, "we did better than that blowing up the reefs with dynamite!"

When we got closer, though, we could see that the blast, set off a few hundred feet overhead, had caused spectacular damage. In the center, the old *Nevada* was afire, the flames blending eerily with the scarlet fever color of her paint. All around her it was a scene of smoking, flaming ruin. Ships were listing and sinking, five going down as we watched. The submarine *Skate* and the cruiser *Independence* looked like junk yards hit by a tornado. For many miles out from Point Zero, funnels, masts, and radio antennas were snapped off or twisted, drooping like palm trees in the wake of a hurricane. Steel plates were bent, buckled, and blown away. No single explosion had ever caused but a fraction as much destruction to a group of ships.

The main job of the salvage ships was to save as many as possible of the burning and crippled vessels for the Baker-Day underwater shot, about a month later. With our hoses going, we dashed from one ship to another, dousing the flames with water and foam. If a ship was listing, we put pumps aboard and started pouring the water back into the sea. And when we were finally finished, we helped to remoor the array in the somewhat different pattern wanted for the underwater test. A number of submarines were submerged at various depths, held in place by cables slung across the bow and stern, the cables being secured to the bottom by an anchor at either end.

The afternoon before the Baker-Day shot, the submarine *Sea Raven* came corking back to the surface, as if in a final break for safety. We managed to pin her back to the bottom, but were ordered to stand by at the site through the night, in case the submarine broke loose a second time. When we finally got permission to leave, at about 5:30 in the morning, we were among the last ships to vacate the lagoon. As the *Conserver* steered for Enyu Passage, a seaman noticed a commotion aboard the U.S.S. *Gasconade,* a target ship anchored to starboard. Someone was waving his arms and a flag was rapidly being run up and down.

"Looks like the goats don't want to stay," said the seaman as we gathered to watch. Everyone was supposed to have been taken off all target ships long before. Word was sent to the captain. He studied the situation briefly, then said, "We better take a look."

With the bomb already in its arming cycle, our little salvage ship held up her exit and cut across bows to investigate, paying no attention to the busy signals from the flagship asking why we were changing course. We would scarcely have been surprised if the Warden, who often had given the impression that he considered the entire Bikini operation his responsibility, had signaled the flag to mind its own business. As we neared the *Gasconade* we counted three Navy men at the rail. We quickly put a boat into the water and picked them off the Jacob's ladder, pulling them aboard as the *Conserver* became the last in line toward the passage.

The three were badly shaken. The boat that had been assigned to take them off the *Gasconade* had been late. Not spotting them immediately—for they had then left the appointed place on the ship—the crew of the pickup boat assumed somebody else had reached them first, and kept going. As the trio had watched the departing fleet get smaller and smaller, with no one coming for them, they realized with growing desperation that they were going to be sacrificed along with the pigs and goats. Running the flag up and down didn't help. All the target ships had their bunting out as part of the test, and there was no reason to be watching to see if any were moving. That our falcon-eyed seaman on the *Conserver* saw it was the sheerest accident.

While it was Baker-Shot that was supposed to put this "sorely stricken human carousel" out of business, we retired only a few miles this time. Experience had built confidence. The air burst had been expected to blow Bikini Island away, while actually, not even one of its palm trees had disappeared. We came about, and as the countdown began steamed slowly back toward Bikini. Since the blast would occur under water, out of sight, nobody wore dark glasses, as before, and there was no turning of backs or holding hands over the eyes. We lined the rail and silently stared off at the indigo sea stretching away to the north. There was no sound except the steady chugging of the ship's engines. Flying fish broke from the bow wave and skittered interminably above the swells.

The countdown ended.

A long moment passed, and then a vast plug lifted lazily out of the ocean before us. As it slowly rose higher and higher, at the same time growing fatter, streaks of color appeared in the sides, and ships were drawn into the towering mass. We could see them riding up end first in the water, black specks that reminded us of raisins in a cake. Out away from the stem, the ships missed by this space-filling hydraulic lift seemed to sit curiously still and out of scale in their Lilliputian tininess.

A mile high the column broke, and as several million tons of ocean tumbled back to earth, the lagoon vanished in fog and spray. Out of it unfurled the bar stool cloud that by now had become the hallmark of the atomic explosion. As the cloud vaulted upward the air began to clear of the water saturating it and we could see the ships that had been so still, now wildly pitching and plunging as a succession of great concentric waves rolled against them from the center of the blast.

The ships were still rocking when a flight of planes from the base at Kwajalein swept through the cloud. We could hear the voices of the crews as they reported in detail what was happening to the ships and gave the readings from their fallout monitors. A moment later, drone boats ran through the battered array, checking radioactivity on the surface. In a half hour the level of radioactivity was low enough for safety, and the salvage ships plowed forward to start recovering the animals and instruments from the target vessels still afloat. It was these, more than anything else, which would tell the big story of the test's outcome. The instruments were numbered in the thousands, measuring stresses, heat, wind velocities, radiation, and so forth. There were 25,000 radiation recorders alone.

It had been estimated that if we recovered 10 per cent of the instruments it would be enough, giving all the data needed. But it turned out that instruments which should have been close together in their readings were often far apart, because of unforeseen variables in blast and contamination patterns. It therefore became a matter of getting back as many instruments as possible and striking averages in the figures. So the work of instrument recovery went on for days.

The job was complicated by the surprising inconsistency of contamination effects. Some areas of the ships were so "hot" they couldn't be approached, while others, often nearby, showed no contamination whatever. For safety as we gathered the instruments, the hot areas of the decks were encircled with chalk by monitors who preceded us aboard with Geiger counters. Inside each area they marked the safe tolerance time for it.

It took a while to get used to these phantom limitations on movement. On the battleship *Utah* there was a hot spot near the gangway. Since this was where people tended to congregate, a guard was posted over it, to keep them moving. One day a visitor stopped on the forbidden spot to talk.

"Don't stand around here," ordered the guard, full of authority. "You're standing in a five-minute area. Move on!"

"How come you're standing here?" asked the visitor, bridling.

"I'm outside the chalk mark," replied the guard. He pointed to the line, passing a few inches from his toes.

"I didn't know radioactivity stopped at chalk marks," said the visitor.

This obviously had never entered the guard's mind. He stiffened and yelled, "Hey, monitor!"

The nearest monitor stepped over. "What's the trouble?" he asked.

"Isn't it safe for me to stand in this spot?" asked the guard.

"How long you been here?"

"An hour or two."

The monitor held his counter on him. He was red-hot.

"That's what I like about my shipmates!" howled the

guard. "Nobody tells me anything!" With a yelp he bolted for the showers, the only known way to remove the contamination.

We also went after the instruments on the ships that were sunk, and this task offered other hazards in addition to radioactivity. On the slick, listing deck of the aircraft carrier *Saratoga*, I lost my footing and slid into the superstructure. The crash which dented my helmet was heard topside. "What're you doing down there?" asked the phone man after I assured him I was okay. "You trying to take off just because this is an aircraft carrier?"

Recovering the instruments fastened to the buoys pulled under by the sinking or capsizing of the ships was the trickiest problem. The water itself showed little radioactivity, but the sandy bottom was hot. So we were lowered only as far as necessary to reach the buoy with a pair of bolt cutters. Suspended in mid-water, we snipped the instruments loose and were hauled back up without touching the bottom. At least that was the idea. Some of us, finding it awkward to work hanging by a line, let go of it for the few moments it took to cut the instrument loose, then washed away the telltale sand from our shoes before returning to the top. Unfortunately, the pen-sized dosimeters fastened all over us, especially those on the lower leg, gave the game away. Despite the resulting chewing out, it was hard to take seriously a danger that couldn't be seen.

Then, all at once, readings began to rise. The attitude toward radiation now shifted to the other extreme. There were wild rumors about what radiation would do to a man. Sterility, falling hair, blindness—these were only a few of the fates in store for the man exposed to this mysterious new enemy.

With each of us as nervous as a boy in a graveyard at midnight, all sorts of sinister meanings were read into commonplace things. Leaning over the side of the *Conserver* one day, a crewman saw a big blob of green in the water. He called others to see it. The alarm was spread to the bridge. The bridge notified the flagship, and in moments a flock of monitor boats were alongside, dipping assorted instruments into the water. Was this coloration some new phenomenon produced by the explosion? There wasn't much doubt about that; the question was, what was it?

In the excitement, a fuzzy-faced sailor sidled up to me and muttered that he was the cause of it all. "I dropped my dye marker over the side," he confided. Each of us carried one of these at his life preserver.

A few days later, at dusk, a strange light was seen coming off the bottom of the lagoon, glowing brighter as dusk gave way to a moonless night. Again excitement swept the ship. The spot was marked with a buoy until morning, when the Warden called the monitor boats back to our side. While the monitors gravely tested the water, the light died out, adding to the mystery. Finally somebody confessed that he had dropped a flashlight over the rail. The water had provided the conduction between battery and bulb that turned it on.

The radiation readings changed again, heading downward. Now it was widely decided that the monitors didn't know what was going on and that, since they didn't know this, they also probably didn't know whether radioactivity was really harmful. We began to discount its effects.

Then Skosh died. Skosh was Doc Schmidt's little dog. Doc had picked him up in Japan, naming him after the Japanese word for small. It was Doc's belief that since all divers were dogs, dogs could be divers. Skosh was the kind often seen on the stage in dog acts—black and white, with short, slick hair—and he had been quick to learn what Doc wanted of him. He was a real sea dog. He loved to swim, and he added to the *Conserver*'s local fame with his feats of swimming between the ships, towing a light line for exchanging messages. "The smartest guy they got on the *Conserver* is the dog," was a frequent comment.

Skosh would put his forefeet on the rail, waiting for the

harness Doc had made for him. He was lowered over the side by a ring at the shoulder, his feet going well before he hit the water. When he arrived at the other ship, a waiting crewman put a hook down to the ring and lifted him aboard. His reward would be a steak, saved for him by the cook. It was said that Skosh got more steaks than any sailor in the fleet.

Skosh gave every indication short of oral testimony that he was a diver at heart. He went through the recompression chamber, clearly pleased by the experience, and spent all his spare time hanging around the diving locker, showing a discriminating taste in his social preferences. Doc was working on a watertight suit with special breathing apparatus for him, when he died.

Doc found him one morning as he came up on deck to ask if he was ready to dive—for Doc talked to Skosh as if he were a crew member. Skosh's bed was a coil of mooring lines near the diving locker. When Doc spoke, the dog didn't move. Bending over him, Doc saw that his tongue was out and that he had been foaming at the mouth. Doc called for a Geiger counter, which showed that the coil of lines was red-hot with radiation, doubtless from sagging into the water while in use to secure the *Conserver* alongside target vessels.

Radiological teams wanted to examine Skosh's body, but Doc wouldn't hear of it. That evening he was given the traditional sailor's burial at sea. He was put into a cut-down sea bag, with a projectile inside to give it weight, and taken to the fantail. With all hands looking on glumly, Skosh was placed on a slab and slid over the rail. "There goes the only guy the captain couldn't break," somebody observed bitterly, while others masked their feelings with profanity. For Doc, no guise worked—he was openly broken up.

Skosh had been killed by radioactivity. For the first time, we had seen what the invisble danger could do. Everyone became acutely radiation-conscious again, getting himself checked and rechecked. This included the Warden. "How about giving me a check?" he said to a passing monitor one

evening as we sat waiting for the nightly movie to start on the
fantail. He tried to appear joking, a rare state for the Warden.

The monitor held his counter close to the Warden's body.
It pegged the meter, the needle going all the way over against
the pin. It clicked so hard that the monitor jerked the headset from his ears, leaving it dangling from his neck. He tried
another counter, thinking there was something wrong with
the first one.

"What's the matter?" asked the captain. "Instrument not
working?"

"Just a minute," stalled the monitor. He moved off to one
side a few feet. "Would you mind standing up and coming
over here, sir?" he asked.

The captain came over. The counter now showed no reading. The monitor held the instrument to the chair, which
had been brought out from the wardroom for the movie.
Back to the pin leaped the needle, the clicking pouring noisily
from the earphones. The chair was red-hot. "Who the hell's
the bastard that wants to see me sterile?" roared the Warden,
rolling a baleful eye at those around him.

The chair had been taken from a target ship, against the
rules, and had been carelessly set down in the wardroom.
Happily, the Warden knew nothing of this. He merely
glowered at the offending seat a moment, then seized the chair
with both hands and violently hurled it overboard, accom-
panying the action with language not usually heard from the
captain of a ship. He turned to the exec and said, "Go ahead
and start the movie without me." He stalked off, and wasn't
seen throughout the picture. It was the first time he had been
known to miss a movie.

On nights of the weekly beer ration, the Warden held his
ground at the movie against uncommonly trying conditions.
Since nothing alcoholic may be brought aboard a Navy ship,
we were supposed to drink our beer on a barge brought alongside the *Conserver* for that purpose. But after the movie began, with the fantail in darkness, the beer drinkers would

come aboard and join the audience, sipping their beer as they watched the picture, throwing the empty cans over the side. One night after a can had sailed past the captain, sitting in the wind offside, he was seen to wipe his face. It was realized that what he was wiping off was beer, emitted by the can as it went by. The beer drinkers were inspired by this to leave a little extra in the can each time, gradually increasing the sacrifice to see how much it would take to get the captain to move.

The sacrifice was futile. Showered afresh by each passing can, the Warden patiently wiped the beer from his dripping face and went on watching the movie as if nothing unusual was going on. When I discovered what was happening, I said solicitously, "Sir, some of the sailors seem to be getting out of hand. Do you want me to stop the movie?"

He swabbed the beer from his eyes and looked up at me as if I had suggested something indecent. "Chief," he said coldly, "if you don't like the picture, you don't have to watch it, you know."

The captain was a stubborn man, but behind this behavior was something more than ordinary cussedness. If he objected to the beer showers, it would have meant recognition that there was beer aboard. This, in turn, would have obliged him to make an issue of it, for the sake of a regulation that he didn't think much of. Besides, it would have interrupted the movie for him.

The Warden was less indulgent toward other types of potables. The crew had now called on our skill in making raisin jack, the art we had gratefully salvaged from the *Nickajack Trail*. In the chain locker they installed a number of five-gallon jugs filled with distilled water, originally intended for the ship's storage batteries. Into the water had been introduced assorted fruits and sugar. The sturdy atmosphere that arose with the fermentation process, speeded by the tropic heat, caught the captain's nose one torrid night as we passed on one of his frequent tours of the ship. He stopped and sniffed suspiciously.

"That's a terrible smell, Karneke," he said.

I could only agree. "It sure is," I said, aping the captain's look of puzzlement.

He opened the door to the locker and squinted into the darkness. "Smells like garbage," he said as he got a full load of the conditions inside.

I agreed again, squinting along with him.

"Get me a flashlight," said the Warden.

I relayed the word to a crewman hanging anxiously on our heels. As we waited, the captain said, "What the hell's garbage doing up here?"

"I'd sure like to find out," I replied sternly.

The crewman arrived with the light, and I passed it to the captain. He played the beam around the interior of the locker, shining it on a jug with a cherry floating on top. "By God, it is garbage!" he exclaimed. "They're throwing the garbage up here in the chain locker, and they got some of it in the battery water."

I took over the initiative, leading the way to the jugs and examining them with an elaborate show of baffled interest. "Beats me, Captain," I said at last, shaking my head.

"Have the cook get up here and clean this place out," the captain ordered.

The crewman hurried after the cook, who appeared promptly. As he passed me I muttered in his ear, "I think the captain's found the raisin jack." It wasn't much warning, but at least it gave him a few seconds to meet the situation resourcefully. I could feel him recoil in the darkness.

"Cookie," said the Warden, "do you know what your mess cooks are doing with the garbage from the reefers?"

"Well, sir, I suppose they're taking it back on the fantail with the rest of the garbage, like they're supposed to," replied the cook.

"That's what you think," retorted the captain. "They're throwing it up here in the chain locker." He waved at the open door. The cook said nothing, effectively giving the impression that he was speechless; he was, but not for the reason the captain thought. The Warden snapped, "I think you can handle it from here!"

"Yes, sir!" said the cook, a little too quickly.

"Yes, sir," I heard myself chiming in.

As the captain turned to go, he left us with an enigma. With a leering chuckle at me, he said, "They thought they could put something over on me, eh? They can never fool an old sea dog."

What he meant by that we didn't know—and to this day I've never been able to decide if the Warden really knew what was going on in the chain locker of the *Conserver*. At any rate, we felt it prudent to get rid of the raisin jack. This we accomplished painlessly the next evening, with a premature party in the afterhold, covered by the thunder of hoofbeats in the horse opera overhead on the fantail.

Skosh's death brought about a general tightening of precautions against the danger we couldn't see. We divers, who had the responsibility of assessing the explosion's underwater work, were cut to ten minutes in our time on the bottom. With visibility still murky from the upheaval of the sea floor, a diver was often forced to come back up before he had found out much. One ship appeared to have a break in her middle, but the first diver down had to return before he could make sure. It was decided to put a man down and have him traverse her full 600-foot length alongside—a job for me. But this would take longer than ten minutes. To help speed me on my way, the *Conserver* was moored toward the stern of the sunken ship, so that my lines led in the direction I would be going from bow to stern, instead of dragging behind and holding me back.

For additional safety, the monitor cautioned that I should

keep up on my toes as I made my dash—no small feat with shoes that weighed eighteen pounds each. This technique would reduce contact with the half million tons of radioactive silt which had been blown off the bottom, leaving a basin a mile across, and which then had fallen back into the sea, forming a hot carpet several inches deep.

Not to lose even a few seconds, I hit running when I reached my sprint course, 180 feet down, taking off like Skosh on his swims between ships. By leaning forward almost horizontally and with my forward-leading lines helping me, I made good time. But I still had some distance to go when I heard from the phone man, "Your ten minutes are about up," he said.

"I don't have much more," I panted. How much more, I still couldn't see. I plowed on, kicking up clouds of lethal silt behind.

"Your ten minutes are up," said the phone man.

I kept going.

"Your time is up," repeated the phone man urgently.

"I'm about there," I gasped. I stalled him by adding, "There's very little silt here."

"Okay," he said doubtfully.

The ship's screws loomed out of the murk, and I gave the word they were waiting for topside. When they lifted me off the bottom, I had been there twenty minutes, twice as long as I should have been.

While they undressed me after I reached the top, coming up by the usual stages because the water itself was safe enough, the monitor casually checked me over, examing the radiation meters I had been carrying. Those on my lower legs, carried inside the dress near my feet, had been driven off the scale. The monitor didn't seem concerned, so I didn't worry about it. I headed for the showers and after a half dozen of them, showed clean.

On my way out I looked to see what the monitor had written in the log about my leg exposure. The entry read 175 roentgens, more than one thousand times the safe level! I thought it was a mistake—that he had meant to write milliroentgens, the normal terms of measure. A milliroentgen is only one one-thousandth as much as a roentgen.

"No, that's right," said the monitor indifferently. "One hundred and seventy-five roentgens." Seeing that I was upset, he added, "You know of course that it takes 500 roentgens to make sure you're dead."

This was small comfort. It meant that, mathematically, I was close to half dead already. "Hey, this isn't good!" I exclaimed.

"No, it's not good," he conceded easily. "I'll make a full report on it." After a pause, he said, "It's not too bad, though —it's only in your legs. Otherwise it would be very serious."

"Only in my legs . . . !" Further words failed me. I had visions of my legs dropping off, as the minimum result. I thought of what happened to Skosh. I dashed up to the bridge and let the Warden know I was packing enough radioactivity in my legs to illuminate all the watch dials in the world. His reaction was more in line with what I felt the circumstances called for. First he shied away from me. Then he rushed an alarm to the flagship, which ordered me sent at once to the U.S.S. *Haven,* a hospital ship. There, even as they received me at the rail, they tapped me for a blood sample. "Do you feel bad?" asked the head doctor.

"I feel great," I replied.

This seemed to upset them. In the examining room they stripped my clothes off, substituting a white gown, flung me out on a table and went to work like attendants in a well-run gas station. They kept taking blood samples, rushing them off for analysis.

During a lull, I sat up and remarked to a corpsman, "The doc seems to be pretty shook up."

"You think the doc's shook up—you should be shook up," replied the corpsman.

"Why, what's wrong with me?" I asked.

"You don't have enough white corpuscles."

"What's that mean?"

"Radioactivity—it's killing you." He studied me closely. "You're getting white," he said. He grabbed my shoulders and hauled me back to horizontal. "Lie down," he commanded.

The white corpuscle count appeared to be the chief criterion for measuring radioactive damage, and mine seemed to have been drastically depleted. If the count went lower, I would be done for in hours. Attendants stood by to give me new blood as a last hope.

At the same time, other symptoms of disaster, supposed to go with diminishing white corpuscles, were looked for. None could be found. It was at length decided that the only possible explanation for the absence of these parallel symptoms was that my white corpuscle count wasn't really low—for me; I hadn't had many white corpuscles to begin with.

They kept me overnight, and next day released me back to the *Conserver*, with instructions not to dive for a while. The medics kept a close watch on me for two years. First, they checked me every day, then once a week, and finally once a month. They never found any changes.

After my bout with radiation, the order was issued to get all divers out of their suits as soon as possible after they were brought up because of the radioactive silt that clung to the dress. To expedite this, the diver untied his shoes and unfastened such other things as he safely could while he sat on the diving stage decompressing on the way up. This procedure nearly lost us Mike Holchek, the master who had come out to relieve me. Mike was on the stage, about twenty feet down, when he suddenly phoned, "Bring me up real quick!"

This was unusual behavior for Mike, who was not one to panic. "What's wrong?" asked the phone man.

Mike didn't answer. We learned why moments later as we pulled him up. His helmet was loose from his breastplate, and he was hanging onto it with both hands. Somebody had forgotten to put the safety catch in place on his helmet lock, and while he was preparing his hose connection for fast uncoupling, he accidentally tripped the lock. Pushed by the air under it, the helmet shot upward, nearly getting away from him. If it hadn't been for Mike's rare presence of mind in calling to be pulled up an instant before the inrushing water drowned out his phone, we wouldn't have known he was in trouble. And two would have died at Bikini instead of only Skosh.

15. "Soft" Duty

In the coastal waters of the United States, the Navy maintains a series of ranges for the study of assorted underwater phenomena and the testing of weapons used below the sea. The ranges are variously equipped, according to purpose, the instruments sitting on the bottom, suspended in mid-water, or held on the surface. There are hydrophones to listen to fish and other creatures of the ocean; magnetometers to check underwater magnetic fields; gadgets to record temperatures, to measure pressures, to tell direction, speed, and variability of currents, and so on. All have a bearing either on the triggering of subsea weapons—as, for example, sound sets off the acoustic mine—or on their behavior after they are fired.

Tending these undersea laboratories or helping with weapons testing provides the Navy diver with a peacetime occupation. It is duty one never asks for, although it is considered soft—by those who have never done it. The description "soft" will never be heard from the diver who has gone down after torpedoes fired in test shots, as at the Keyport Torpedo Station in Puget Sound, off Seattle, where I was assigned after Tiburon. The torpedoes were fired in varied simulations past lines of instruments which were rigged along the way

to tell how the shot behaved. At the end of the run, each
torpedo was supposed to come to the surface, so that it and
the $50,000 load of instruments it carried in lieu of explosives
could be recovered.

Quite often, however, the torpedo failed to appear at the
end of the run, sinking to the bottom. This brought us divers
into action. For the man who went down to find the torpedo
there were several things to keep in mind. As he groped in
the darkness, working by feel, he could accidentally start up
the propeller. This could get him torpedoed, the fish coming
about erratically and charging him. Or, more likely, the propeller blades, honed to razor sharpness to help ensure a true
course, could cut him to pieces. This happened to one diver
as he was putting a line around a torpedo. They found his
helmet two weeks later containing what was left of him.

But the torpedoes that simply lay on the bottom were tame
compared to those that drove themselves into the mud, auger-
ing their way in by the propeller. Sometimes the torpedo
would keep going for fifteen or twenty feet, kicking out mudballs behind. These mudballs provided a means of tracking
it in the darkness, and when the mudball trail had led the
diver to the buried torpedo's lair, he would call for a probe,
a steel rod about ten feet long with a line through an eye at
the near end, as in a sewing needle. With the probe he carefully poked around the hole, hoping that the propeller had
run down. Having located the torpedo, he next undertook
to wash it out with a high-pressure nozzle, warily working
from behind in case the torpedo sprang back to life. It might
turn on him, of course, but there was nothing he could do
about this possibility. It was a little like going into a
hole after a wild animal of unpredictable habit.

Still, none of the torpedoes I dived on showed other than
peaceable character. All lay quietly dead on the bottom, remaining lifeless throughout the work. So it was with no unusual sense of adventure that I drew the job one day of going

after a torpedo that had sunk mid-course. Where it lay on the bottom was routinely established by the range boat, using a magnetic drag, the same as is used in locating sunken treasure. The spot was marked by a buoy, and over the side I went.

I sank in mud up to my knees, and for all I was able to see I might as well have been blindfolded. I got down on all fours, as if I were looking for a collar button, and almost at once raked a hand against a big hunk of clay rolled up in the ooze. At last I had a torpedo that promised some excitement. "I found a mudball," I called with elation.

"Good, you've become a regular torpedo hound," replied the phone man encouragingly. "Trail those mudballs! We'll keep track of you by your bubbles."

I crawled forward and found a second mudball, then could find no more. "I seem to have lost the trail," I said.

"That's because you've changed directions," the phone man returned. "Turn to your left."

I turned left. In a moment I put my hand into an opening in the mud. I felt around the edges and reached deep inside. "I got it," I called. "I found where it went in."

"Okay, stay right where you are. We'll send you a probe."

Soon something metallic banged against my helmet. I swung a hand around in the darkness overhead and clasped the rod. Good shooting by topside. I rammed the probe into the hole and a few feet inside felt it strike something hard. "I think I feel the torpedo," I said.

"Okay, stick your probe into the mud beside you, and we'll send you a tunneling hose," said the phone man.

The hose arrived. I took the nozzle and lined it up on the hole. "Make sure you got the right direction of this torpedo," the phone man cautioned. "Make sure you're back of it."

"Yeah, I know," I replied impatiently. I was inclined from experience to regard all sunken torpedoes, including those that were buried, as harmless scrap metal. "Just turn on the pressure up there," I called. "I'm all set."

The nozzle thundered and pulled back in my hands as the water came on. The spewing jet blasted out a trench that soon had me standing well below the bottom as I directed it toward the hidden torpedo. All at once there was a clanging sound, instantly followed by a sort of whistling scream and a shock wave of water rolling against me. The whole ocean seemed suddenly to be filled with sound and movement. I swung the nozzle toward another quarter.

"I think I hit the torpedo—something's happened," I reported tightly, as abruptly all was quiet once more.

The pressure went off the nozzle, and the phone man called excitedly, "Hey, Chief, are you all right?"

"I'm fine," I said shakily, controlling a personal internal movement. "Why?"

"The torpedo just broke surface," said the phone man.

"It can't be this one," I said. "It's still here. I'll check and see."

"Be careful," the phone man pleaded, as I got hold of myself and warily felt around for my scrap-metal friend. The torpedo above could well have been another one. So many had been fired and lost in these waters that spare ones were turning up all the time. We had even found one from World War I days. There was no question of this one being harmless. It was run by inertia—a flywheel spinning some 10,000 revolutions a minute, long since spent. Modern torpedoes are driven by compressed air, chemicals, or electricity.

But the torpedo that had popped to the surface was no relic; it could only have been the one we were after, for I could find no sign of it. Several things could have caused it to take off—the propeller starting up, the ejection of air, or the blowing of ballast.

As I was being undressed a little while later, the tender remarked admiringly, "What a torpedo hound you turned out to be! You scare 'em right off the bottom!"

I saw no reason to mention how close it had come to being mutual.

While diving for torpedoes was our primary work at Keyport, there were other things to do as well. We had equipped two surplus army trucks with portable gear, and with these we gave diving service to all activities in the region, civilian as well as military. In Puget Sound's crazy quilt of islands and waterways, it was usually quicker to go by truck than boat.

We were frequently called on to recover the bodies of drowned swimmers. These Red Cross dives, as we called them, were a thankless business, for nobody likes you for bringing up a dead body. People seemed to think that because we were divers we should somehow recover the victim alive, even though the tragedy might have happened hours before. "There must have been *something* you could do," they would say accusingly, often in the eloquent language of silence.

The grief-stricken relatives would press the diver who found the body for graphic details of the death scene on the bottom. What was he like? How did he look? Sometimes we sensed that they felt a subconscious responsibility for the tragedy, and in their guilt used this morbid probing as a way to punish themselves. Then they made the diver listen to a long eulogy on the deceased, coupled with a recital of how he happened to have been swimming. Usually this turned on some freakish circumstance which would never have come about but for the sheerest chance.

We got so we almost hated to find the body. We tried each time to conceal the identity of the diver who brought it up, but this invariably failed, as did the efforts of the authorities to keep the public away from us.   .

The drownings consistently had one thing in common: the victim was an "expert" swimmer. Thus the accident was all the harder to accept. How could it have happened? We heard this question over and over. The answer to why good swimmers drown is easy: Only good swimmers take chances. They become overconfident. Then, in their surprise when things go wrong, they panic.

Overconfidence is also what gets the skin diver into trouble. Because it takes very little skill to become proficient with his equipment, he is under an illusion of safety. The truth is that the man down in a Scuba outfit is up against the same problems—undergoing the same physiology—as the hard-hat diver who, unlike the other, has had long training in what he is doing. And such differences as there are hardly favor the Scuba diver. He is entirely on his own; there is no crew tending him. He has no telephone to call for help if he gets into trouble. He has no lifeline to be pulled up by, and no hose bringing him an inexhaustible supply of air. On top of all this, he generally knows little or nothing about his environment. He is only vaguely aware that the rules by which nature allows him to be there are narrow and rigid, and that the penalty for breaking them is swift and final. It is hard for him to take seriously, for example, that if he is down for any length of time he must go up by the same decompression tables as the diver in a suit, or risk the bends. Failure to realize this is the real story behind the deaths of many skin divers.

One drowning during my stay at Keyport was a little different from the others. It occurred at a resort beach, about fifty miles from our station, on a weekend. The sheriff had first called the Naval Air Station on Whidbey Island but for some reason the divers who responded weren't able to go down. This was quite unusual; the only reason I could think of was that the water was too deep for their equipment. Puget Sound contains some of the deepest inland water in the world. It may be five hundred feet or more only a few yards offshore.

"Round up the divers," I phoned the diving locker after taking the call. "This is going to be a deep one."

In minutes we were off, pushing our truck to the limit to keep up with the sheriff, out in front with siren screaming. People stared in wonderment at this apparent celebrity treatment for a bunch of guys in a drab GI truck. They would have understood even less if they had known that we were on our way to find someone at the bottom of the sound who was already long dead. Death seems to invite racing even though it is already the winner.

It was late evening when we reached the scene. The usual crowd was on hand, surging against the police line thrown around us as we pulled up and quickly began unloading our gear. "I hope you brought your helmets," someone called.

We soon learned that it wasn't deep water that had kept the other outfit from diving. They had come without their helmets. The man in charge, an old friend I hadn't seen since our days in Australia, was blustery with embarrassment. An audience of at least two hundred had excitedly watched the first crew get their man into his suit, then open and reach into the chest marked HELMETS and find none.

"What do you want me to do—lend you a helmet?" I asked sympathetically.

"No—Christ!" he pleaded. "Better let the job look beyond our capability."

This it certainly was, technically. "Okay," I replied, "we'll go ahead and do it."

"You'll do it, and no one will ever forget that we are the only diving outfit in the whole Navy that goes on a job without helmets," he said bitterly.

It was an unusual distinction, at that. "How did it happen?" I asked.

"You wouldn't believe it," he said. "Neither would anybody else." He pointed out that they seldom got a diving call at the air station, and when this emergency had come in, their regular gear was scattered. Not to lose time, they had grabbed an emergency outfit from the storeroom, along with the chest supposed to contain helmets. "When we opened the damn thing, it seems somebody had decided to use it to store rags and spare gear," he said.

The drowning victim was a fifteen-year-old lifeguard who had gone for a swim of his own—taken a chance—after the beach crowd had left at the end of the day. He probably had been hit with a cramp. He had been heard to scream.

After we had made several dives, it seemed unlikely that he would be found. The area had been artificially created, and a pine forest startlingly grew out of the bottom, full-grown trees thrusting up to meet us as we descended. The trees hid all things that sifted down among their branches and they were a suicidal hazard to our lifelines and air hoses.

Then we found him. He was caught in the limb of a tree, and as always with the drowned, stiffened in the attitude in which he had been challenging death in the final moments of life—knees bent, arms as if grappling with something. Draped on the shoulders of the diver who brought him up, he looked alive, inspiring false hope in the crowd watching from a distance, though they knew he had been gone for hours. We quietly handed him over to others and tried to do a fade-out.

We had gotten back into our regular clothes and were having coffee in the coffee shop when the crowd got to us. In the forefront were the dead boy's parents and his uncle. "But how could he drown?" they begged over and over, holding out their hands in appeal. "He was a lifeguard!" If only they could understand that, it seemed, life would be easier.

We couldn't tell them that the boy had drowned *because* he was a lifeguard, not in spite of it—that this had led him to take the chance of venturing into the water alone.

On another day we turned underwater plumbers. There was a hurry-up call from Fort Flagler, located on an island in the sound, that they were without fresh water. The six-inch pipe bringing it over from the mainland had been snagged and broken by a ship's anchor. We added plumbing tools to our diving gear on the trucks and hurried over, reaching the island by bridge. A waiting officer pointed to a small cargo vessel tied up nearby. "You'll be working from that little Army ship over there," he said, directing us to her side so we could put our equipment aboard.

An Army ship? Everybody knows that the Army operates on land, using wheels; and that the Navy operates on the water, using boats. "What's the Army doing with ships?" I asked with a puzzled grin.

"What's the Navy doing with trucks?" he retorted, making things even.

We learned more about the fleet of small, round-bottomed freighters operated by the Army Transportation Corps. During the war these craft had done probably their biggest work running supplies among the Pacific islands in support of the B-29 assault on Japan. We were not alone in not knowing about them. The services themselves hardly knew of them, making it hard for the little ships to maintain themselves. Suspicious supply officers didn't lightly fill requisitions for outfits they had never heard of.

The water in this part of the sound was remarkably clear, and to the kibitzers above, we made a fanciful scene against the snow-white sand of the bottom as we went about our work. We did exactly the same things as plumbers do in more usual places. We threaded pipe, moved it around, fitted it together. The only difference was that we wore diving suits.

After a day or two, the bright cheerfulness of our surroundings was made the more so when the fish accepted us. They followed us like blackbirds after a plow, feasting on the sand crabs we kicked up in our wake. Most of them were halibut, looking like pieces of flying carpet as they fluttered after us. Soon they were waiting for us each morning, swarming in from all directions as we hit the bottom. In the evening they followed us back to the descending line, seeing us off to the top.

The fish would learn better than to trust us humans. The cook remarked one evening at chow, "It's a shame you fellows have to eat this frozen fish when there's all that fresh halibut swimming around on the bottom."

"We can get you some very easy," I volunteered, taking the hint.

At the close of work the next evening, when I reached the descending line to go home, I opened my toolbox and set it on the bottom. I unscrewed the knife at my belt and quickly stabbed it down through the backs of a half dozen of the faithful friends who as usual had seen me to the line, throwing their twitching forms into the toolbox. The fish seemed stunned at this treachery, scattering just about the time remorse suddenly stayed my hand. I couldn't have felt lower.

Fresh fish gave the cook a chance to shine, and he delightedly served them for the evening meal, only to be taken aback that I didn't touch them. "What's the matter?" he asked curiously. "Don't divers eat fresh fish?"

"I'm just not hungry for fish tonight," I said. I have not been hungry for them since then. And I have never thought much of spear fishing.

Lousy as I felt that evening, it was worse yet next morning when the fish scattered at our descent. They never again came close during the rest of the job, watching us distrustfully from far out on the perimeter. It was good to get the job done and leave the area.

If anything we did at Keyport came close to being routine, it was diving for things lost into the water. This is a big part of all diving activity, Navy or civilian. All sorts of objects are dropped from ships being berthed. Passengers leaning over the rail let go possessions they ordinarily have no trouble holding onto. The people on the dock do the same. The ship's movie operator drops a can of film. The gang watch loses his pistol. A set of keys plinks to the bottom. Whatever the bother, it is usually well to get these items back, each for its own reason. Lost keys may mean the changing of a large number of locks. A pistol must be recovered, if only to establish that it was lost and not stolen or otherwise conveyed into the wrong hands.

This kind of diving was interesting mainly for the extra things one found. In a dive at Bremerton one day this "bonus" took an extraordinary form. What I was after primarily was a pair of chipping hammers, each with fifty feet of hose attached, lost by a work party chipping paint from the seaward side of a Navy ship tied up at a dock. When I had found the hammers and started them topside, after first raking up four or five other pieces of hose, I sat down on the bottom to wait for word that the hammers were safely over the side above. Some sort of line—or several of them— seemed to entangle me. One strand drifted languidly past my faceplate, a deeper shadow in the darkness. Another lay along my back. I carelessly pulled them away, not thinking much about it. But they kept coming back. It was a little like fighting a big spider web. From their soft, soggy feel, these old lines must have been down here a long time, I reflected. Probably it was the current that kept carrying them against me.

When word had come that the hammers were safely aboard and I was ready to start up, something seemed to be holding me from behind. I brushed at it, without effect. "There's some old line giving me trouble," I said into the phone.

"What kind of line?" asked the phone man.

"It's some old chunks of hawser, I think."

"Are you getting clear?"

"No. The damn things seem to be floating all around me," I said. "Pull me up slowly and I'll know just where I'm being fouled."

They started to pull, my lines going taut. Something still tugged at my shoulders. "It beats me," I said. "These lines are floating but they seem to be holding me back."

"We'll keep pulling," said the phone man. "Let us know if you're okay."

I rode slowly up through the water, feeling strangely weighted down. A moment before I broke surface the phone man yelled in terror, "Karneke, what's the matter with you?"

"Why?" I asked.

"There's a big octopus on you!"

My head was now out of the water, and the first thing I saw was the crew noisily coming at me with upraised boat hooks. The octopus was sitting on my shoulders, its long tentacles draped up over my helmet and trailing down along my body. From the way it felt now that we were out of the water, it must have weighed hundreds of pounds. The onrushing crewmen with their flailing boat hooks apparently unnerved the octopus as much as they did me. There was a whipping of tentacles past my faceplate as he let me go and dropped into the water behind.

"You're too late, Karneke," somebody yelled. "He got away." The crew thought I had brought up the octopus deliberately, to terrorize them. They changed their minds only after we found the tips of two tentacles under my belt, where the animal had fastened on to me as I sat on the bottom.

The chronicle of Keyport days must include the incident of the innocent sailor, especially told for those who may not have known about the fresh, unworldly qualities of those who follow the sea. In Liberty Bay one day we were diving for torpedoes and had stopped for noon chow when a civilian yachting party hailed us. They explained that they had never seen divers in action and wanted to know if it was all right to look on. We were flattered to have people interested in our work and invited them to join us. When they were tied up alongside, they first had us come aboard to see the yacht, after which they all came over on our lowly diving boat. With ladies present, we watched our language and did our best to be well-mannered hosts. We served coffee, and while the diver scheduled for the first dive after chow was being dressed, I explained each step of the procedure and the purpose of the equipment.

As I talked I became aware that our engineer, a bright-eyed, apple-cheeked youngster of eighteen, was motioning to me from offside. "I want to talk to you, Chief," he whispered when he got my eye. He looked strained.

Maybe there was something wrong with the compressors, which could mean the embarrassment of not being able to perform for our guests. I excused myself and stepped to his side. "What's the trouble?" I asked in an undertone, leading him out of earshot. "The compressors not working?"

"No, it's—it's nothing like that," he said, swallowing. "You know I was aboard the yacht . . ." He gulped again.

"Yes, what of it?"

"I was looking at the engines."

"That's nice," I said impatiently. "I know you're an engine man, but tell me about it some other time. Was there anything else?"

He shifted to the other foot and pulled himself together. "Chief, this is what I wanted to tell you—this lady was showing me around, and . . ." He stalled again.

"So what?" I prodded. I was anxious to get back to our guests.

"She took me up forward and showed me where the cabins were. I saw some bunks and she wanted me to come in. She acted real funny." He studied his feet.

"And what did you do?" I asked with rising interest.

"I told her I was only interested in the engines," he gulped.

Now I swallowed. "What did she say to that?" I asked keenly.

"She said to come in anyway. She said something about wanting to see what kind of stuff I was made of. I told her I had to get back to the boat." He looked at me for approval. "Did I do right, Chief?" he asked stoutly.

I studied him long and wonderingly. "You did right," I said firmly. "Now you go down and take care of the engines. I'll send a diver over to check that cabin."

The United States Navy obliges.

16. Near Miss in a Rescue Chamber

Since the specialty of a submarine rescue vessel is to rescue submarines, it keeps in sharp trim for this function with frequent drills. At least four times a year the vessel goes through an S-51 exercise, a code designation by appropriate coincidence the same as the name of a former submarine which was lost. A submarine hides on the bottom in a simulated sinking, its engines dead. Using sonar, the rescue vessel locates it. By submarine telephone, transmitting through the water as radio transmits through the air, the rescue vessel phones in to the crew of the submarine that they have been found. "We're right over you," they are told.

A diver from the rescue vessel takes a cable down and attaches it to a pad eye in the center of one of the submarine's two escape hatches. (If the water is too deep for a diver, the submarine releases a rescue buoy, which floats up through the water, unreeling a cable from the submarine.) The diver returns to the top, and the diving bell—officially rescue chamber—is reeled down to the submarine on the cable. With three or four passengers aboard in addition to its crew of two, the bell is tightly seated on the hatch, so that no water can enter. The hatch is opened and the passengers on the bell

188

climb down into the submarine, from which in turn three or four crew members climb up into the bell. The hatch is closed. The bell is disconnected, and back up the cable it goes, putting its exchange passengers aboard the rescue vessel. The crew of the "sunken" submarine is now considered to have been rescued.

Next is to recover the submarine itself. Divers take hoses down and attach them to fittings on the hull which lead to the submarine's ballast tanks. The air pumps aboard the rescue vessel are started. Air flows down the hoses and into the tanks, blowing out the water and displacing it with air. The submarine becomes buoyant and floats to the surface. Mission completed.

An S-51 exercise starts at about eight o'clock in the morning, and the idea is to have it done by noon. One of the passengers who go down in the bell to board the submarine is usually the squadron commander. A successful operation requires that the submarine be brought to the surface without spilling the commander's coffee as he sits aboard having lunch.

A key element in such a submarine rescue operation is of course the bell. The bell has two chambers, an upper and a lower, with a hatch in the center of the deck separating them. The upper chamber is the passenger compartment, with room for seven in addition to the two operators. Here also are the controls, the air motor, and the air supply and exhaust air vent. The vent and the air supply are connected to hoses leading to the surface. Fresh air comes in at the supply and the used air flows out the vent, in a natural circuit, at the same pressure as in the open atmosphere. With four-inch-thick solid steel walls to hold off the squeeze of the sea, there is no need to put extra pressure on the air, as for the diver in a suit.

In the lower chamber, much smaller than the upper chamber—about three feet by three feet—are the reel for the cable on which the bell rides up and down, and the fair-lead for the cable. In the lower sides are the ballast tanks, arranged in a circle around the hull.

Used in an actual rescue for the first time in the *Squalus* disaster off Portsmouth, New Hampshire, in 1939, the bell is still being modified with a view to improvement. This means it is continually being tested, to see how it works with the latest change; the crew at the same time keeping in practice, and new operators being trained. When it isn't an S-51 exercise, it may be a false seat exercise. In this, a big steel plate simulating a submarine escape hatch lies on the bottom to receive the bell in place of the submarine itself.

The bell marked YRC-10 (Yard Rescue Chamber) was new, carrying all the latest modifications. My new ship, the submarine rescue vessel *Coucal*, was ordered to take YRC-10 out to deep water off San Diego, California, and give it a false seat test. But before going for the big one, we decided to give the bell a check in close, to see if the more obvious things were functioning. It was lucky that we did. We went out into the bay a little way and left the bell tied up alongside the *Coucal* while we went to lunch. When we came back an hour or so later, the bell was gone. It had snapped the two mooring lines that held it to the side of the ship and was hanging near the bottom by its retrieving cable.

We pulled the bell up and found that water had leaked into it from the bottom through an open valve, flooding the upper chamber and causing the bell to sink like a filled bottle. After we hoisted the bell out of the water and drained it, we made sure that the valve was tightly closed. Then Chief Bill Rainey and I lowered ourselves into the bell through the 20-inch entry hatch on top, to find out what was causing the leak. As a first step, we experimentally flooded the main ballast tank. Water at once rose into our chamber through the hatch. To stop the water, we sealed ourselves in by closing the entry hatch over our heads, relying on the air around us, trapped at atmospheric pressure and being compressed, to keep the water from rising. Then we opened the hatch in the deck to have a look at the action of the fittings and reel in the lower chamber.

As we opened the hatch to this section, we routinely reported the action into the telephone, just as the diver reports his activities from the bottom. We gave little thought to the absence of any acknowledgment. This was unfortunate— for the telephone was out of order and they hadn't heard us topside. And topside, for their part, wasn't giving it much thought that they weren't hearing from us. We were, after all, a couple of chiefs and should know what we were doing.

As we stood looking innocently into the lower chamber, unaware of the treachery of the phone system and the resulting situation, we heard someone jump onto the top of the bell, soon followed by a hissing sound overhead. At the same instant, water came gushing up at us like an artesian well. Somebody topside, at last curious that he wasn't hearing from us, had cracked the entry hatch to investigate. Out rushed our air, and up came the water.

Bill and I grabbed the hatch wheel and pulled the hatch back into place, overcoming the would-be do-gooder on top who had lifted it, just as the water reached our shoulders. In another second or two, it would have been too late. The water-filled bell would have snapped its mooring lines once more and plunged back to the bottom, and what the water didn't do to us would have been accomplished as the suction of the outrushing air carried us slamming against the steel top, leaving us wedged in the narrow entry hatch.

With the helpful fellow above struggling harder than ever to remove the hatch, we spun the wheel tight to hold it, hanging on with all four hands. There we stood in the water, arms over our heads, looking at each other. It was a time for one of those Dear Mom letters.

"It's only a matter of time till he gets some reinforcements up there," Bill said. Even as he spoke, there was another thud on the hatch. "See what I mean?" Bill added. "Now that they know there's something wrong, they'll get the hatch open come hell or high tide."

I nodded glumly. "Got any ideas?"

"No, but we better get some fast," Bill answered. "We'll drown like rats when they get the hatch off."

Yelling was no good; they couldn't hear us through four inches of steel.

"Let's try giving the emergency diving signal," Bill suggested.

"With what?" I asked. We had no tools with us.

"I got a wrench in my pocket," Bill said. He took a hand off the hatch wheel and drew the tool from a back pocket. He gave the hatch four groups of four sharp raps. The strain on the wheel topside was released. We heard one man jump off, then the other. The bell was raised out of the water and soon we were back on the wonderful, dry deck of the *Coucal*.

The valve which we thought we had closed proved to be faulty, and was repaired. The phone was restored, and the bell otherwise made ready for the main test in deep water. The captain said there would be doctors and other top-ranking submarine people interested in submarine rescue techniques on hand to see the operation. Some would be aboard the bell to make the descent with us. Priding ourselves on the appearance of our equipment, we went out of our way to get the bell spruced up for the visitors. We made it shine like a fire engine, and for a final touch painted the inside an aseptic white enamel for the benefit of the doctors.

Then, with our guests aboard, we steamed out to Coronado Roads, to a point where the water was 200 feet deep. The dummy submarine escape hatch was lowered to the bottom. A diver went down and attached the bell's downhaul cable to the hatch. The communications line into the bell was hooked up. The two hoses—one to bring in air, the other to carry it out—were secured to their respective openings in the top of the bell. The emergency retrieving cable was fixed in place. The bell was ready.

Bill Rainey and I boarded first, climbing down through the narrow hatch and standing by at the controls as our guests followed through the hole one by one. There were five of them, plus two spare operators who were making a training run, giving us a full load. They made an intimate group as they stood around the perimeter, heads thrust forward into one another's faces under the low curve of the sides. Bill Rainey was on the motor; I handled the buoyancy manifold and the communications.

We made a final check. Then I flooded the ballast tank, and down we went, Bill taking up the cable on the reel as we dropped. The needles on the pressure gauges told of our descent and as they climbed, I noticed water seeping in around the hose fittings. I didn't pay much attention to it—there was always a little water here and there from condensation and small, sneaky leaks in fittings.

We reached the bottom and made the seat with the dummy hatch without trouble, sending up a running account of the operation over the telephone. Then we reversed the procedure for the return trip.

The downhaul cable, disconnected when the seat was made, was reconnected to the hatch's pad eye. The bolts holding the bell to the hatch were removed. The hatch to the lower chamber, through which we worked to make and unmake the seat, was closed, and we announced on the phone that we were ready to start up. Bill Rainey, working the motor as before, slacked off on the cable to let it start to unreel, allowing the bell to rise. I watched the pressure gauges, waiting for the needles to begin swinging back the other way, indicating we were on our way up. Nothing happened. The bell wasn't moving.

"What seems to be the trouble?" topside asked when they didn't hear that we had started.

I had no answer.

"There's water coming out of the motor exhaust," Bill said. The motor was dead. Water was also coming in at both the air intake supply and the air exhaust vent—much more so than when we came down. I reported this disquieting information topside, meanwhile feeling the questioning eyes of the passengers.

"There's probably some condensation in the hoses, or a little leakage in them," came the reply hopefully. "Drain your air supply."

I opened the valve regulating the inflow of air—and got not air but water. It poured in. Before I could cut the valve off, we were standing in water over our ankles. And no air came with it. Our only air now was what we had in the chamber. With nine of us breathing it, we would fast be turning the place into a gas chamber filled with deadly carbon dioxide. Apparently the pressure of the water 200 feet down, six times that of the atmosphere—or eighty-six pounds per square inch—was forcing water into the hose at the couplings, occurring every fifty feet along the way from the *Coucal* above. I told topside what was happening—no air, only water coming in.

"What do you intend to do?" they asked helplessly. I had hoped they would have some ideas on that point themselves.

"I feel we have some positive buoyancy left," I said, acutely mindful that the margin, if any, was close. One more shot of water from the air supply could make the difference, destroying this last remaining hope. "The only thing preventing ascent is that the motor is flooded and isn't working," I went on. "I think if we disengage the motor and try to come up on the brake, we can probably make it. I'm afraid to try the air again. If we get any more water in here, we'll lose our buoyancy. Let me know if it's okay to go on the brake, and if we are far enough away from the ship."

They would know from our bubbles—what was left of them—where we were in relation to the *Coucal*. If the brake didn't hold and the bell popped up like a rubber ball, the ten-ton projectile it made would stow in the bottom of the ship. If the impact didn't kill us, the ship sinking on us would.

There was no assurance, however, that the bell would go up at all, even though we disconnected the motor. The reel might still not pay out the cable. Then we would be held down by the dummy hatch underneath, to which the cable was attached. The hatch weighed five tons. This weight, added to that of the bell, also made it doubtful that we could be hauled up by the emergency retrieving cable.

While we waited for the answer to my proposal, one of the passengers, a doctor, broke the fascinated silence of his companions. "Are we in trouble, Chief?" he asked. He was standing with his hands braced against opposite sides of the chamber.

The CO_2 must have been getting to me, for I replied peevishly, "No, Doctor, but *please* keep your dirty hands off the white paint!"

Topside reported, "We can't be sure of your bubbles, but go ahead on the brake. We'll be waiting for you. Good luck."

I told Bill, "Disengage the motor and lie on the brake as hard as you can, in case we start shooting up." To the passengers I said, "Everybody stand by. We're going to come up on the brake, and we may come up a little fast." I turned back to Bill. "Okay, start slacking off."

Bill released the brake. I glued my eyes to the pressure gauges to see if the needles moved, telling us we were on our way. The needles stood still. Our last hope seemed to be gone. We didn't have much longer—maybe five minutes. Everybody was already groggy from the poison he was breathing.

Suddenly, then, the needles began to spin wildly. "I think we're moving," said Bill with relief. "As a matter of fact, I think we're moving pretty fast." He bore down on the brake lever.

"Slow her down," I said urgently. The needles were spinning so fast I couldn't see them.

"I can't," replied Bill. "I'm holding as hard as I can."

Smoke began to roll out from the brake. Fire would make short work of what oxygen we had left. I reached over to give Bill a hand at the brake. As I did so there was a moment of weightlessness, followed by a jarring sound. The gauges stood still, indicating we were on the surface. "Good work!" came a voice on the intercom speaker. I passed the happy word to the passengers, making it official, and in a few moments the hatch came off, letting in the freshest air I had ever breathed.

"Man, did you come up!" exclaimed one of the tenders, grinning down at us through the hatch. "Damn bell shot clear out of the water." This would account for the weightlessness and the jarring sound—the first when we reversed course in the air, the latter when we fell back into the water.

The captain was on hand to greet us as we climbed out. "How'd you enjoy your trip?" he asked the guests genially.

"Well, Captain," said the doctor I had cautioned about keeping his hands off the paint, "I know we were in some kind of serious trouble down there. Water was pouring in on us from all directions, threatening to drown us like rats. I don't think the chief realized the seriousness of our situation —all he seemed to be worried about was keeping the white paint clean."

17. Hell-Fire and Deep Water

The water off Lanai, Hawaii, is deep and blue, the kind often shown on picture post cards. On this day, though, we had small eye for these beauties of nature. The work before us was helium diving. In this a number of new hazards are added to the normal dangers of deep-sea diving.

Proficiency in helium diving, as in the operation of the bell, is important in a submarine rescue, because with helium the diver can go down deeper than with ordinary air, greatly increasing the range of possible rescue. Ordinary air, breathed under pressure, gives the diver "raptures of the deep." This is a form of intoxication, which grows worse as the pressure increases. Like alcohol, it destroys the diver's coordination and his ability to think straight. In short, it leaves him in no condition to be on the bottom of the ocean, let alone work there. For this reason, 300 feet is considered the practical limit for an air dive.

The mischief is caused by the concentration of the air's two main components—nitrogen and oxygen—which takes place under pressure. Nitrogen, making up about 80 per cent of the atmosphere, causes the intoxication. Oxygen, accounting for the other 20 per cent, has a toxic effect.

197

The answer to the problem is an artificial breathing mixture, in which the nitrogen is entirely displaced by helium and the oxygen is reduced below its content in nature, while at the same time being kept variable for different depths. Being inert, the helium mixes with the oxygen but does not combine with it, thereby keeping the chemical balance of the mixture. In other words, the helium is a kind of filler, like the sawdust in dynamite.

To breathe this mixture on the surface, with its low oxygen content, would kill a man. When he breathes it on the bottom, he thrives on it. He stays alert. He can work harder, longer, and more efficiently; and he is good for 565 feet down, nearly twice the limit with air.

The advantages of helium in deep diving were established in theory back in the twenties. How much of it there should be in relation to the oxygen was worked out under simulated conditions at the Naval Gun Factory, at Washington, D. C., in the thirties. By the time the *Squalus* was sunk, enough had been learned about helium diving to try it out in the salvage work of that disaster. This left no doubt of its usefulness, just as the bell proved itself in the rescue of the thirty-three survivors.

But along with the advantages of helium diving there are also disadvantages. A lot of special equipment is needed. The helium and the oxygen are necessarily furnished in bottles, each in its own, so that the two components can be mixed in the proportions needed for the particular depth at which the diver is working. The deeper the dive, the less the oxygen. A cylinder of the mixture holds only about seventy-five cubic feet, which would last only two minutes or so if it was sent down through the same open-circuit arrangement as is used in the ordinary air dive. At this rate, it would take thirty cylinders to keep the diver on the bottom for one hour. Small salvage craft could hardly carry enough gas for a day's diving.

A method was therefore worked out to recirculate the mixture in the diver's helmet so that he could use it over and over instead of exhausting it into the water. The core of the problem was to rid the mixture of the carbon dioxide it picked up as it passed through the diver's lungs. After long and frustrating experimentation, the solution was found in the form of an absorbent carried in a canister fixed to the back of the diver's helmet. The principle of the absorbent is roughly the same as that of the filtering agent in a gas mask. As the charcoal in a gas mask filters out the gas in the air drawn in, so the absorbent in the diver's canister removes the carbon dioxide from the helium-oxygen mixture as it passes through. The arrangement extends the life of a cylinderful of the breathing mixture from two minutes to two and a half hours. Just enough new mixture is metered down to the diver to make up the small deficiency caused as his body uses it up. He uses his regular air only to valve himself down and up, and to control his buoyancy.

But there was a strict price for the advantage of the absorbent, a flaky material known by the commercial name of Shell-Natron. The material is fiercely caustic, and if any water enters the canister with it, the diver gets a preview of hell. His lungs are seared, his eyes scorched, his face blistered. And, with the sea pressing in all around, it is in the nature of things that some water should get inside. Even with the tightest possible fittings and the most rigid vigilance, it happens.

Helium diving being what it is, and since most actual submarine rescues call for the use of helium, at least half of all training dives are required to be with helium. The purpose is to build confidence in its use, but this confidence is slow in coming. It hadn't yet come to us as we prepared for a day of helium diving, there in the cobalt water of Lanai Roads, about two miles offshore. And before the day was over, I'm afraid we lost ground.

I had made helium dives before, but I had never been able to shake the memory of an accident I had seen on my first practical experience. Two minutes after the diver reached bottom, he called that his faceplate was fogging up. As he was being brought to the top, he cried out helplessly that he couldn't see, and was hanging onto the diving stage with one hand. There was a scream, and a moment later he blew to the surface, unconscious and salivating heavily. Although no one ever determined for certain what went wrong, it appeared that he had gotten carbon-dioxide poisoning, either because his recirculating system failed, letting the CO_2 build up in his helmet, or because the absorbent failed to absorb.

While the vision of this affair lingered in my mind, I tried not to show my uneasiness. My job was to convince the others by example that helium diving is a sound, safe practice. I began by saying that I would make the first dive.

"Karneke's being pretty brave—diving on his own gas," somebody gibed, referring to the fact that we each analyzed our own breathing mixture, to see if the oxygen percentage was right. This is done ashore, because the instrument used for the purpose is fluid-operated and the least motion of the ship will throw off the readings. It is hard enough at best to know to the necessary fine point just what the percentage is. It keeps changing with pressures and temperatures. All that can be hoped for is an average not too far off the mark.

Getting dressed for a helium dive, involving much special procedure and equipment, adds further to the diver's apprehensions, and I felt the old uneasiness as the helmet was lowered over my head. With the canister and the other modifications, the helmet for helium diving, together with the breastplate, weighs 103 pounds, compared to fifty-six pounds for the ordinary helmet and breastplate. It is so heavy that a block and tackle is used to hoist it into place, and then hold the weight off the diver while the dressing is completed. After the helmet came the Shell-Natron canister, bolted on behind. While I worried if they were making the connections tight enough, they turned up the bolts with a wrench. Then they hit the wrench handle with a rawhide mawl, with much wear and tear on my eardrums. But it all spelled security.

Gloves were put on my hands and cemented to the suit to make a watertight fit. Any slight leakage at these points would mean moisture joining the circuit through the corrosive absorbent in the canister—with disastrous results. My helmet was locked up and then, with the air shut out, came a loud hissing as circulation of the breathing mixture began.

A voice blasted in over the phone, the words big chunks of sound amid the hissing. "Are you okay—ready to go over?"

"Yeah," I answered deceitfully.

"Okay, we're going to stand you up." They hauled on the block and tackle, and slowly up I came, looking like some inert monster from another planet. Because of the three hundred pounds of equipment on me, I had been dressed directly on the diving stage. When I was more or less vertical, the diving stool I had been sitting on was taken away. I was tapped on the ankles to spread my feet for greater stability. My arms were positioned against the side supports of the stage and I was hoisted over the side.

As I was being lowered toward the water, I felt that my suit was overinflating. This posed a fleeting dilemma: Should I say something about it while there was still time? Or should I take a chance that the valves would be all right once I got into the water? This, after all, was where they were meant to operate, not on the surface. I decided to keep going. I didn't want to cause anyone concern, especially since, as the master, I was supposed to inspire confidence in the others. This decision was a mistake. As I reached the water, I flattened out and lay helplessly spread-eagled on the surface. I floated off the stage and drifted like a bloated fish. I hit the exhaust valve with my chin, but no air was exhausted.

"Spill your air," came the order from above. "You're overinflated."

"I can't," I said sharply, wondering if they thought I would let this happen deliberately. "The valve seems to be stuck."

By now, with the gas continuing to flow, my suit resembled a well-inflated tire—and held the air about as well, too. With my cuffs sealed no air could escape there, as normally happened during overinflation. When the man on the gas finally got it cut off, the suit could burst any moment. Then there could be several more reverses. In this horizontal position, the 100-pound helmet could crash down on my head. There would probably be a dose of fire from the canister at the back, as the absorbent reacted to the water getting into it. Then, in bad shape from the burning, my buoyancy gone, and 300 pounds of equipment encasing me, I would probably drown.

I had wanted to demonstrate that helium diving was nothing to worry about. Instead, by my decision to pass up a timely warning of malfunction, I was putting on a performance that seemed likely to drive a group of good men out of diving altogether—if not clear out of the Navy.

The stage was maneuvered back under me, as a fisherman puts a net under a trout, and I was brought back aboard. I was laid out on the deck, face down, and my faceplate was quickly cracked. The air went out with a whoosh and the strait-jacket grip on my body was gone. As I lay ignominiously on the deck, I expected to hear comments to the effect that here is the master, showing us how, and he can't even get himself into the water; and other suitable observations. But there were none—only silence, which only made things all the more embarrassing.

With my ego as well as my dress deflated, I was hauled upright with the block and tackle and put back on the stool. The crew lifted my helmet off and disassembled the exhaust valve to see why it had stuck. They found that a diaphragm had become inverted from the pressure, causing it to block the port. The valve was repaired, and once more I was ready for the water.

"Do you still want to go?" the diving officer asked anxiously.

"Yes," I replied weakly.

The diving officer wasn't fooled. "Are you sure you want to make this dive?" he asked, knowing that a scared diver is an unsafe diver.

"Yeah—I'm okay," I repeated, trying to sound convincing.

As I stepped off the stage and started down the descending line, slowly giving myself more air as the pressure increased, I felt like a man who knows he is walking into an ambush but can't turn back. More than usual I brooded on the things the helium diver thinks about, his apprehensions sharpened by the fact that most direct control over him is in the hands of others. Would the valve go wrong again? Were the fittings at the Shell-Natron container tight enough? Was my gas mixture right?

The gas, especially, is on the diver's mind. Being lighter than oxygen, helium sometimes leaks out of the bottles, bringing up the oxygen percentage in the mixture. This change of balance between the two, with the oxygen percentage too high, can mean oxygen poisoning. Is the man in charge of the gas on the ball, cutting in the right cylinders with their diminishing oxygen percentages as the depth increases?

Meanwhile, it was taking a long time to get to the bottom, 325 feet down. At last, my feet sank into the sand. "I'm on the bottom, and I'm all right," I said into the phone, as much to reassure myself as those topside. I was startled at the falsetto sound of my voice, having forgotten that in a helium atmosphere, less dense than air, the vocal cords vibrate against less resistance, with these unsettling results. To the crew topside the man down on helium sounds like Donald Duck.

"Check your valves and go on circulate," said the phone man.

I closed my control valve, putting me back to breathing the mixture as metered down to me under control from above. The low rumble in my helmet changed to a high hiss as the mixture circulated through the small orifice between my hel-

met and the absorbent canister at the back of my helmet,
driven by a jet nozzle.

Soon I noticed that I was getting light. I hit the chin button on my exhaust valve to let some of the gas out, reducing
my buoyancy. The valve did not exhaust. I was back to the
old trouble I had had at the top—only down here, with the
whole ocean above me, the problem promised to be a good
deal more awkward. I was already floating off the bottom,
and with my left hand I instinctively grabbed the descending
line, anchoring myself by the 250-pound weight holding the
line down. If I blew to the surface, I would explode like those
fish brought up from extreme depths. At least I had the good
luck not to have wandered away from the line, as I would
have done if the trouble at the top hadn't made me more
wary than usual. I told topside of the situation, explaining
that the exhaust valve was stuck again.

This was bad news. "Are you sure you can't exhaust?" the
phone man asked.

"Positive," I answered. "How about cutting off my gas?"
My suit was getting as tight as a drumhead.

A moment passed. "Okay, we've cut off your gas," said the
phone man.

This gave me but a temporary reprieve. It meant only that
my suit wouldn't go on inflating, finally exploding. I couldn't
go up. The gas trapped in my suit, opposed from the outside
by a sea pressure of more than 270 tons on my body, would
expand as the pressure eased off on the way up—eased off at
the rate of one atmosphere, or twenty-seven tons, every thirty-
three feet. This would explode the suit as surely as if the gas
had continued to come into it. But neither could I stay where
I was. With the gas cut off, I was getting no new breathing
mixture and the old was fast going stale. It was no longer
being circulated through the purifying absorbent in the canister, for the hose that brought in the gas also supplied the
pressure to the jet nozzle that kept it circulating. I had ap-

proximately twelve minutes to live before the carbon dioxide got me.

For a few moments after the gas was cut off, ending the sharp hissing in my ears, the world seemed uncannily silent. Then I was suddenly aware of new sounds which I had never heard before, coming out of the darkness from all directions. They were the sounds of the sea: the grating and clicking of fish, the snapping of shrimp—all blending in a great chorus of static. I never realized how noisy this supposedly silent world of the ocean was. In a deep-sea diving suit, with the noise of the valves overriding other sounds, there is no chance to find out.

The welcome voice of the phone man broke in. "Stay calm, Chief, so you won't burn up your oxygen too fast." He knew that when one is excited, his oxygen consumption goes up.

I felt I was doing as well as the next fellow under the circumstances. Then, abruptly, it struck me that I had stopped breathing. This may have been suggested by the absence of the sound of gas circulating in my helmet, subconsciously associated with breathing. I slapped my hands to my ribs to see if they were moving. At the same moment, for no reason except to keep in touch with me, the phone man asked, "What are you doing now?"

"I'm checking to see if I'm breathing," I answered impulsively.

There is generally an assumption topside that the man on the bottom, whatever the conditions, is a little out of his mind —which, in fact, he often is, because of the unnatural stresses on him. At this answer from me, topside was sure I had slipped my moorings from the CO_2 build-up. "Yes, Chief," said the phone man soothingly, "you're breathing all right. Just be calm now. We're going to turn your gas back on."

"Why?" I asked nervously, the vision of an exploded suit before me.

"Listen carefully," said the phone man as the hissing of the gas began again.

"I'm listening." I never spoke a purer truth.

"Take your diving knife and slit your left glove, so the gas can exhaust through your glove. Repeat that and let me know what you're doing."

I repeated the instructions, at the same time unscrewing the knife from my belt and starting to carry them out. I knew that no water would get in at the slit so long as the pressure inside the suit exceeded the pressure outside.

"Be careful, don't cut your hand," the phone man cautioned. When I had made the cut, he said, "Now put your hand with the slit glove on your control valve."

I did this, lifting the hand to the valve at my chest. "Don't raise your hand any higher, or the water'll get in," the phone man warned. He still wasn't taking any chances that I knew what I was doing. The water would come in if I raised the hand higher because the air would rush out.

The instructions continued. "Now with your right hand hold onto the descending line, and with your left slowly start ventilating and see if you're exhausting through your glove okay."

I already had a death grip on the descending line. With my left hand I slowly opened the valve, letting more gas into the suit and increasing the pressure. A bubble squeezed from the slit, then more of them; the slit began to fizz like soda water. I would be alive for a while yet. "Yes, I'm exhausting through the glove okay," I reported.

"Fine," said the phone man with relief. "Now go on circulate."

I closed the control valve. This put me back on the recirculating system, with just enough new gas coming in to make up what little my body took out of it. "Back on circulate," I said.

The phone man acknowledged. "Now stand by to come up," he directed. "We're going to pull you up slowly. Be careful and don't lift your left arm above your control valve."

This reminder was reinforced by one I carried with me.

Despite all my efforts to prevent it, water was seeping through the slit in my glove. Not much, but it wouldn't take much. I could feel its chilling presence on my forearm, a whiff away from my Shell-Natron. "Ready to come up," I said.

I was a long way from being out of the woods. If the position of my hand with the slit glove was accidentally changed, as from a jerk on the lines, my suit could be quickly flooded. As I was being pulled up by my lifeline and air hose toward the waiting stage sixty feet above, I concentrated on keeping the hand exactly in place at the valve, while with my right arm I warmly embraced the descending line. I kept up a running exchange with the phone man on my progress.

"Look out for the stage," he cautioned when I should be getting close to it.

Just then my helmet banged against the bottom of the stage. "I guess you're there now," said the phone man, before I could reply. "We heard you hit it. Are you okay?"

"I'm okay—but it's going to be a little rough getting on it with one hand," I said.

"We'll hold you there steady while you ease onto it. Take your time." He cautioned me again about the left hand. The encroaching water was now well above the elbow.

Gingerly I managed to gain the stage. "I'm all set," I said.

"Fine, we're going to give you your first decompression stop, then we'll bring you right up, because we're going to give you surface decompression."

"Why surface decompression?" I asked, not thinking.

"You want to play around with that hole in your suit till you get a dose of Shell-Natron?" the phone man retorted.

After standing on the stage for about two hours, watching the gas fizz from the slit in my glove, and desperately hoping the water would rise no higher on my arm, I was pulled up and swung back aboard the dry, friendly deck of the *Coucal*. I was greeted with unusual cordiality. I had never seen the crew so happy to see me—nor had I ever appreciated until now what a fine bunch they all were. Even for those I hadn't known well I now felt a glow of warm good will. They flocked over me solicitously, speedily working together to get me out of my ponderous equipment and into the recompression chamber, using only about one minute of the allotted five-minute time limit.

In diving, all is well that ends well, but we had more than a safe ending to show for this experience. The dive established that there was a basic flaw in the exhaust valve's diaphragm, which again had folded over and blocked the port, as it had done on the surface. As a result, a new type was developed, and what happened to me can't happen any more.

18. The Gentle Art of Defusing

In war, certain explosives are placed to explode at a later, more convenient, time. The other side tries to see that they don't by removing the fuses. In few lines of work is an education in one's job more desirable. To invert an old saying, in this work what you don't know will hurt you—it will kill you.

That I needed to know a lot more about fuses, described by the dictionary as "a mechanical or electronic device to detonate an explosive charge," I first realized when I retrieved the spilled depth charge for the destroyer at Pearl Harbor. I was reminded of it all over again each time I was called upon to dispose of some piece of underwater ordnance.

The opportunity to get some schooling in the subject came in 1951. I was back at Pearl Harbor, assigned to the *Coucal*, which at the time was taking part in a torpedo testing program. It had been discovered with considerable concern that our torpedoes weren't going off as they should; too many were proving to be duds. To find out why, among other things, the torpedoes were being fired against a cliff, and then recovered for study. To go after those with exploders in them, a new diver had come aboard who was a specialist in handling explosive ordnance. He had been trained at the Explosive Ordnance Disposal School, at Indian Head, Maryland, long known for being the home of the Naval Powder Factory.

The EOD school, new to me, had been set up soon after the Battle of Britain, when many good men died in disposing of delayed action bombs, men who would have lived had their skill matched their valor. The purpose of the school was to teach men from all branches of the service—the Army, Navy, Marines, and Air Force—and from friendly nations as well, to disarm the explosives of all nations, friend and foe alike, from bullets to blockbuster bombs. More recently nuclear weapons have been added. When and if a warhead packed with hydrogen falls among us and fails to explode, there will be a man to call who will try to see that it doesn't. He will have been trained at Indian Head.

Our Indian Head alumnus on the *Coucal* said the school was looking for volunteers, especially among those with diving experience; there was work for them in Korea. In taking explosives apart it is no less important to have your heart in the work than it is to know how, so attendance at the school was on a free-choice basis. I asked my commanding officer for a transfer to Indian Head. The request was approved, and by January I was going to school again. I had attended more than a score of the specialized schools run by the different services during my naval career. My subjects ranged from how to man a field piece, as taught by the Marines, to how to kill bugs, as taught by the Army, earning me the rating of DDT expert, or Bug Man.

At Indian Head, since I already knew diving, the first part of the course, I started right in with fuses and the mechanics of detonation.

Although we worked with everything that explodes from a dozen nations—in the water, on land, and in the air—my particular interest was mines. These are among the most effective of weapons, and the hardest to combat. With no other weapon can so much be accomplished for so little. With mines you can lock up the enemy in his ports, leaving neither men nor equipment behind to keep him there. Moreover, with some modern mines, the effect on the enemy is psychological as well as physical, for he can never really be sure whether they are present or not, no matter how much he sweeps the water.

The science of these underwater weapons has come a long way since the old contact mine, which did its work only when it was bumped into. Today we have the "influence" mine. Lying on the bottom, it works either on magnetism or sound. The magnetic mine senses the ship's presence through a small coil which picks up the radiations of the ship's magnetic field. The acoustic mine does its detecting through a highly sensitive microphone. What either mine does, once it has sensed an approaching ship, depends on a computer inside, which programs and controls its action with a precision far sharper than that of human faculties.

A ship throws out dozens of sonic and magnetic waves. These travel in different directions at different strengths and speeds, and differ from ship to ship, no two vessels having exactly the same pattern. And the pattern differs with the areas of the earth, those thrown out at the equator being different from those in the Arctic, and so forth. The scriggle they make on a graph is called the ship's signature—appropriate because it is as varied as the way people write their names.

While the magnetic mine tunes in for the ship's assorted magnetic radiations, the acoustic mine listens for the creaking of the hull, the waves slapping against the sides, the swishing of the bow wave, the gurgling of the wake, the sounds of the motors and mechanism. Out of this montage of sound and radiation, the mine may be programed to pick out a single detail—which may be peculiar to that particular target—and explode. And there is usually no way to set off this ambush by trickery. The magnetic mine is not prone to be fooled by a magnetic field artificially created, such as a piece of metal dragged behind a mine sweeper. The acoustic mine listening for the beat of a certain propeller has ears for nothing without the same frequency.

So the influence mine waits—silently, patiently, in total command of itself and its assignment. It may be months, but no matter; it asks nothing—neither food nor water nor visits from the USO. Then, at last, here comes something of promise. The mine alerts itself, maybe for the fortieth time. It tenses. It waits. Yes, this is it. It holds for the moment of maximum opportunity—and the headlines tell of another ship sinking, perhaps mysteriously from the midst of a whole flotilla which was already nearly past the point of the explosion.

So there may be suspicion of sabotage. Everybody looks at everybody else a little suspiciously. If it happens in a harbor, despite repeated sweepings, the inclination is to close the port, for it seems to mean nothing that the enemy hasn't been seen around for a couple of months, or that many ships have come and gone in that time without incident.

But for every mine developed, no matter how ingenious, there is a defense, based on how the thing works. For the influence mines of World War II, these defenses were worked out through the efforts of disposal men, many dying in the process. What they learned the hard way, we studied at Indian Head, along with the variations on the basic types that kept showing up. In class, the instructors stressed the importance of making only the right moves; it was better to make none than the wrong ones. Live cowards were preferred to dead heroes. If a man was blown up for playing Fearless Fosdick in the effort to recover some new, unknown mine, the damage went well beyond himself. Such a mine might not be found again for a long time. Meanwhile, for want of a defense against it, ships would be sunk and men killed.

To develop the right outlook toward the work, along with making the student an expert at it, no effort was spared. In class we studied charts and diagrams and soaked up lectures, delivered in the simple, salty language of men who spoke from experience as well as theory. Then we went out to the "Bone Yard," spilling over with actual specimens of most of the world's explosive devices—rockets, V2s, shells, bullets, incendiaries, bombs, grenades, blockbusters—and applied what we had learned in the classroom. When we made a mistake, the fact did not pass in silence but was advertised by the explosion of a miniature charge, impressing on us that under real instead of simulated conditions we would be dead.

When we had learned to disarm mines on dry land, we learned to do it in the water, where we would be doing it for keeps. The practice water was the Potomac River. If you could disarm a mine in the Potomac, you could do it anywhere, for the water makes the supposedly muddy Missouri as clear as a trout stream by comparison. In the Potomac it could be guaranteed that the diver would never see even the dimmest outline of what he was doing.

For all this, the Potomac seemed pretty tame to be coming back to after sixteen years, and for this attitude it came near to closing me out at full circle, reminding me that the rules hadn't been changed while I was away. We had put in about three months in dry-land studies, and one day after class Instructor Dusty Malone said, "All right, I'll see you men down at the river tomorrow morning at nine o'clock." The final phase of our training was about to begin. To me Dusty said as the class filed out, "Well, Bubblehead, you made some pretty good grades in Russian influence mines. Here's where we find out if you cribbed or not."

"Why, what's up?" I asked.

"We got a Russian mine out here in the bottom of the river," said Dusty. "It's fully armed. We'll see if you can disarm it."

"What type is it?" I asked, trying to catch him off guard.

Dusty looked shocked. "You think the Russians are going to tell you what type they're putting out?" he demanded. "That's for you to find out."

"Okay," I said, grinning faintly, thinking he was probably trying to throw me off when he said Russian. I got out my notebooks and boned up on all known mines, including Russian. I went to the back of the classroom and carefully went over the specimens we had there. In the Bone Yard I further refreshed my mind. By the time I got to the river next morning, I was in good shape on the subject.

On the diving barge at the river's edge I found Moose Call, a first-class diver I had known in the fleet years before.

"What're you doing in this outfit?" Moose asked. "I thought all you master divers were out there where the water's deep, terrorizing first-class divers."

"I'm becoming a mine disposal expert," I said. "I could ask you the same question—what're you doing here?"

"I'm a diving instructor," said Moose. "My job is to put you TNT clowns down and try to bring you back safely. What're you going to do here today?" he asked.

"I'm going to attack an unknown mine as my final test," I answered.

"Boy," said Moose, "it's a good thing it doesn't have any real high explosive in it! They blow me up every day down here."

"How's that?" I asked, mildly disquieted.

Moose pointed to a cubbyhole in a corner of the barge. "See that June bug hole over there? Dusty'll probably tell you about it when he gets here. He goes in there and the mine tells him everything you guys on the bottom are doing. The instruments are wired to the mine circuits. You do anything that alerts the mine, Dusty can tell. You do anything wrong, he knows about it before you do." Moose was describing the electronic monitoring system that told how the mine was being influenced by the man in the water.

Moose lowered his voice. "As an old-timer, let me give you a hint," he said. "Take any metal out of your pockets. A lot of them get caught that way." He told of one diver who mysteriously kept being blown up, until it was discovered that his brass belt buckle wasn't really brass but iron with brass plating. "This mine can tell," said Moose confidentially. "Make one mistake and you can't say next time you'll keep your pockets empty—there won't be any next time. You better take your wrist watch off, too."

Clearly Moose still thought of me as a diver only and himself as instructor. Also, it was an opportunity to tell a master diver something.

"This watch can go deeper than I can," I replied lightly. "It's nonmagnetic."

Moose scowled. "I know you're a master diver, Karneke, but you know these mines can hear, too."

Besides wondering from this remark if the unknown mine was acoustic instead of magnetic, as I had first gathered from Moose's helpful hints, I was impressed by his knowledge. "How come you know all this?" I asked. "You're not a disposal expert."

"Neither are you guys," Moose retorted. "That's what blows me up every day—you guys goofing."

Moose was beginning to shake my confidence. I was starting to wonder if we were missing something in the classroom when Dusty Malone arrived, and we got busy on the day's diving. There were twenty or more mines in the river— from Britain, France, Germany, Russia, Japan, any country that made them—planted all over the bottom. They included acoustic mines, magnetic mines, and combinations of both. There were pressure mines and several experimental types. All were connected by submarine cable to Dusty's monitoring panel in the corner cubbyhole, but to the divers their locations were unknown. Each man was directed to his particular mine by hand signal on his lifeline. No telephones could be used. The magnetic metal in the mike could set off the magnetic mines, the conversation the acoustic mines.

The first man down promptly got into trouble. Moose came rushing out of Dusty's monitoring quarters. "Quick," he said, "Dusty says this guy's about to blow himself up!"

I reached Dusty's side just as a needle swung sharply on its dial, bearing out his prediction. A dull bang rolled up from the water, confirming the instrument. Then came the emergency signal from the diver to be brought up.

"It's going to be a good day," observed Moose drily. "They started killing us off with the first one."

The first "casualty" broke surface and was helped aboard. He looked bewildered and shook his head dumbly at questions, his ears still ringing from the blow to his eardrums by the concussion from the explosion.

"Well, Dusty," said Moose as the first man was led aside, "who you want me to put down next?"

Dusty glanced at me. "How about putting your old buddy down?" he said.

"Glad to," answered Moose, a little more eagerly than I liked. When I saw him and Dusty wink at each other, I knew there was skulduggery afoot. I may have been a hero at diving but I was new at this, and the opportunity to humble me would be greatly tempting.

"By the way, Master," Moose asked evilly, "you got your suit with you? Or would a standard number size be good enough?"

I had had my deep-sea diving dresses custom-tailored, back when I made first-class diver, and I had never been able to live it down, but I hadn't expected that the story would have followed me all the way to Indian Head. I decided to play it straight. "You know I would never have a shallow-water diving dress tailor-made," I replied with dignity. "What kind of rig you going to put me in?"

"We'll put you in a Jack Brown-type outfit," said Moose. This is roughly the same as a deep-sea dress except that the diver wears a mask in place of a helmet and no air goes into the suit. The idea is to combine the lightweight advantages of the skin-diving outfit with some of the protection of the deep-water rig. The Jack Brown rig was nonmagnetic, but this told me nothing; all strange mines are approached with nonmagnetic equipment.

It was with a little of the feeling of a novice that I slipped into the muddy darkness of the river, running heavy with the outbound tide and giving me a lot of turbulence to contend with. The milling currents shoved me this way and that like a rush-hour crowd, making it hard both to detect the directional signals on my line and to follow them. Still, I seemed to be on course and making progress, when I felt the pulls of an emergency signal. I returned the signal and struggled back along my lines toward the barge. I figured that a ship was coming by overhead.

"What happened?" I asked as I was hauled aboard. I saw no ships around.

"We're having a hard time giving you signals," said Moose, "and searching for the mine is not real important in this dive. But what is important, we got a mine out there, and my job is to try to get you on it."

"What's so special about it?" I asked suspiciously.

"It's a Russian mine," Moose replied pointedly.

"I know how to attack a Russian mine," I said, glad to have this confirmation of what I was going after.

Dusty Malone came out of his monitoring booth. "Here comes Dusty," said Moose. "He'll tell you."

Dusty looked concerned. "We want you to attack an R-1," he said.

"You taught us how to do that," I replied.

"Yes, but I didn't tell you about a new way to attack it. Chief Custis has worked out a method that he thinks is a lot safer, and we want to try it. Instead of having you waste all that time searching for the mine in this tide, we're going to send you right out to it." He explained the new method of attack.

"How close was I to the mine?" I asked Moose Call.

"About halfway," said Moose.

"I could hardly feel your signals," I reminded him. Further out I wouldn't feel them at all, probably.

"Then what's your suggestion for the best way to get out there?" Moose asked.

I thought a moment. "The best way," I said, "is not to worry about signals. I'll follow the line out to the mine. You'll know by the instruments when I'm getting there and what I'm doing."

This proposal was agreed to by everybody who should have known better, and disagreed to by the one man who could be forgiven for not knowing better. This was Frank Moore, a classmate of mine who was learning diving as well as disposal. "You know," he said disapprovingly, "this is the kind of stuff you say people get hurt doing. You always say never dive a man unless he can signal every few minutes."

"That's true," I conceded, "but in this case I'm going down myself, and I know what the conditions are."

Frank Moore was not convinced. "You can goof—the same as anybody else," he said. He listened with a deepening frown as I went on with my plan.

It was understood that Moose was to follow my progress in the water by my bubbles. "If the bubbles don't move, assume I'm in trouble," I said. "Pull me up or get somebody to me."

"Okay," said Moose, sharing some of Moore's doubts. "Get back in the water when you're ready."

I put my mask back on, tethered my nonmagnetic tools by the strap at my wrist, and with the aplomb befitting a master diver went back into the water, sliding down the cable tied to the mine somewhere out in the Potomac's midstream. When I reached the bottom, I gave my lifeline a single pull to signal my arrival there. Then I gave it two pulls to say that I was on my way. That ended my communications.

Following the cable by picking it up and placing one hand before the other, I found myself passing through what could only be described as an underwater dump. I stumbled against hunks of scrap iron, tin cans, old tires, tubes, tree stumps, tangles of wire—none of it good for my lifeline and air hose. The lines could be fouled. My air could be pinched off, or the hose cut. Another problem which grew as I progressed was the increasing pull on my lengthening air hose by the tide sweeping across it. I leaned almost flat into the water and bulled on, occasionally digging my hands into the bottom. My suit was squeezing me tighter, indicating that the water was getting deeper, making it necessary to keep opening my valve for more air. This worried me—the water wasn't supposed to be that deep. But I kept going, a kind of to-hell-with-it feeling coming over me. At least, conditions couldn't get any worse—or so I thought.

I estimated that I was getting close to the mine. I decided I had better stop worrying about the diving part and start using the prescribed approach procedure, requiring that I control my breathing pattern in such a way as not to resemble a ship's signature. With the currents buffeting me and less and less air coming through my hose, this was not easy. But I bore in mind that in a real-life situation my life could depend on it.

Then I felt the mine. The effect on me was electric. I instantly forgot all my troubles and with intense concentration started the disarming procedure. In my mind's eye I could see Moose Call and Dusty topside, electronically following my movements. I was determined to make none of them wrong. In a few moments I was finished. I backed off to take a deep breath of relief, unaware that in my intensity as I worked I had been holding my breath. No air came. Strangling and gasping, I reached for my air valve—it was already spun wide open! My air flow had stopped entirely. Something had happened to my hose, or the air compressor topside had quit.

I gave my lifeline a pull to begin the emergency signal,

then remembered that I had canceled the signals; no one would be paying any attention to tugs on the line. For the first time in my years as a diver I was truly on my own.

Somehow I must get to the surface, some sixty feet above. By its fast release mechanism I dropped my belt with its fifty pounds of lead, then tore off my mask and desperately began swimming upward. After a time that seemed eternal, there was still no thinning of the darkness. I was getting nowhere. Something seemed to be holding me. I stopped kicking and discovered I was still standing on the bottom. I bent over and clawed the area at my feet. Circling my ankles were the belt and its leaden weight. The heavy canvas of my suit had insulated me from feeling it sooner as I struggled to go up. I always hated these suits—"suicide suits," we called them. They were like a strait jacket. They gave the effect of a deep-sea suit without the benefit of air inside and a helmet on top. I stepped out of the belt and started up once more, my wits beginning to fade.

It occurred to me that I wasn't breathing. "Why don't I breathe?" I asked myself confusedly. I inhaled deeply, filling my lungs with Potomac River. I spewed it out and took in some more. I became a water-breathing creature, dreamily trying to remember why this wasn't supposed to work, and reminding myself to be sure to tell the others about this important discovery.

At last I saw a faint dawn, growing rapidly lighter, and I popped into the brilliant light of the air-breathing world. But my brain was growing dark, and with the twilight still left to me I realized that the barge I had dived from was on the other side of the universe. The crew wouldn't be looking for me, and I could neither swim the distance nor call across it. Sudden peace came over me, and I gave up. Far away, as if it were happening to someone else, I felt strong hands taking hold of me and lifting.

When I came to, I was in a boat, with Frank Moore sitting over me. He hadn't been impressed by my reassurances that

I wouldn't need signals and had taken to a boat as soon as I went down, following my bubbles. He had been within arm's reach when I came up, and he gathered me in just before, like all good sailors, I went to sea with the tide. Frank joshed me about pouring barrels of water out of me. "What're you trying to do—drink the river dry?" he asked.

There had been nothing wrong with my hose—except that it was hopelessly fouled. But it wasn't this that had kept me from getting air. We had underestimated the amount of resistance 500 feet of hose of this small diameter would put up to passage of air through it sixty feet down. The gauges all indicated that there was more than enough pressure behind it to keep the air flowing to me.

Besides, wasn't I a master diver, of great experience and reputation? This idea, which in its ultimate extension would mean that a really good diver needed no air at all, had nearly gotten me killed by the river I had left sixteen years before as a beginner.

I was still learning.

19. Not All Mines Have Horns

A cold wind swept across Korea's Wonsan harbor as we bore down on the mine, bobbing like a big apple in the distance. To the uninitiated, it could pass for something about as harmless, rather than a destruction machine with more than 600 pounds of high explosive in its steel belly, well able to sink the biggest battleship afloat.

I knew that in theory 200 yards was a safe distance to shoot at mines. How much closer this crew had been approaching in practice I didn't know, but with my reputation as a big man in mines, just out from Indian Head, I wasn't going to embarrass myself by asking, preferring to leave it up to the crew. Besides, when people have been doing something successfully in a certain way, it was a principle in good standing to let them go on doing it that way. As we neared what must be the critical point, I picked up my camera and casually said to the coxswain, "Tell the men to shoot when they get to the usual distance. I'll take some pictures."

I mounted the transom and, managing a precarious foothold on the bouncing deck, began focusing on the mine. In the well, a half dozen Garands were brought into position, ready to spurt armor-piercing bullets at the target. I expected them to shoot any moment, but nothing happened. We were getting so close to the mine that even through the camera it looked big. Not more than seventy-five yards separated us. I called to the coxswain, "When you guys going to shoot?"

Instantly there was a crash of rifle fire, with immediate, cataclysmic results. In my exposed position it felt as if I had been swung on with a boom. I pitched to the deck, and as I lay stunned amid the pieces of my camera, the water that had gone up with the explosion broke in a storm over the boat. Distantly I could hear an alarmed voice on the radio, "Cowhand Five, are you all right? Are you all right?" The flagship told us later that they couldn't see us for five minutes.

Far out all around us as I crawled back into the well, the steel began to rain down. The blast from an exploding mine is expended upward, in the direction of least resistance, and we were well inside the cone formed by the falling fragments. It was much safer in here than out on the 200-yard perimeter where the shooting was usually done. As we emerged from the downpour of water and metal, a crewman wiped the moisture from his face and said to me, beaming with admiration, "Boy, you must really know your mines! That other chief would never think of going in this close."

I started to say something but checked myself. Besides, it was true that I knew more now than a little while earlier. In fact, we all knew more. It was adopted as standard practice thereafter to go in this close before opening fire. The other destructor boats did the same. It made for greater safety, better shooting—more efficient performance all around. It was more exciting, too, helping to keep morale up.

The job of the destructor boats was to follow in the wake of the mine sweepers and dispose of what they swept up. Wonsan was a key enemy stronghold, containing his main railhead on the west coast, and the object was to keep the harbor clear of mines for a possible UN invasion. The mines hung under the surface, moored by a hook which unreeled to the bottom by a wire. Arming was done hydrostatically—that is, from the pressure of the water as the mine sank to its pre-scribed depth after being planted. As the sweeper passed above, dragging its sweep gear, it cut the anchor wire and the mine came to the top, theoretically disarming itself as the pressure came off. We in the destructor boats first took a good look at it. If the mine was a new type or showed modifications from a known kind, we hauled it in for study—so it would no longer be unknown. If, on the other hand, the mine was al-ready known, as was usually the case, we shot it. Depending on where the bullets hit, the mine blew up before us or it sank to the bottom, where it might or might not explode from the impact with the ocean floor. In any event, it was safely out of the way.

The sweepers worked the water like tandem plows, and sometimes a sweeper would find itself surrounded by loose mines cut adrift by the sweeper ahead. All it could do then was to cut off the engines and drift helplessly, hoping it didn't bump into one of the mines, or vice versa. If a mine had failed to disarm itself as it came to the surface, which hap-pened more often than not, it took but a light rap to set it off. In this crowded togetherness, the destructor boats were limited in what they could do to help. We couldn't risk shoot-ing to get rid of the mines. We could only dash in with a long wire, hook it through the lifting pad eye of the mine, and tow it off where we could deal with it on our own terms. Some-times, when mines suddenly seemed to be bobbing to the surface everywhere, we rushed from one to another, as busy as a one-armed camper pitching a tent in a high wind.

In shooting at the mines, the holes were put as near the water line as possible. Assuming the mine didn't explode, the waves washing up the sides did the rest, sloshing water through the holes and sending it down. If the sea was calm, we raced the boat around the mine, kicking up our own waves.

One memorable time we decided to try something new. This was to back the boat up to the mine and as we pulled away at high speed, throw water on it with the propeller. As the coxswain heavy-handedly slammed the lever back to reverse the engine, he broke the throttle linkage mounted on the same lever. With the engine roaring out of control, the boat shot back toward the mine at full speed. A second or two before it wouldn't have mattered any longer, the coxswain threw the tiller hard over and the boat slid past the mine on a sharply curving course with barely room to spare. Unfortunately, in his enthusiasm to throw the tiller over, the coxswain had jammed it in place. We now had nothing to say over where we were going, or how fast we were going to get there.

As the boat raced backward on a mad circus around the mine, the frozen rudder pulled the circle steadily tighter. At the same time, the mine was being drawn toward us by the whirlpool churned in the center, and tending to move with us in pursuit. We stood watching the mine like the rabbit regarding the python.

"Somebody better do something quick!" someone finally yelled, delivering a line you can always count on in a situation that needs no one to speak for it. Specific recommendations remained lacking.

The engineer spoke up. "I'll cut off the valve from the fuel tank," he shouted. "That'll stop the engine in a couple of minutes." There was a scramble to find the valve, only to discover that in the conversion of this former landing craft to a mine destructor boat, the valve had been blocked out of reach by the special equipment bolted aboard. There was no way to get to it short of tearing the boat apart.

Meanwhile, our fortunes continued to decline. Now water was getting into the rifle holes in the mine, causing it to ride lower in the water; and as the water line crept up, more water got into more holes, accelerating the mine's disappearance into the depths. This raised the prospect that the mine would rearm itself and then explode, because our bullets had triggered the firing mechanism.

"Get on the squawk box and call for help!" I ordered the radioman.

"Shall I call Mayday first, Chief?" he asked, referring to the international distress call for aircraft and ships.

"Mayday, hell!" I yelled. "Tell them we got a jammed rudder, a runaway engine, and we're circling a mine!"

The call went out, and in a few minutes destructor boats were converging on us from all sides, hoping to get a towline to us, to pull us out of danger. Just before the first reached us, some inspired genius among us tore off his life jacket and stuffed it into the engine's air intake vent. The engine strangled and died. The propeller spun to a stop and, with steerageway gone, the boat drifted out of the circle, away from the mine. With a large audience gathering around us, we could only grin foolishly—but we didn't mind too much; we felt very lucky.

Not all floating enemy mines had reached the surface because of the sweepers. Some rose to the top by accident or, it was suspected, by design—the Geneva Convention against floating mines notwithstanding. One drifter which we encountered quite often was the M-26, a Russian type of particularly unstable habit. A sharp rap with the knuckles was enough to set it off. Like other moored mines, the M-26 was supposed to disarm itself automatically when it came to the surface, but this it usually failed to do—because, said the Russians, the Koreans didn't assemble it properly. Like the devil, all mines are popularly believed to have horns. The M-26 had none. This made it the more dangerous, because it was sometimes mistaken for a buoy.

One day we spotted a patrol boat dead in the water toward shore, the crew waving to us to come over. As we approached, our lookout in the bow suddenly whirled and vigorously motioned to the coxswain to hold off. The coxswain stopped the boat, throwing it into reverse.

I called to the lookout, "What's the trouble?"

"That patrol boat over there's tied up to a mine—an M-26!" he cried feelingly.

I brought up my binoculars and, sure enough, the patrol boat was moored by a short line to the most erratic floating explosive in Korea. A passing shift in the current, sending the boat brushing even lightly against the mine, could set it off. That this hadn't already happened could only be freakish luck. "Stay here," I told the crew. "Let's put the raft into the water." The raft was made of shock-absorbing rubber, making it safer for the final approach to a mine.

The raft was launched, and Eaglehoff—generally known as Eagle, at first because he was such a poor shot at hitting the mines, and later because he got so good at it—volunteered to help me paddle. As Eagle and I came gently alongside the patrol boat, the crew surveyed us questioningly. "What's the matter with you guys?" asked the coxswain. "You think we got cholera, or something? Nobody here's been ashore."

"Don't get excited," I said as calmly as I could. "It's worse than cholera—you're tied up to a mine."

The coxswain glanced at his mooring. "Don't kid me, Chief," he said. "We're not fresh from the States. I know a mine has horns. I've seen plenty since I been here. You people on the mine sweepers are always trying to scare people. We got a dead engine and we were lucky to find this buoy, because we were drifting toward the Commies on the beach."

"You've been lucky, all right—luckier than you think," I said, narrowly watching the fluctuating space between the boat and the mine. If it closed entirely and the boat nuzzled the mooring, there was little doubt we would all be blown to kingdom come. "You don't mind if I go and release you from that thing?" I said.

The coxswain shrugged. "Okay—if you think it's a mine. Suit yourself."

Eagle and I eased our raft over to the mine. I carefully untied the line from the pad eye where it had been fastened and gently let it slip free. The patrol boat drifted slowly away, and when a healthful hundred feet or so separated it from the mine, I signaled our destructor boat to come over. Our boat was one of those with an expert engineman aboard. These were spotted throughout the destructor boat fleet so that, in a sea of mines, no one among the sweepers and ourselves was long helpless in case of an engine failure. Radiomen were similarly distributed among us, for the equally vital matter of keeping communications open.

Our engineman was quick to get the patrol boat going again, and as it pulled away, the crew looked back at us as if we had done them a dirty trick. When they were safely out of range I suggested, as an afterthought, that we ought to let them know that the mine might go off when we started shooting to sink it, so they wouldn't be caught off guard.

"Hell, no!" objected Eagle. "If this is one that only sinks, they'll think we're really nuts! It'll prove they were right about its being a buoy."

For a minute or two, as we stood off and pegged bullets into the mine, we were grateful to Eagle; it looked as if the crew of the patrol boat would get away unconvinced of a recent hard fact of their lives. Then, with our ninth bullet, the sea shuddered; it humped its back, and out of a great circle ripped across the waves leaped a geyser 200 feet high. When a mine explodes, everybody for ten miles around knows about it, and as the shock wave crashed against the ears of our departing friends, now about a thousand yards away, they took off their hats and waved. They were convinced.

Most of our work to keep Wonsan harbor clear of mines came under range of the enemy's shore guns, and this made for extra stimulation. To my destructor boat one afternoon came a radio call from a sweeper. "Cowhand Five, this is Cowhand Three. We have a mine fouled in our sweep gear. Request assistance."

Normally, when a mine became fouled in the sweep gear,

the solution was simply to cut the gear loose and replace it with new equipment, rather than run the risk of blowing up the boat and crew by trying to disentangle it. We guessed that something had gone wrong so that Cowhand Three couldn't follow this procedure.

Before we could acknowledge the call, the listening enemy on shore answered for us. "This is Cowhand Five to Cowhand Three," came a voice in precise English over the loudspeaker. "Please stand fast. We are sending you one six-inch shell. Ha, ha!"

The enemy knew that with a mine hung up in its sweep gear, Cowhand Three wasn't able to move, and after letting him stew for a few moments, the enemy added the further taunt, "Cowhand Five to Cowhand Three, do not get impatient. Making sure of your range before sending assistance."

Now the sweeper was heard from. "This is Cowhand Three to Commie assistance. Please hurry so we can determine what direction assistance coming from, so we can return favor." When there was no immediate response, our man on the sweeper followed up mockingly. "Chicken! How would you like some nice Willie Pee?" This was phosphorus, a poisonous, inflammable element that eats into the flesh like acid, allowing nothing to stop it.

The enemy replied disrespectfully, begetting a return commentary from Cowhand Three in language not widely considered suitable for wireless communication. When he finally had run down, the Communist answered smoothly, "Very sorry, cannot understand you. Please repeat all after son of . . ."

These exchanges of courtesies might or might not end up in gunfire. There were restraints on both sides. The enemy knew that our small boats were hard to hit, at three to five miles out, and he hated to waste ammunition. Also, to shoot meant to give away his position. On our part, we were backed up by a good-sized fleet of destroyers, cruisers, and even battleships, standing by outside the harbor, ready to plaster any spot that showed a gun. Also, we had spotters aloft in aircraft, keeping a hawk eye out for enemy emplacements. The spotters were continually calling out the grid co-ordinates for various positions, keeping the enemy under a strain. He was not disposed to add to it by revealing where he was.

This time, though, there was reason to believe that the enemy might shoot. "The sweeper is in pretty close," said Lieutenant Edwards, who that day happened to be working with me rather than commanding his own boat. "They may have decided to use a tank gun." Such a weapon could be quickly moved, keeping its whereabouts hidden. We pointed our destructor boat toward the troubled Cowhand Three and opened the throttle.

The strained faces of the sweeper crew relaxed as we came alongside. No matter how dangerous a situation is, it seems the moment the experts arrive—before they have turned a hand—it becomes safe. It was my job to make the dive, but Lieutenant Edwards insisted on going down himself, and he wasted no time getting into the water for a preliminary look. The mine was caught in the otter, the part of the sweeping mechanism nearest the sweeper, placing the explosive directly underneath the boat.

Edwards soon returned. "How about the nail?" he said.

I knew from this that we had another highly sensitive mine on our hands. This one had horns. A couple of pounds of pressure on one of these, which are made of lead, and it would break. Inside the horn, a thin glass vial filled with acid would be broken. The acid would run into a cup containing a pair of electrodes, and up would go the mine, taking both boats with it. It was remarkable that a horn hadn't been broken when the mine first became fouled in the sweep gear.

To make the mine safe, all that was needed was an ordinary carpenter's nail of a certain size. We had discovered that with the nail, the arming mechanism could be locked out just as effectively as with the special pin developed for the purpose but which, because it was classified, was hard to get. We got the nails in the ship's carpenter shop, and carried a big supply in our tool bags. I handed a nail to Edwards and he ducked back below.

An added incentive to work fast besides the critical condition of the mine was the temperature of the water. The average survival time in it, without waterproof clothes, was five minutes. Edwards was wearing a frog suit, which made him good for only a little longer than that—provided the paper-thin rubber of the suit wasn't ripped, letting the water in.

A flash bloomed on shore, and a moment later a shell gouged a towering divot out of the water nearby. "I see why the lieutenant wanted to get into the water," remarked a crewman. "He wanted to get where it's safe."

I was tempted to shake him up by telling about the nature of the mine under us but stifled the impulse. This was no time to have somebody panic. Lieutenant Edwards reappeared amid the choppy waves. "How about some pliers?" he said, his teeth chattering. "I'm going to unshackle the mine." This meant the nail was in place and the mine safe.

"Hand Lieutenant Edwards a pair of pliers," I sharply instructed the man who had been belittling him.

He handed Edwards the pliers as another shell splashed a few yards away. "They're shooting at us, Lieutenant," he said anxiously.

"Are they trying to make trouble for us?" said Edwards with gentle irony, going back down with the pliers.

More shells came in. "In case you hadn't noticed it, Chief," Eagle put in sarcastically, "they're shooting at us."

"What do you want me to do about it?" I retorted. "Go over and stop them?"

"We would if we thought you could," somebody gibed.

The mine popped to the surface, followed by Edwards.

"Jeez!" it was remarked. "A nail in that thing! Is that what's making it safe?"

"Yes," I said. "Just a nail."

To avoid shore fire, the decision was made to sweep at night, under the sheltering cover of darkness. This raised a new problem for the destructor boat crews in disposing of the mines; they couldn't see to shoot at them. One solution was to paddle up to them in our rubber raft and hang an explosive charge on the pad eye, setting it off by hellbox from the destructor boat at safe range. We decided to give this procedure a trial run by daylight. At the sight of our next mine, I called for a volunteer to help me paddle over to it. The crew exchanged glances, no one coming forward.

"Come on, now," I said, "if there was any danger I wouldn't be going myself."

The last man I wanted stepped up. It was Jones (although this was not his real name). Jones' eyes glared at each other across his nose, and he seemed always to be in an uphill battle to keep them open from overweighted lids. Jones had the look of a cross-eyed owl fighting sleep. More important, he didn't seem too bright at times. There were better choices for an approach to a live mine.

When we got up to the mine, coming in upcurrent, Jones stopped paddling just as I was ready to grab the pad eye. We tried again, and he did the same thing, shipping his paddle at the crucial moment and nearly causing me to fall into the water as I lunged at the mine. After several cycles of this pantomime, I said to my oarsman, with a slow burn, "All I want is to get hold of the pad eye."

"I know, but I don't want to ram the mine," Jones replied querulously. He turned his head away to bring a heavy-lidded eye to bear on me. "You don't want me to blow you up, do you?"

I turned this answer against him by saying, "All right, then I'll paddle and you grab the mine."

We changed places, but Jones was as reluctant to do his new job as the old one. He would hold out his hand to grab the pad eye but at the last moment couldn't quite bring himself to go through with it. "Goddammit, grab it!" I bellowed as we approached the mine for the sixth time. Jones was so startled that he nearly fell out of the boat, grabbing the mine to save himself. After that there was no holding him— he became the best mine grabber in the whole destructor boat fleet.

One moonless night, with all hell on the loose, following the sweepers as usual, we heard a familiar call on the radio. "We think we cut one. Watch for it."

We dimly spotted the mine in the darkness and put over to it by raft. What we found appeared to be something new. The mine was only a fraction of the normal size, and it had fewer horns—only three instead of five or more. At least this was our impression. With falling flares blindingly bleaching out the night, followed by bombing and strafing runs; with wheeling searchlights knifing the darkness, gunfire flashing between ships and shore batteries, shells plowing the water everywhere—with all this going on, it was possible to make a mistake. Less uproar and confusion were not one of the advantages of nighttime mine disposal. It was hard to be sure of anything; no one printed programs.

The radio crackled again. "We're cutting many mines now —we're in a heavy mine field. Watch for them."

There was no time to debate what to do about the new one. We hung a charge on it and blew it up.

Next day, making a routine report of the night's work, we were told Intelligence had information that the enemy was introducing a new type of mine in the area. The description tallied with what we thought we had seen and destroyed the night before. We were ordered to recover one of the new mines for study at all costs.

A couple of nights later, the lookout sighted one bobbing in the wake of a sweeper. Rather than try the ticklish business of taking it apart in the darkness, Lieutenant Edwards and I decided to moor it and come back in the morning. We tied a long line to the mine and after two hours of pampering labor, being especially careful not to bend the horns, had it anchored in the lee of a friendly island. It was then two o'clock in the morning and we were badly bushed, but it was good to have gotten one of the new mines so soon. Intelligence would be pleased. We looked forward to completing the job by daylight.

After a few hours' sleep, we were back. The mine had disappeared. We searched the area where we had left it and then cruised up and down in front of the island, on the off chance that the mine had been washed ashore. This water was considered no man's land, and it was unthinkable that after we had plucked our prize from under the noses of the enemy, we should lose it.

A voice rolled out from a megaphone somewhere on the heights of the island. "Are you sailors out there looking for a mine?"

The seven of us in the destructor boat brought our guns up. "Who are you?" I shouted.

"I'm an Army spotter," came the reply. "That mine you're looking for—you don't have to worry about it no more. I sunk it."

We looked at one another with long faces. The lieutenant cupped his hands to his mouth and called back, "Did it have three horns?" The fellow could be mistaken. There were a lot of mines around.

"Yep, that's the one," the voice on shore returned proudly. "Those Commies must be running out of materials. They're not putting as many horns on as they used to." Hearing nothing more from us, he demanded, "Don't you sailors know how to say thank you?"

"Thanks," called Lieutenant Edwards. "Thanks a lot."

"Don't mention it. The Army's always glad to help the Navy, any time."

Next day there was a general alert on for the new mine. Any ship sighting it was ordered to take no action against it but to report the find to ComMineRon Three—Commander

Mine Squadron Three. Intelligence told us the mine was probably directed at the small boats of the mine sweeping and destructor fleets, to put an end to our disposal activities. It was imperative that we get our hands on one before they caused us heavy casualties.

All craft became leery of any floating object. A ship signaled that one of its boats had seen a "small buoy," possibly with horns on it, and gave the location. Our boat was dispatched to investigate, Edwards and I making the final approach on the rubber raft. Once more there were the telltale three horns. Whether or not the mine was armed we had no way of telling, since the type was unknown. I dived below and unshackled the mine from its mooring, letting it come to the surface.

"Now that we got it, what are we going to do with it?" I asked as I climbed back on the raft.

"We've got to take it apart, that's for sure," said the lieutenant.

"We can't do it here," I said, glancing apprehensively toward shore. "We'll have to get it to one of these beaches." I indicated the islands in the opposite direction.

Edwards wasn't sure. "One thing about these beaches, they're all mined," he said.

"Let's go to one that the North Koreans haven't been on yet," I suggested.

"Remember, the ones they didn't mine, we mined," Edwards cautioned. "These islands have changed hands so many times that nobody really knows what's safe any more."

"I got an idea," I said. "How about getting hold of the Army and seeing if they can help out?"

The lieutenant shook his head. "Remember the help they gave us on the last mine," he said with a rueful grin. "If it hadn't been for that, we wouldn't be sitting here under the guns with this one."

I was trying to recall something the Army had taught us about land mines. "It was something unusual about them," I mused.

"I remember!" exclaimed Edwards. "Land mines are not effective below the high-water mark. Flooding makes them inert. Let's call and find out when low water is."

We tied a 200-foot line to the mine and paddled back to the destructor boat. The radioman learned that low tide was at 1400. Edwards looked at his watch. "That's about two hours from now," he said. "That'll give us time for a banker's lunch. Let's have a sandwich."

As we ate our sandwiches, a crewman pointed toward an island with a broad band of sand along the edge and observed, "That looks like a nice beach over there."

"Yeah," replied another, "some litterbug got there first, from the way it looks. It's covered with oil drums."

Edwards studied the shoreline closely. "What do you think of that beach, Chief?" he asked.

"By the debris, the high-water mark seems quite a way up," I said approvingly. The wider the tideland, the more room we would have to work in, since any land mines planted there would have been drowned out—if the lieutenant remembered his land mines correctly.

"After we eat, we'll pass up and down in front a few times and see if anybody shoots at us," said Edwards. "If not, we'll try to beach the mine there."

No shots were fired, bringing us to the problem of the best way to get the mine ashore. "Remember the school procedure, that any safe method is a good method, and any remote method is a safe method," said the lieutenant.

"Yes," I agreed. "The problem is how to get that mine on the island remotely."

Edwards scratched his head. "We can only go to the high-water mark—and even that's a calculated risk," he said. "Then we'll have to shorten our line."

I looked at the long combers curling in toward the beach. "We've got enough surf action to tumble the mine," I pointed out. This would almost certainly break a horn, causing the mine to explode.

But it was no good being dainty about it. First with the boat, then with the raft, shortening the line to twenty feet, we towed the mine in as close as we could before there was danger of tumbling. Then we abandoned all pretense at sticking with the classroom injunction to use remote methods, and came to intimate grips with the situation. We jumped into the breakers and, in water up to our waists, walked the mine in by hand, using the surf to help us along. We grasped it by the pad eyes and as each roller swelled around it, providing lift, we moved the mine several more feet on its way. Our boat lay far off, some of the crew keeping their eyes the other way.

When the mine at last lay high and dry, we badly needed a breather. It was a warm, bright day, and Edwards looked around for a place to get out of the sun. "Let's sit under that tree over there," he said, wiping the sweat from his brow and pointing to a tree among the oil drums a little farther up.

"Yeah, and get our feet blown off," I said. "Remember, this place is full of land mines."

So we lounged alongside our inscrutable friend. I pulled a cigar from my shirt pocket, inside my foul-weather gear, and lighted it. This was an old habit of mine after a hard piece of work.

The lieutenant thoughtfully watched the smoke drifting around the mine. "At least there's one advantage in being here, Karneke," he observed philosophically. "You can smoke a cigar without getting criticized for it." It was generally held to be poor form to smoke in the presence of high explosives.

The pay-off part of the job—to make the mine safe—was still before us. "What do you think is the best way to take it apart?" Edwards said as we got to our feet.

"There's one good thing," I parried. "We're both here. We don't have to walk ourselves to death while we're coming to an agreement what to do with it."

Ordinarily, only one man goes up to the mine at a time. He takes a look at it, then reports what he sees to the second man, waiting at a safe distance in the background. The second man then takes a look at the mine while the first waits. When the two agree on what they see—sometimes only after many trips—they decide on the procedure to use in disarming the mine. This way, if the mine blows up, the surviving second man may reasonably assume that the procedure used by the late first man is not the right one.

But how, in these limited quarters, could one of us absent himself?

"One of us could go out in the rubber raft," Edwards suggested.

Neither of us thought much of this idea. Now that we were cooled off, it would be chilly paddling back and forth in the wind offshore, fighting the surf. Also, while we had escaped hostile attention from the enemy up to now, this going and coming would only tempt him further. Under the circumstances, especially since we hadn't gone by the book thus far, we agreed that it would be all right to break a few more rules. We both stayed by the mine.

"I wonder which of these fittings we should take off first?" Edwards muttered as we broke out our tools.

"How about a little eeny-meeny-miney-mo?" I said.

"Look, Chief, we're supposed to be experts," Edwards chided. "How about a little more scientific approach in deciding which it should be?"

"Okay, what's your guess?" I asked. Subconsciously, each of us was leaning on the other to decide the first move.

"Let's try this retaining ring in the top," Edwards said. "It looks the easiest to take off."

"All right by me," I answered. "I'll hold it while you turn." I handed him the screwdriver.

In a moment the ring was off; we relaxed slightly. Beyond the ring was what we took to be the arming mechanism. With the sweat beading out on our faces again and breathing heavily, we silently detached and lifted this out. Next came the detonator and booster—the detonator sets off the booster, the booster sets off the main charge. We pulled these out. It was all over.

I relighted my cigar. With the detonator in one hand and the booster in the other, I squatted beside the mine while Edwards took my picture. On our way back to the boat, carrying these sensitive parts in our well-padded pockets, the lieutenant suddenly said, "We forgot something. You should have taken the cigar out of your mouth. Now we can't show the picture."

"We sure ruin a lot of pictures that way," I said. We laughed, dispelling what was left of the tension.

From a study of the parts we brought back, Intelligence was convinced that the small, three-horned mine was specifically designed to get the little boats of the UN mine disposal fleet. By our quick action in recovering one, we learned to deal with the new mines before they scored a single victim. This success was credited to the alertness of everybody in looking for one—and to a lot of luck.

Just how lucky Lieutenant Edwards and I had been we learned from the colonel in charge of Army spotters on the island, and who had been responsible for the UN mines planted there. The colonel could hardly believe it. "That beach was covered with land mines—ours and the Commies'," he exclaimed. "You had to walk a special path through the mine field, marked out by those oil drums. There was no other access." The colonel shook his head. "I don't understand it," he repeated.

Lieutenant Edwards spoke up. "Sir," he said tactfully, "as you know, land mines are rendered inert by tidal action."

The colonel clearly indicated that he wouldn't have put any money on it.

On our next assignment, we got a chance to do something for the Army, returning the favor the Army thought it had done for the Navy in the matter of the first small mine we had captured—only this time there was no confusion. Aboard our support ship, Lieutenant Edwards and I were summoned by the operations officer, who explained the problem. At an island about an hour away, a mine had somehow floated across a reef into a cove and sunk, causing worry to a certain unidentified Army activity on the island. Our job: get rid of the mine.

As we rounded a point of the island and came into view of the cove, we saw an Army man waiting for us on the beach. He animatedly waved us off, pointing into the water at his feet. We hove to with the destructor boat outside the reef, and Edwards and I went in the rest of the way by rubber raft, crossing the reef at a low place. While the Army man kept a finger trained on the water, we paddled alongside a little makeshift pier fashioned from oil drums and planking. The mine was easily visible in the clear water, resting on the sand about fifteen feet below. Why its presence so upset our Army friend, who proved to be a major, we understood as we looked up the heights rising steeply above the cove. There, in a pocket among the crags with trails snaking up to it, was a big Army camp of some sort, complete with a small Stars and Stripes fluttering from a pole. It was all so well camouflaged that although we had been past here many times, we had never suspected there was anything on the island but an occasional Army spotter. The camp was almost straight above and not more than a hundred yards from the cove with its explosive egg, which looked like an M-26. The troops had spotted it that morning, the major explained, as they looked down after breakfast. If it blew up, it would wipe out the camp.

"I guess it won't be much trouble for you experts to take care of it," said the major.

"There should be no problems," agreed Edwards. "Just get your men back to a safe place, and we'll blow it up."

The major was startled. "Blow it up!" he echoed. "Look, if we want something blown up, we don't need the Navy to do it. We would have done it ourselves long before this instead of sweating for you Navy people to show up."

"Why can't you evacuate the men?" I asked curiously.

The major turned on me. "We didn't ask you people to come over here and tell us how to run the war," he declared loudly. "We were told you could make the mine safe and take it out of here. This is why you were asked over."

"We'll do our best, Major," said Edwards patiently.

We paddled back to the boat for our frog suits, and when we returned to the cove we delicately suggested to the major that he put his men in the safest possible place.

"They're as safe as they're ever going to be," said the major, making it clear by his tone that he had heard enough on the subject.

We suggested that he and a sidekick who had shown up leave the immediate area. This effort was more successful, the two withdrawing.

I slid over the edge of the raft and down to the mine. It was a modified M-26 with a rubber cover over the arming mechanism so I couldn't tell whether it was armed or disarmed. There were dents in the sides, undoubtedly made as the mine bounced over the reef. I returned topside and Edwards went down for a look, seeing the same things I did. From the beating the mine had taken in crossing the reef, we felt that either the firing mechanism had been proven safe, or it was faulty from improper assembly. Since we couldn't know which it was, we assumed the worst: that the mine had armed itself as it sank and was in its most hazardous condition. The least jar could set it off. We sat on the raft pondering what we could do, finally deciding that our only choice was to put a long line on the mine and try to pull it out to sea. Whether this could be done without accidentally blowing it up was a matter for speculation.

We explained the circumstances to the major, who by now was back on the beach. We reopened the sensitive issue of evacuation for his men. "You'll have to get them to a safe area," said Lieutenant Edwards bluntly.

"Listen," replied the major grimly, "after we get all these men up here, do you think we're going to move them?" He answered his own question. "No!"

"In that case," replied Edwards, "there is nothing we can do for you." He swept an arm toward the heights. "We will not work on a mine with all those people sitting right above it."

"Then it looks like we'll have to get some new talent," snapped the major.

We saluted and paddled away. "From the look on the major's face," I remarked, "he thinks we're chicken. He doesn't know that we could tie a wire on the mine and pull it away from far enough out so there's no danger to ourselves." If it worked, we would be heroes. If it didn't work and the mine went off, we would still be heroes, because we tried. "He doesn't know we're passing up a chance to be heroes that couldn't miss."

Back at our support ship, things were not as usual. The officer of the day met us as we came aboard. "The commodore wants to see you, Lieutenant," he said ominously.

Edwards hesitated. "Chief, you might as well come along," he said. "He'll probably want to see you, too."

I waited discreetly outside the commodore's cabin while Edwards went in. The curtain parted a moment later. "Come on in," said Edwards, his face giving no hint of the weather inside. The commodore, who had heard from the major, quietly listened to our story. He agreed that we had acted intelligently. "But," he said, "this is the Navy's responsibility, and needless to say," he went on, measuring each of us meaningfully, "it rests on you." He let this penetrate. "All I've got to say is, get back into your boat and get back over there!" His inflection was such that he had no need to add that this was an order.

"Aye, aye, Commodore!" said Edwards, saluting.

As we again set out for the island, the man in the bow griped, "Hey, Chief, it's getting close to dinnertime. We'll all be doggone hungry by the time we get back."

"By the time we get back you may not feel like eating," I answered gloomily. I had visions of the camp above the cove being smeared over the rocks.

Edwards joined me. "That last remark—I hope it's not prophecy," he said. He gazed meditatively at the deck. "We'll give the mine another close look," he said. "Maybe there's something we missed. Then we'll decide what's the best thing to do, and then we'll do it. It's no use talking to that fellow on the beach any more. He's won his argument."

We hove to with the destructor boat at the same point as before. The rubber raft was put over the side, and Edwards and I paddled back across the reef to meet our responsibility. The major and his pal were waiting, keeping smugly silent. "I'll go down first," said Edwards, slipping over the side. Through the clear water I watched him swim around the mine a couple of times, inspecting it closely. He came back up and as he broke surface, went back down again, as if he had had an afterthought and wanted to take another look. Finally back aboard the raft, he took off his mask and said, "Okay, I thought I saw something different but I guess not. How about your taking a look?"

I found the same things as the first time—nothing new. There was still no reason to doubt that the mine was armed, or to think that if we banged or jarred it, it wouldn't go off.

"You know," said Edwards, "if we could pull the mine straight up, very gently, so it wouldn't touch anything, the arming mechanism would probably disarm itself; it looks in good working order."

"That's probably right," I said. "But how do we lift it?"

"We could do it with a couple of oil drums," said the lieutenant. "Let's ask the major if he can get us a couple."

The major willingly obliged, having a pair of GIs lash them together as we directed and put them into the water for us. We tied a short line to the drums and by this towed them out to the destructor boat for rigging with a pulley slung underneath. Then we towed the drums back to the mine, trailing 2,000 feet of sweep wire behind us. We floated the drums into position directly above the mine. We put the wire through the pulley underneath the drums, and I carried the end of the wire down and fastened it to a pad eye on the mine. We were ready.

We paddled back to the boat and from the safety of nearly a half mile began pulling on the line. If things worked as they should back at the mine, it would lift off the bottom for a certain distance, the drums being held stationary to this point by the weight of the mine. Then the direction of the force would shift to a point midway between the vertical pull of the mine and the horizontal pull of the towline and the drums would start moving with us, the mine swinging along underneath. Once started, it was critically important that we keep going, in order not to drop the mine back to the bottom, where the impact would set it off.

All went as planned. Far out to sea we cut the mine loose. In a minute or so the ocean quaked, rumbled, and ripped open for the ejection of a great climbing column of water, propelled by some 600 pounds of high explosive. Back on the beach stood the major, a lonely figure as the shock wave rolled over him. He never knew that we had done nothing to make the mine safe before we lifted it away, or the risk he was taking in staying on the beach. He would have been the first to go.

"Shall we go back and ask him if the Army doesn't know how to say thanks?" a crewman growled. At that moment, as the water tower collapsed, the major waved to us. "Good enough," grunted the crewman. "The Navy is always glad to help the Army any time."

Not long afterward, another of the small mines was found. "This one should be ideal to take apart," someone remarked as we looked it over. "It's brand-new. It's drifting nice and free, and it's right near the beach where you've been taking the others apart."

I didn't like it. The combination of these favorable factors added up to too much coincidence. We knew that the enemy, frustrated by us in their plans for the small mine, had been watching us take their handiwork apart, and I suspected they were cooking up something to dispose of us disposal experts. "I think we better back off and sink this one," I said. "Get your rifles ready."

At the first shot the mine exploded, rocking the startled riflemen back on their heels. "Say, Chief," said the man who had found all things ideal a little while earlier, "you don't suppose those Commies would be so dirty as to booby-trap one of these things, do you?"

It was my last trip in Korean waters. I had a feeling I couldn't have been going home at a better time.

20. Ground Zero in the Water

One of the things that help the explosives disposal man to go up to a big piece of ordnance, as opposed to a small one, to make it harmless is that there are no degrees of death. The blast from either package, large or small, travels 27,000 feet a second—18,700 miles an hour; and with you standing right by it, it hasn't far to travel. Still, as my plane droned down the Atlantic seaboard from Indian Head, I felt more than the usual apprehensions at being off to take an explosive device apart. The device in this case was nuclear—a nuclear depth bomb.

It was to be tested, and if it didn't go off, there would be a great deal of urgency about getting it back. An ordinary depth charge, lying unexploded on the bottom for ships' anchors to drag against, is bad enough. A live atomic charge is unthinkable. Leaving it on the bottom would also risk compromising a top defense secret of the time. And it would be imperative to find out why it didn't go off, so that the fault could be corrected.

In theory, though, failure had been made technically impossible. In developing the bomb, the Navy realized that anything less than total reliability was impermissible. This applied to timing as well. It must go off at a precise moment—no sooner and no later. The well-being of a whole fleet, not just a single ship, could depend on it, for the damage radius would be in miles instead of yards. To ensure this kind of performance, twelve triggers had been built into the bomb, the extra ones really being back-up devices. If the first trigger failed, there were eleven more down the line to make it go.

Unfortunately, this multi-triggering complicated things for the disposal man. If the impossible happened and all twelve triggers failed, he faced twelve chances of the bomb exploding rather than only one as he worked to disarm it. We instructors in mines at Indian Head had been kept abreast of this special weapons development, and one of the designers couldn't understand why we didn't seem to appreciate their efforts to make the bomb foolproof.

"Nearly all dead disposal men were killed by foolproof devices," I had told him. The extra foolproofing built into this one gave me less rather than more comfort as I now headed for the test. I couldn't help thinking, too, that if the developers completely believed in their work, they wouldn't be having me come down.

Since it obviously wouldn't do to kick a nuclear charge off the fantail, the way ordinary depth charges are launched, the new bomb was designed to be dropped from an airplane. The first thing therefore was to find out how it stood up under impact with the water in an air drop. I was asked point-blank if I thought I could disarm it, in case there was failure. With other nuclear devices under test, provision is made to disarm them remotely, or to make them safe to approach for the purpose. This would not be feasible with an air-dropped depth charge. There was no other way than to have a man enter the water and turn off the arming switch by hand.

"I can disarm it all right," I assured them. "There's only one question in my mind—whether the pressure of the water will tighten the seal around the switch so much that I can't turn it." I suggested that before the air drop was made, we lower the ballistic envelope into the water and try the switch.

The envelope was put into the sea, and then the nearest diving facility was called to put me down to it. This raised an awkward security problem. The secrecy of the development had been so well kept that even most of those taking part in it didn't know what was going on. They told of rumors that an A-bomb was to be tested somewhere in the vicinity, never suspecting that this was their own project. The diving crew was insulted when they apparently weren't trusted to be told what was on the bottom, and learned that another diver was to make the actual dive. They concluded that what we were after was treasure of some sort.

They were protesting their wide experience and inflexible honesty when I walked in. The diver in charge was Mac Connery, an old acquaintance.

"Karneke!" he exclaimed. "What the hell are you doing here? Are you on a treasure hunt or something?"

I replied evasively, revealing nothing. Connery leaned close. "These guys don't trust us," he muttered. "Then what the hell are they doing putting *you* down?"

"This is not a treasure hunt," I said. "It's just some scientific test they're making."

Connery looked at me cynically. "Okay, Doctor, I believe you. You're on a scientific expedition." He paused, disgust on his face. "But don't feel bad if I don't tell anybody. They'll think Connery's gone nuts."

I could only go along with the rib, grinning passively.

Connery began to be less sure. "So I guess you're testing some special type of instrument?" he asked.

"As a matter of fact, yes," I said.

The civilian scientist in charge of the project, who had let me deal with Connery, came back into the room. "Will you be able to make the dive all right?" he asked with a trace of impatience.

"Yes, Doctor," I replied.

Connery was a savvy fellow, quick to size up a situation.

Hearing me address the other man as Doctor, he got down to business. "Okay," he said, "how do you want to be dressed?"

"I'll wear a Number Two suit," I said.

"What size hat?" This was the takedown for divers who thought they were pretty good. I let it pass. When I was dressed and ready to go, Connery asked, "Okay, anything special we should know?"

"Nothing. Just use the standard diving procedure—the standard signals."

Connery was a long way from realizing that a serious moment of science was at hand. He still suspected hanky-panky. As he was ready to close my faceplate, he whispered slyly, "Do you want us to drop you a line on the other side of the boat?" This signified the diver's traditional arrangement for sending up his personal percentage from the bottom.

"It won't be necessary," I said. By the look on Connery's face as he swung the faceplate closed, I knew that he was still doubtful.

As it turned out, the dive was anticlimactic after the problem of keeping security raised by the divers. The disarming switch gave me no trouble, easily turning to the safe position. Connery and his visiting divers probably still think there is treasure there.

Then came the actual tests of the device by dropping it from an airplane. These all went well except one. When the explosion failed to come in a few seconds after the device hit the water, the two dozen or so of us watching through binoculars from the bridge of the control ship knew there was something wrong. "Well, we know that at least some of the triggers aren't working," someone remarked dryly as the seconds ticked away.

"In a few more seconds the next trigger should pull," came the hopeful reply.

But nothing happened. "Shouldn't it have gone off by now?" it was asked. "You don't think we got a dud on our hands, do you?"

I tensed. A dud meant work for me, as the stand-by diver on the project.

The seconds became minutes. Now it was even doubtful where the device had hit. By the shadows cast on the bridge, the ship was swinging, and the circles in the water made by the impact had disappeared among the waves. Someone observed that the dye marker fastened to the device should afford a clue.

"But we can't go maneuvering over the spot, looking for a dye marker," it was hastily protested.

"I'll get hold of the sonarman and find out if the sonar buoys are picking it up," it was volunteered.

The sonar operator replied from his shack that he wasn't able to pick up any of the buoys. "Anybody up there on the bridge know what frequencies the sonar buoys are set for?" he asked.

There was an exchange of glances. "Well, the sonarman ought to know that," it was commented. "What's he asking us for?"

It was now silently accepted all around that there had been a boo-boo. All eyes came to bear on me. "We won't worry about that now," said the man in charge. "We got a diver with us." To me he said, "How long do you think it would take you to find it?"

"It's a big ocean," I pointed out.

I was momentarily saved from further commitment by a dispute as to the location of the drop. Everybody was pointing in a different direction. The shadows on the bridge showed increased swinging of the ship, borne out by a long curve in the wake. The melancholy truth was, nobody had much idea any longer where the device had hit the water. One of the cooler heads observed placatingly, "There's no reason to panic yet. We still have one more back-up device to go."

But a full couple of minutes had now passed. If the last trigger was going to work, it would have to be soon. Conversation stopped, everyone staring desperately out at the distant water. A few skeptics turned away, already giving up.

"I'm sure glad I'm not a diver," someone observed glumly. He and I were two minds with a single, perfectly matched, thought.

Then the ocean rose to the sky in a mighty upheaval. Everybody slapped everybody else on the back, joyfully shouting he knew all along it would go. Their happiness was nothing compared to mine.

For the remaining tests, the cause of the skip in the triggers was found and corrected—and everybody knew the frequencies of the sonar buoys.

The final phase of the tests was to see how the depth bomb behaved in a crash. There conceivably would be times when the plane carrying it, taking off from its carrier, would slam back to the deck or into the drink. Other times the plane might unavoidably bring the bomb back from a mission, unable to get rid of it. There could be a rough landing as the plane came in with its unexpended load. If the bomb didn't go off in any of these circumstances, would it be safe to approach it to make sure that it didn't?

To get the answers to these questions, the fully armed device was given simulated crash treatment by launching it from a high-speed rocket sled in the desert. We watched from a blockhouse far off as the bomb went looping and bouncing through the air after being cut loose from the sled, finally coming to rest somewhere in the sand beneath a cloud of dust. We were as elated as a boy with a new bag of marbles that it didn't explode. The order was given that no one was to leave the blockhouse until the all clear was sounded—as if it wouldn't have taken tear gas to get anybody out. Attention turned to the question of what condition the bomb was in.

This speculation ended when someone remarked with a glance in my direction, "We have this Navy special weapons disposal representative with us. He's supposed to check and tell us if it's safe."

There was a conference to decide how long it should be before I set out. "What do you think, Chief?" I was asked.

"Any time delay is a safety factor," I replied starchily, conforming to my academic associations. Translated, this meant, "As long as we don't go near the thing, it's safe." I was tempted to quote the old bomb disposal line, "Wait a couple of years and I won't be in this line of work." I recommended that we wait at least ten minutes.

"Don't you think a half hour would be better?" someone countered.

"It will be just as safe in ten minutes as later," I said. The bomb could be cooking itself off, and I remembered the rule of thumb that heat-sensitive explosives do what they are going to do, one way or the other, in about ten minutes.

After much debate, it was decided, nonetheless, that I should wait a half hour. That would look a lot better in the record than ten minutes if things went wrong. When the half hour was up, it was announced, "The bomb disposal man is going out to check the device. All other personnel will remain in the blockhouse."

I had donned a special white suit, with gloves and canvas puttees, all disposable in the event of contamination. As I was ready to leave the sheltering walls of the blockhouse, the others seemed embarrassed, feeling they should say something. "Is there anything we can tell you that will help?" one asked. "I guess it's not necessary to tell you to be careful," said another.

My jeep, waiting outside, was loaded with disposal tools and was equipped with siren and red light, which I hardly needed. Disposal men are sometimes heard to talk of wanting only one thing if they must go: that it be with a man-sized bang. As I drove off under the hot desert sun, I consoled myself with the thought that if this was to be my time, I would go not only with a respectable bang but under circumstances that made me remembered a little while. Then I got down to more positive thinking. Mentally, I reviewed the things that could have happened to the bomb from the beating it had taken. If luck was with me—if there had been no damage

—my problem would be simple: I would turn the arming switch to the safe position, and that would be the end of it. I considered what I would do if, on the other hand, luck was not with me and the switch could not be turned.

Some 200 yards from the bomb I parked the jeep and walked the rest of the way. If the bomb was in a sensitive condition, the vibrations from the vehicle, transmitted through the ground, could set it off. I tried to approach with a brisk, professional manner, showing concern but not nervousness. I knew I was under close scrutiny through high-powered binoculars from the blockhouse. I assumed that movie cameras with telephoto lenses were trained on me, too, so that if the bomb exploded, there would be a record of my moves up to the last moment. I had seen such movies. Projected in slow motion, they clearly show the pattern of human disintegration. First, the hat goes off, then the arms . . . the legs . . . and the rest of you. The effect is of a sawdust doll flying apart.

A few feet from the bomb came the strange awe that always takes hold of me in the presence of armed ordnance. Now it lay at arm's length. I am okay up to now; the bomb has admitted me to this proximity without going off. I realize that it probably never will if I don't touch it. The urge not to do so has the pull of the tides. It is total fascination in reverse. I wait awhile. I walk around it, heart pounding, sweat streaming down my face. I see that my luck is not good: the disarming switch is bent beyond any possibility of turning it. Nothing else shows which might be of help in making the bomb safe. There are no wires, no parts which might be removed—all are sealed inside.

But I must do something to show my distant kibitzers that the bomb is safe, or show that I am doing something to it to make it so. I must get intimate with it; I must touch it —that is the key. I lie down beside it—to get my racing system under control, and to listen, with an ear against the side. I hear nothing, and the silence is as ominous as if it were ticking. I get up and lean over the bomb, weaving right and left and closely inspecting it from all angles. I put an ear down to it and run my hands over the surface. I make myself master.

I glance at my watch. I have been here ten minutes. I hold up an arm to the blockhouse and walk away.

Before I could get the jeep turned around and headed back, I was met by a great rush of vehicles—jeeps, cars, trucks—racing out to the bomb like sailors scrambling ashore on their first liberty in a South Sea port. All waved at me as they passed, looking happy and relieved. They knew as well as I that I had done nothing whatever to change things where they were going, but it would be hopeless to stop them. They had seen me put my hands on it; that was enough.

Only the janitor was left at the blockhouse, all others having found a pretext for going out to the bomb. He poured me a cup of coffee. "We got all kinds of it here now," he remarked, looking around the empty room. He wanted to talk. "You know," he began, "I been working here a long time, and I think you're the bravest guy I ever saw."

"Why do you say that?" I asked.

"All each of these guys talked about while you were out there was the part he had made for the bomb, and how he hoped it wasn't his component that failed the test. They didn't seem to have much confidence in it. You didn't make any part of it, but you went out there and showed that they were all okay." He went over to a porthole and took a look through the binoculars. "It's just like you said—it's safe," he called. "They're banging it around now and taking it apart." He came back to the table and refilled my cup. "What I want to know," he said, gesturing appealingly, "is how did you know it was safe?"

"I'll let you in on something—I didn't," I said. He stared at me in shock as I sipped my coffee. "It's a funny thing," I went on, in a sudden realization. "You're the first one who's ever asked me that question."

Epilogue

"I wonder what Karneke's doing now?"

"I hear he's a computer engineer."

"A computer engineer! What's a bubblehead know about thinking machines?"

"I guess it's natural. Divers got no brains, so they have to work with machines that do."

One of my old shipmates told me about this conversation. He said he couldn't believe it when he heard what I was doing in civilian life—it was so far from diving. Actually, the two are not far apart at all. During the twenty years I was in the Navy, electronics came into wide use in diving. In the beginning, we used the old rural-type, hand-cranked telephone, with the diver wearing a headset receiver. In the end we were using what amounted to underwater hi-fi, complete with tone and volume control and transducers in the helmet. Where once we had used a copper wire dragged across the bottom to locate objects, we now used underwater television. Electronics told how much oxygen and carbon dioxide the diver was receiving, and in many other ways has made diving a highly sophisticated business. Electronics has also been applied to ordnance, with fusing and firing systems controlled by what are really small computers.

While these changes were taking place, I was making a hobby of studying them. And by the time I got out I had a good start in the field of electronics.

So you see, all you bubbleheads, it makes good sense that I am now happily ensconced as a senior systems engineer with Remington Rand Univac.

Made in the USA
Lexington, KY
06 May 2019